Visual Journeys Through Wordless Narratives

Also Available from Bloomsbury

Children's Language and Multilingualism, Gillian Wigglesworth and
Jane Simpson
Children's Literature in Context, Fiona McCulloch
Literature in Second Language Education, Piera Carroli

Visual Journeys Through Wordless Narratives

An International Inquiry with Immigrant Children and *The Arrival*

Evelyn Arizpe, Teresa Colomer and
Carmen Martínez-Roldán

*with Caroline Bagelman, Brenda Bellorín, Maureen Farrell,
Martina Fittipaldi, Giorgia Grilli, Mireia Manresa, Ana Ma. Margallo,
Julie McAdam, Neus Real, and Marcela Terrusi*

BLOOMSBURY

LONDON · NEW DELHI · NEW YORK · SYDNEY

Bloomsbury Academic

An imprint of Bloomsbury Publishing Plc

50 Bedford Square	175 Fifth Avenue
London	New York
WC1B 3DP	NY 10010
UK	USA

www.bloomsbury.com

Bloomsbury is a registered trade mark of Bloomsbury Publishing Plc

First published 2014

© Evelyn Arizpe, Teresa Colomer and Carmen Martínez-Roldán and Contributors, 2014

British Library Cataloguing-in-Publication Data
A catalogue record for this book is available from the British Library.

ISBN: HB: 978-1-7809-3758-8
ePDF: 978-1-7809-3724-3
ePUB: 978-1-7809-3776-2

Library of Congress Cataloging-in-Publication Data
A catalog record for this book is available from the Library of Congress.

Typeset by RefineCatch Limited, Bungay, Suffolk
Printed and bound in Great Britain

Contents

List of Figure Permissions

Notes on Contributors

Evelyn Arizpe is a Senior Lecturer at the School of Education, University of Glasgow and is the Programme Leader for the M.Ed. in Children's Literature and Literacies. She has taught and published widely in the areas of literacies, reader-response to picturebooks and children's literature, including Mexican children's books. Evelyn's publications include *Children Reading Pictures: Interpreting Visual Texts* (Routledge, London, 2003) and *Reading Lessons from the Eighteenth Century* (Pied Piper, Lichfield, 2006), both with Morag Styles. She also recently co-edited *Picturebooks: Beyond Borders of Art, Narrative and Culture* (Taylor & Francis, London, 2013) with Maureen Farrell and Julie McAdam.

Caroline Bagelman is a PhD student at The University of Glasgow. Her dissertation explores the ways in which picturebooks can act as socially transformative texts. Engaging with students' responses to picturebooks within the Visual Journeys project has been a highlight of her research experience at the University of Glasgow.

Brenda Bellorín is a researcher, critic and editor of children's literature. She coordinated the Study and Documentation Centre of the Banco del Libro – the Venezuelan children's literature and reading promotions institution – and has collaborated with the publishing houses Ediciones Ekaré and Fondo de Cultura Económica. Currently, Brenda is a PhD candidate at the Department of Didactics of Language, Literature and Social Sciences at the Universitat Autònoma de Barcelona, where she also engages in GRETEL's different research projects and teaches on the MA on Books and Literature for Children and Adolescents.

Teresa Colomer is a Professor at the Department of Language, Literature and Social Sciences Education at the Universitat Autònoma de Barcelona. She is the Director of the international MA on Books and Literature for Children and Youngsters (organized by the UAB and the Banco del Libro from Venezuela), as well as the Director and Coordinator of the official interuniversity MA on School Library and Reading Promotion (UAB-UB). She is also the Principal Investigator of the research group GRETEL. Teresa is the author of approximately 200 publications, a member of different councils for educational magazines and she runs various courses and conferences on teacher training. She has received several international awards and is one of the leading scholars in children's literature.

Maureen Farrell is a Senior Lecturer in the University of Glasgow, School of Education. She has been a researcher and teacher, working in schools and FE colleges for 12 years before becoming a teacher educator. She has been a Programme Leader and Associate Dean with responsibility for all ITE programmes and is on the teaching team for the M.Ed. in Children's Literature and Literacies. Maureen gained her PhD in Scottish Children's Literature in 2008. Her research interests and publications are mainly in that field.

Martina Fittipaldi has a BA in Literature by the Universidad Nacional de Salta, an MA in Language and Literature Didactics by the Universitat Autònoma de Barcelona and an MA on Books and Literature for Children and Youngsters, directed by Dr Teresa Colomer. She has been a teacher at secondary education and also a mediator of the National Reading Plan of Argentina. As a researcher, she has published articles about reading and literature. Martina is a fellow researcher and a PhD candidate at the Department of Language, Literature and Social Sciences Education at the Universitat Autònoma de Barcelona.

Giorgia Grilli is a tenured Researcher and Instructor in Children's Literature (Department of Education, University of Bologna). Her PhD dissertation was published as *Le Public Schools Britanniche tra Mito e Realtà* (Clueb, Bologna, 2003). She is also author of *Myth, Symbol and Meaning in Mary Poppins: The Governess as provocateur* (Routledge, New York, 2007), in the series 'Children's Literature and Culture', edited by Jack Zipes (with a foreword by Neil Gaiman). Giorgia translates both critical essays and children's and young adult literature and writes about topics concerning children's literature on a regular basis in specialized magazines in Italy, and in the literary supplement of a national newspaper (*Tuttolibri*, 'La Stampa').

Mireia Manresa has a PhD in Didactics of Language, Literature and Social Sciences from the Universitat Autònoma de Barcelona. Her doctoral dissertation about reading habits, directed by Dr Teresa Colomer, has been recognized with several awards. She is currently combining secondary-school teaching with teaching in the Department of the Didactics of Language, Literature and Social

Sciences at the Autonomous University of Barcelona, as well as training secondary-school teachers. As a researcher, Mireia is interested in children's and young people's reading habits, including digital literature and literary education.

Ana María Margallo is a lecturer at the Department of Language, Literature and Social Sciences Education at the Universitat Autònoma de Barcelona. She has been a teacher in secondary school for 20 years. She is currently investigating how literature can be useful for the integration and acculturation of immigrant children. Ana María focuses on projects in which students acquire literary competences and is interested in the ways in which adolescents move from juvenile literature to adult reading material, as well as in digital literature for children.

Carmen M. Martínez-Roldán is an Associate Professor in Bilingual Bicultural Education at Teachers College, Columbia University. Her work on bilingual children's literature discussions has been disseminated through more than 25 publications targeting both academic and teacher-practitioner audiences. She was elected as Chair of the Literature Special Interest Group for the American Educational Research Association (AERA) for the term 2012–13. She was also appointed to serve as Co-Chair of Area 9, Text Analysis/Children's, Young Adult and Adult Literature for the Literacy Research Association (LRA) for the 2012–14 term. In 2012, Carmen received the Mid-Career Award for outstanding research in teaching and teacher education by Division K of the American Educational Research Association (AERA).

Julie McAdam is a University Teacher within the School of Education, University of Glasgow. She has developed and worked on undergraduate and postgraduate courses on Initial Teacher Education in Scotland and the Middle East. Together with Evelyn Arizpe and Maureen Farrell, she has been involved in projects associated with the use of picturebooks to promote learning in diverse classrooms. Julie is currently working on two Comenius-funded projects that are looking at how to support teachers working with New Arrival Children across Europe. She has published on learning communities, the use of culturally responsive pedagogy and the use of children's literature in the classroom. She is currently studying for her PhD and is committed to supporting educators work with children's literature to take social action.

Neus Real has a BA in Catalan Studies from the Universitat Autònoma de Barcelona and a MA in Literary Theory from the University of Birmingham. In

2004, she completed a PhD on Catalan Studies with a thesis, a part of which was distinguished with an award in 2005 (Premi Fundació Mercè Rodoreda). Currently, she is a Lecturer at the Department of Language, Literature and Social Sciences Education at the Universitat Autònoma de Barcelona. Neus' research has focused on Catalan women writers from the 1920s and 30s and she is now investigating digital literature for children.

Marcella Terrusi has a PhD in Children Literature and is a teacher of History of Picturebooks at Isia-Urbino (School of Art and Design) and a researcher with the Department of Quality Life at the University of Bologna. She collaborates with the Bologna Children Book Fair as Master of Ceremonies at the Illustrator's Cafe. She is active in the Italian IBBY section (International Board on Books For Young People) and she participated in the Biennial of Bratislava International Jury as the Italian Member in 2009. She is author of *Albi illustrati. Leggere, guardare, nominare il mando nei libri per l'infanzia* (preface by Antonia Faeti), the first Italian monograph on picturebooks.

Foreword

As an artist who enjoys expressing ideas through the medium of the picturebook, probably the most common question I'm asked, particularly by those outside the world of writing and illustration, is: *who are these books for?* In particular, people tend to assume that a picturebook might be tailored specifically for a certain group of readers, particularly young children, as if one is presupposing a number of possible receptions, a known level of interpretation in advance, and thus writing or drawing accordingly, even a little prescriptively. In my case, nothing could be further from the truth, if only because half the time I don't even know what I'm doing! I'm just fascinated by certain kinds of stories told through hand-made images, and I want to see what they look like. And I often have no idea how a book might travel or into whose hands it might fall once the final illustrations have left my table.

Being an artist is like living in quite a strange bubble that way: when working creatively, I never see my readers, I'm alone in a small room jigsaw-puzzling ideas together, experimenting with words, pictures, layouts, formats. It's not possible to think about an audience, I'm so distracted by the idea of a particular image or story that, above all other considerations, just seems *interesting*. Not just for me, but possibly for other people too. And importantly, interesting in a *different* way for each person, whose experience of the world is quite removed from my own, who may know things that I don't and find meanings I'm blind to. Who are my books for? They are for as many different people as possible. I just trust that we all have something extremely valuable in common: an unpredictable imagination.

As an illustrator, I wasn't always aware of this. I started out with the youthful ideal that, as an artist, I had a duty to show people things, to 'illustrate' ideas, implant objects or messages into the minds of others, to convey some kind of special truth, and this is often how painters or writers are mistakenly represented. Eventually, through the rigours of work and experience, failure and success, I realized that any good act of creativity is fundamentally an act of sharing and co-creation. It's based on generosity, humility and trust. As a creator, you provide a little architecture, build some imaginary walls, add a few furnishings, then wait for an anonymous visitor to arrive: should they accept the invitation, any real meaning can only come from their own hearts and minds. The reader is not so much the recipient of ideas; they are a conversationalist, enjoying a language that transcends the ordinary boundaries of daily chit-chat. All we need to do as creators and readers sitting together in the imaginary guest room is look at things and wonder about them openly. There is not a fixed meaning that needs to be unearthed like an archaeologist finding bones; all interpretations are alive and well, and changeable too.

Among a general readership of my own books, two groups have consistently provided the most fascinating and unexpected feedback: children, and people from other cultures (that is, not a monolingual Australian suburbanite like myself). Children for their honesty and free-roaming interpretations, and the fact that they tend to look carefully at concrete details in pictures, where adults are often overly preoccupied with understanding meaning, too quickly searching for big concepts and 'isms'. People from other cultures offer a similarly unexpected view, particularly as my work has been widely translated; it's interesting to see how images refracted by one experience are received through the lens of another. *The Rabbits*, about Australian colonization, is a popular story in Mexico, as it also relates to Central American history; *The Red Tree*, a book about overcoming loss or trauma, was considered in Japan to be a response to the recent tsunami disaster, even though painted a decade earlier. What this points to is the cross-generational and cross-cultural potential of narrative imagery, particularly where it's uncluttered by context or specific references, and universal in nature.

Those two reading groups, the young and the culturally diverse, intersect of course in the case of immigrant children, in many respects an ideal audience for a book like *The Arrival* (if any such thing exists) for several reasons. First and most obviously, the absence of specific language leaves it open to all, not just by avoiding English (my own language) but also by ignoring levels of literacy education too, depending entirely upon pictures for meaning. I was interested in returning to an original state of observation, a pre-literate state. In the absence of linguistic experience, we have all been in a situation of dependence upon visual intelligence, making connections between things without the convenience of written or spoken meanings, and hopefully we continue to do so throughout our lives. At times, we must remind ourselves that meaning can be personally constructed, not just received from elsewhere; children and migrants know this acutely, and we have much to learn from them. It's at once a position of disability, to not be able to read the world because of age or cultural difference, and also of heightened ability, a privilege. It means you can be unfettered by the constraints of recognition, the automatic filing system that might stop us from really *looking* at things. In my book *The Arrival*, I was not so much interested in imagining the life of a migrant, as much as looking at how a migrant must imagine life. How we make sense of the world, how we ask questions, how we make connections: this is more important than knowledge.

That kind of open reading is necessarily an automatic process, however, and does need to be learned and sustained through education. Books by themselves are not living things, they are static objects that mostly live in the dark. They don't automatically expand imagination or understanding, they need to be opened and read, in the broadest possible sense, sometimes an uncommon privilege without help from teachers and academics.

One of the problems of creating a wordless book in particular is that it can be too silent to even court attention. Additionally, illustrated books are sometimes regarded dismissively, including by older children who feel their reading has graduated to the level of picture-less prose (as if such levels are natural, rather than cultural conventions). Furthermore, even when someone does read a book, the ideas and feelings contained within it are generally quiet by nature; in order to work they do not shout for attention, they need to be discovered pensively, and sometimes over a long period, and there must be a level of inquisitive interaction that's quite personal. It's here that the work of educators can be indispensable, not in explaining or decoding a book, but mediating the experience of reading by focusing attention, pointing to things that might not otherwise be observed, asking open questions. To go a step further and study children's responses, as here in *Visual Journeys*, is a wonderful continuation of that process, particularly in considering how reading has intellectual and emotional ramifications beyond the pages of a book, and can deeply engage the everyday lives of real people. *The Arrival* has come full circle in this regard: what began as a personal research project of mine to gather real-world immigrant stories and project them into the realm of fantastic fiction is now a work, essentially still in progress, whereby fictional images inspire immigrants to relate their own real-world experiences.

At the end of the day, artists and writers like myself are not just interested in making pictures and stories, we are hoping to connect with other individuals, to share thoughts and experiences. We want to look together at things that amuse, frighten, puzzle and inspire us, to know that we are not alone, and that different people have more in common than we might at first believe. I'm extremely grateful to all the teachers and students who participated in this study and who gave life to inanimate drawings, and also to all the teachers, who continue to build bridges between books and young people, to give value to their thoughts and feelings, and to share their curiosity.

Shaun Tan, October 2013

Introduction

Although we were not aware of it at the time, the starting point of our journey was *The Arrival*. A chance encounter between colleagues at a conference where someone happened to have a copy of Tan's latest book led to a conversation about the possibility of sharing it with immigrant children and finding out what sense they made out of it, and whether and how it might prove to be a good support for learning and for reflection on the immigrant experience itself. This conversation led to further conversations, with other colleagues (some of them immigrants themselves) who were also concerned with research into the teaching and learning of children who were having to cope with the multiple consequences of migration, as well as struggling with literacy in a new language. Linking these colleagues were two firm beliefs: the first, in the power of literature, including picturebooks, to contribute to overcoming these challenges through offering pleasurable and empathetic reading experiences where alternative futures can be imagined; and the second, in the power of shared discussions about literature, in which a secure, hospitable space can be created for exchange and reflection, and which can be part of a socially responsible movement against the intolerance and injustice that immigrants often face on their arrival.

It seems fitting that Tan's words should be at the beginning of this book and that, like the immigrant family in his wordless book, we have arrived at the end of our research journey, having overcome the challenges of crossing a range of borders. Of course, one cannot equate the hardships and traumas of forced migration, or even the emotional and social costs of 'voluntary' migration, with participation in a scholarly research project, but inquiry is always a journey that involves elements of uncertainty and confusion, the need to make sense of new data and to finally arrive at the place where expectations and findings have evolved in order to, hopefully, suggest new paths forward. There are also parallels in the sense of having to overcome the barriers of funding, distance and language as well as academic, social and cultural conventions and theoretical traditions, in order to create a convivial space for shared inquiry that raises questions for further investigations. Finally, just as migration is being transformed by communications technology so that it is now possible to maintain the links between immigrant communities and those in the country of origin, so international research is being transformed by the possibility of exchange through email, videoconference and social networks.

Twenty-first-century language and literacy challenges: A visual response

As host countries struggle to meet the educational demands of ethnic-minority and immigrant children, educationalists in the areas of language and literacy learning have been investigating and proposing novel ways of responding to these demands by looking at new social and cultural theories of language, literacy and multiculturalism. They have explored aspects such as school environment, curriculum, home practices, literature and reading resources. However, because of the urgency to teach children to be able to communicate in the new language, there is often little room to include imagination and creativity or to incorporate the skills, experience and knowledge that the children bring with them.

One of the least explored avenues in both research and practice is the critical use of the visual image. It is evident that we are living in an era where visual images have increasingly more impact on our daily lives, whether they appear on paper or on screen. One of the effects of globalization is that children from many different countries and backgrounds share a visual culture to an extent they have never done before the twenty-first century. Although it is probably true that most children do not spend much time reflecting on the visual images that surround them, there is no denying that they have a great deal of knowledge about different narrative forms and affordances of visual media. Why not build on this experience and knowledge and apply it to language and literacy learning and, in the process, expand that experience and knowledge of the visual image itself? Fiction helps navigate real-world experiences as well as the emotions of other human beings. Good picturebooks about immigration can address these sensitive aspects through the nuances of colour, line and perspective, encouraging reflection as they provide story as well as visual pleasure.

Visual resources, of course, have long been used in language teaching and also in the teaching of reading and writing, given that they can provide attractive stimuli and can sidestep the language and printed word barriers. However, when constructed for didactic purposes, few visual narratives can sustain interest and provide deeper opportunities for exploration and interpretation. Many teachers therefore turn to the riches offered by picturebooks, visual narratives that are created with an aesthetic and playful intent, which make use of artistic and literary features that invite reading and re-reading of their multiple layers of meaning. Yet often these picturebooks are considered useful only as far as the images provide support for reading words, and usually they are abandoned once the child can read 'well enough' or are simply not considered to be for children over a certain age.

Many contemporary picturebooks, however, are not age limited and invite readers to use critical interpretive skills and to reflect deeply on complex issues (following Kiefer, 1995, the compound word 'picturebook' is used here as an indication of the interdependence of word and image that distinguishes these texts and as opposed to 'picture books', which are non-narrative, such as concept books with images). The authors and illustrators of what are known as 'postmodern picturebooks' make use of sophisticated literary and artistic features such as irony, metafiction and intertextuality, challenging even young readers to fully engage with their reading of both text and image and to reflect on the narrative resulting from this interaction. The same can be said for many graphic novels and comics.

Picturebooks (with and without words) have been the subject of literary research by seminal authors such as Bader (1976), Nodelman (1988), Nikolajeva and Scott (2001) and D. Lewis (2001), who have refined our understanding of what picturebooks are and how they work as a multimodal genre where the playful but often complex interaction between the words and the images has the potential to generate tiers of meaning as readers are invited to attend to and move between the response-inviting structures. Together with more recent studies (e.g. Beckett, 2012; Painter, Martin and Unsworth, 2013), they highlight the fundamental demand made by the picturebook on the reader, which is to migrate back and forth between the narratives created by the words and the pictures, crossing the particular boundaries of each media in order to make meaning.

As other studies have shown (Arizpe, Farrell and McAdam, 2013), as well as crossing borders between different modes, picturebooks also encourage readers to cross borders between artistic genres, languages and cultures, as well as urging researchers to cross disciplines such as art and cultural history, semiotics, philosophy, cultural geography, literary theory and visual literacy in order to explore the texts and the responses in more depth. However, the ever-increasing production of picturebooks and the constantly evolving theories around reading visual images, for example as a result of neuroscientific discoveries, means that the study of this genre of children's literature is far from complete.

Research using picturebooks to investigate reader-response or additional language learning has provided plenty of evidence that children can skilfully read texts in which images have a significant narrative role. Even very young children, struggling readers and children at the early stages of learning an additional language can construct meaning from picturebooks with those sophisticated literary and visual features (Arizpe and Styles, 2003). Empirical studies have looked at how meaning-making from picturebooks can contribute to furthering an understanding of literary and artistic features (Evans, 2009; Kiefer, 1995; Pantaleo, 2008; Sipe, 2008); supporting additional language skills (Mourão, 2009, 2012; Walsh, 2003) and negotiating cultures and identities (Coulthard, 2003; McGonigal and Arizpe, 2007; Mines, 2000), including intercultural learning (Morgado, Livingston, Ondráš, Tembra and Blazic, 2008). However, so far, no study has focused on whether and how immigrant children from different backgrounds can benefit in all these areas from looking at and discussing wordless picturebooks.

Wordless picturebooks in particular raise the stakes for meaning-making because, by prioritizing the reading of images, the need for the reader's involvement is heightened. Among the award-winning, internationally known illustrators who have created wordless picturebooks are Raymond Briggs, Mitsumasa Anno, Shirley Hughes, Quentin Blake, Tord Nygren, Chris Raschka, David Shannon, Barbara Lehman, Jerry Pinkney, Istvan Banyai, Juan Gedovius, David Wiesner, Shaun Tan, Suzy Lee, Bill Thomson and Gabriel Pacheco. The affordances of wordless picturebooks mean that readers must take risks with their predictions and understandings, and they must also activate intertextual and cultural knowledge. The lack of language challenges obviously makes them particularly well suited for those learning a new language but this does not mean they are an 'easy' read.

One of the ways in which the challenges of picturebooks, and wordless picturebooks in particular, can be met is through the collective construction of meaning. An interpretative community, led by expert mediation, can enhance reading experiences and responses (Colomer, 2002; Manresa and Silva-Díaz, 2005; Sipe, 1998). Many studies stress the importance of 'literary discussions' or 'literary circles' (Campbell Hill, Johnson and Schlick Noe, 1995; Daniels, 2002; Martínez-Roldán and López-Robertson, 1999; Short and Pierce, 1998) where meaning can be constantly probed, negotiated and revised in the light of contributions from the members of that community. This type of 'booktalk' (Chambers, 1993) is both 'generative' and 'structured' at the same time (Bland, 2013), and thus is particularly valuable for English language learners (ELL)/ English as an additional language (EAL) learners in allowing them to move beyond their interpretations and participate in the construction of meaning. Given the diversity of backgrounds of the children in each context, this also meant that meaning was built on intercultural exchanges.

In the case of literary discussion around wordless picturebooks, it is important to consider the visual literacy skills that the children already have and also how these can be developed, such as the awareness of compositional features (layout, perspective, colour and design among others), and how they have been used by the illustrator to construct a particular story. For children learning a new language, visual responses provide alternative ways of communicating their knowledge, awareness and thoughts that are more consonant with the wordless images; these can include, for example, visual responses, such as drawings, collages, photography. Other media also allow for a different exploration and representation of themes and ideas.

Visual journeys: The point of departure

The research question that led the inquiry was: 'In what ways does participation in visual response strategies and discussions of wordless postmodern texts support recent immigrant children as readers?' Our primary hypothesis was that reading wordless picturebooks with immigrant children from diverse backgrounds and using a variety of oral and visual strategies to encourage their responses could develop both their literacy learning and cultural understanding. We also believed that the inquiry would provide insights both into the knowledge and skills the children were applying in their meaning-making and also into the role this particular literary genre could play more widely in fostering social and intercultural cohesion in the classroom.

The inquiry was therefore designed to draw on the relevant research evidence mentioned above and to respond to the main objective which was:

To explore the responses of immigrant pupils from different backgrounds to wordless picturebooks in order to understand how they construct meaning from visual images in complex narratives about immigration, journeys and the visual image itself with the intention of creating strategies that can develop their literacy skills, as well as help them reflect on their own or others' experience of migration.

This objective was further defined and widened through the following aims:

1. Considering the role of picturebooks in encouraging reflection on the personal, social and intercultural issues involved in the immigrant experience.
2. Creating a 'safe' and stimulating space for these reflections where awareness and understanding can be fostered.
3. Using image-based research tools to obtain responses, which can then be adapted in the classroom as strategies to develop visual, linguistic and intercultural skills.
4. Initiating a cross-national, collaborative research agenda through the creation of a network of inquiry and practice with university-based research teams sharing experiences and learning on reader-response, picturebooks and immigration.

Given the participants, we felt that 'hospitality' should be a key part of the methodology, not only as the overall educational qualitative research approach but also as the sustaining foundation of the research tools. Literary circles or discussions would create comfortable but stimulating secure spaces in which children's oral responses would be welcomed and shared, and visual strategies that could be developed as pedagogical tools would be used to elicit alternative forms of response. Given the previous experience of some of the researchers, the design and methods were based on those used successfully in previous studies but incorporated new methodological ideas to suit the international contexts. The books selected for the inquiry were *Flotsam* and *The Arrival*, two wordless narratives on the theme of immigration and journeys, which were self-reflective in terms of the visual and which offered multiple levels of interpretation and promised to excite readers. This selection was not undertaken lightly because we believe that reading – whether it is text, image or a combination of both – has the potential to foster, to heal and to transform. As Petit writes,

Cada uno de los libros leídos es una morada prestada en la cual uno se siente protegido y puede soñar con otros futuros, elaborar una distancia, cambiar de punto de vista. Más allá del carácter envolvente, protector, habitable, de la lectura, lo que se hace posible en ciertas condiciones es una transformación de las emociones y los sentimientos, una elaboración simbolizada de la experiencia vivida. (Petit, 2009, p. 295)

[Each book that is read is a borrowed dwelling in which one feels protected and can dream of other futures, elaborate distance, change point of view. Beyond the enveloping, protecting, inhabitable condition of reading, what is made possible in certain conditions is a transformation of the emotions and feelings, a symbolized elaboration of the lived experience. (EA transl.)]

We were aware that investigating acts of reading is not straightforward, given these are set within contemporary sociocultural contexts where multimodal texts are part of children's daily lives and are inserted in a popular, often global, culture, which intersects the particular literacy practices and cultural heritage of each individual. In the case of immigrant children, their experience of migration is an undeniable part of the way they view the world and therefore of the way they read. Reading implies a crossing of an invisible border into the world of the book where the rules of reality and fiction, as we know them, do not apply. Reading is also intensely personal and, therefore, as Pennac (1994) rightly reminds us, one of the reader's rights is 'to remain silent'. The research paradigm was therefore based on a qualitative interpretive approach that allowed the act of reading to be examined and understood within these personal and cultural parameters. The approach included an awareness that, while literary and sociocultural theories can help illuminate reader-response events, the data remains slippery, subject to aesthetic reactions, to emotions, to critique, to social mediation and influence of others and to the interpretation of researchers who themselves were subject to the intentional ambiguities and uncertainties of the narratives. In addition, we were working with data in a language that some of the children (and, in the case of Glasgow, most of them) were in the process of acquiring and which evolved in the course of the inquiry. Finally, we were working with young people whose identities were in flux, not only because of their migrant circumstances (i.e. from 'asylum seekers' to 'refugees' or to 'citizens') and because they were children becoming adolescents, in between primary and secondary schooling, but also because the act of reading is itself a transformational process and we are never the same person we were after a profound encounter with a text.

These challenges help explain why the data resisted division into rigid categories and both the data collection and the analysis processes themselves mirrored the idea of border crossings, with all the uncertainty that this implies. It also entailed a negotiation across various disciplines (literature, literacy, language education) and across the epistemologies behind the research traditions of each team. This negotiation was part of our research 'journey', given we all had to cross invisible borders in order to learn from others so that at the end of this particular intercultural exchange we could create something new that would work for all of us and for our particular data.

One final challenge was making the decision to focus only on the response data on *The Arrival* for our collective book. Having looked at and discussed all the data, the teams regretfully decided that it would be impossible to cover both picturebooks in appropriate depth. However, some of the work on *Flotsam* has been published (Arizpe and McAdam, 2011; Walsh, Cranitch and Maras, 2012) and we hope to come back to this data again in the future.

Fellow travellers on the inquiry journey

The initial teams became involved in the inquiry as a result of existing research networks around picturebooks and ethnic-minority literature and literacy education. They were based in universities from four of the major host countries – the UK, the USA, Spain and Australia – in regions that have a particular history of immigration and to which an increasing number of migrants have been arriving in the last two decades: Glasgow, Arizona, Barcelona and Sydney. The three principal investigators had all previously worked in areas relevant to the inquiry and two of them were immigrants themselves. Among the teams, another four were also immigrants, while others had experienced long periods of living in countries different to their native one. The teams drew up a collaborative agenda and a research proposal and proceeded to obtain funding and relevant permissions in their respective countries. Each of these researchers contributed to the project as a whole as well as to particular chapters, and, without their invaluable input, this book would never have been written.

The project was led by Dr Evelyn Arizpe who, along with her colleagues Dr Maureen Farrell and Julie McAdam, were part of the language and literacy team in the University of Glasgow, responsible for, among other tasks, developing the area of children's literature in undergraduate and postgraduate programmes. Evelyn had been continuing her work on picturebooks based on the initial project with Morag Styles, which resulted in *Children Reading Pictures* (2003). Maureen Farrell's area of expertise is Scottish children's literature dealing with issues of language, culture and identity, while Julie McAdam's interest is in literacy and EAL students and issues of social justice. Caroline Bagelman, a student from Canada supervised by Evelyn, joined the project in 2011 while carrying out her doctoral research on picturebooks and food politics. Grants from the University of Glasgow School of Education and from the UK Literacy Association (UKLA) facilitated the project in this context.

At the Universitat Autònoma de Barcelona (UAB), Professor Teresa Colomer, one of the leading scholars in children's literature in the Catalan- and Spanish-speaking worlds, has been leading the research group GRETEL (Grup de Recerca en literatura Infantil i Juvenil i Educació Literària) on a variety of national and international research projects (literacy education, picturebooks, reading habits on paper and screen). Teresa and her team joined the Visual Journeys inquiry within the context of a wider research project on the role of picturebooks to support the education of immigrant children: 'La interpretación literaria de álbumes en el proceso de acogida de los alumnos inmigrantes' funded by the Programa Nacional de Investigación Científica, Desarrollo en Innovación Tecnológica 2008–2011. This umbrella project looked at the literature available as well as the didactic strategies used to explore new forms of pedagogy based on active and collaborative construction of meaning from complex picturebooks (including *Flotsam* and *The Arrival*). Altogether, 108 pupils from 14 classrooms, both primary and secondary, in the province of Barcelona, were involved in the project. This project also included a review of children's books (not just picturebooks) available on the themes of multiculturalism and migration and 50 books were analysed for their possible use in the classroom. Findings from the overall project were the topic of an International Conference in 2011, 'La literatura que acoge: infancia, inmigración y lectura', and appeared, together with some of the work described in this book, in an edited volume, *La literatura que acoge: inmigración y lectura de álbumes* (Colomer and Fittipaldi, 2012).

A large group of researchers worked on the project in Barcelona, some of whom were university professors, senior lecturers and research fellows, while others were students conducting their postgraduate research. Brenda Bellorín, a Venezuelan children's literature researcher and a PhD candidate, and Martina Fittipaldi, an Argentinean researcher and also a PhD candidate, joined the research as fellows. Martina's MA thesis in particular provided a seminal contribution to the Visual Journeys inquiry, through her initial analysis and selection of examples. The core group included UAB staff: Dr Ana María Margallo, a lecturer and experienced literature teacher in secondary school specializing in literature teachers' training; Dr Neus Real, a lecturer whose work focuses on Catalan women writers and Catalan children's literature; and

Dr Mireia Manresa, an Associate Professor and a secondary-school teacher specializing in reading habits and literary education.

Working at Arizona State University at the time as an Associate Professor, Dr Carmen Martínez-Roldán's work involved teaching and conducting research on language and literacy of bilingual learners. Carmen brings a sociocultural perspective to the study of bilingual children's literate thinking – the various ways children construct meanings from texts (literature and digital texts) in English and Spanish, and the contexts that mediate their interpretive processes and discourses in literature discussions. Her work has been disseminated in international and US scholarly journals, such as the *Journal of Early Childhood Literacy*, *Critical Inquiry in Language Studies*, *Research in the Teaching of English* and the *Language Arts*. Her participation on the Visual Journeys project was aligned with her interest in children's responses to literature. She invited graduate student Sarah Newcomer to participate in the project, and together they conducted the discussions in a bilingual, pre-K-8 bilingual school with a population of almost 90 per cent Latino students, 65 per cent of whom were classified as English language learners. Carmen joined the faculty of the Bilingual Bicultural Education programme at Teachers College, Columbia University in New York in 2011, where she conducted further analysis of the children's discussions. She organized a symposium where members of the international team presented some findings of the Visual Journey's project at the 2012 Literacy Research Association conference.

The Sydney team consisted of three academics from the Australian Catholic University in New South Wales, with expertise in different areas. Maureen Walsh's research and publications on visual literacy and multimodal literacy have been focused on multicultural learners in urban classrooms. Maya Cranitch has publications and extensive experience working with refugees and asylum seekers, as well as developing and teaching TESOL Curriculum for diverse groups. Karen Maras' expertise is in the visual arts and her research explores the theoretical bases on which younger and older children come to understand and explain representational meaning in art. They received a small internal research grant from their university and, in collaboration with the Catholic Education Office Sydney, worked with a small group of refugee students from the Sudan. As a result of time constraints and other commitments, their inquiry was mainly focused on *Flotsam* (see Walsh, Cranitch and Maras, 2012); nonetheless, they have generously contributed to this book with their ideas and comments.

The initial teams had already been working for three years when they met Marcella Terrusi from the University of Bologna. Marcella is an expert in children's literature, and in particular in picturebooks, and she worked with Giorgia Grilli, a tenured researcher and instructor in children's literature especially interested in comparative analysis, to carry out the research in schools in Bologna. The final chapter in this book relates the story of their particular journey, and, although they were 'late arrivals', as they described themselves, their enthusiastic contribution was a welcome addition, which added a further dimension to the results of the inquiry.

Although the multiculturality of the researchers, teachers and other mediators could not equal the remarkable cultural range of the children (who originated from at least twenty different countries and spoke some forty languages between them), the diversity of the team members also reflects the new cosmopolitanism of collaborative inquiry as a form of intercultural exchange and learning. Although we worked in two main languages, English and Spanish, this did not diminish the importance of other languages such as Catalan and Italian (and, to a lesser extent, Scots). There were also humorous misunderstandings between different versions of Spanish (Castilian, Mexican, Puerto Rican, Venezuelan, Argentinean and even 'Spanglish') among both the children and the researchers. Finally, extra effort and goodwill were required to grasp the nuances of academic writing in these different languages and translate them into English for this publication.

As we followed the footsteps of the immigrant in *The Arrival* together with the children in the inquiry, we also followed, with great pleasure and satisfaction, the remarkable success of this book together with Shaun Tan's journey towards international fame. During the years in which we worked on the research and the writing, Tan received more and more prizes and accolades, not only for *The Arrival* but also for his other creations, such as the Academy Award for the Best Short Film for the animation of *The Lost Thing* (2000), and the prestigious Astrid Lindgren Memorial Award. Since then, he has produced not only more excellent books, such as *Tales from Outer Suburbia* (2009), but also a series of talks and essays (mostly digital publications) on his work. We have been fortunate enough to attend some of his talks but, most importantly, we feel we are fellow travellers with similar missions to promote curiosity and empathy through words and images.

Tan (2012) has spoken of 'moments of transitional migration' in both books and life when our expectations are challenged or disrupted and how the way we react to these defines who we are. Rather than reacting through apathy, hostility or prejudice, it is curiosity and empathy, or 'the will to find "otherness" actually interesting rather than problematic' (Tan, 2012, p. 31). He says he tends to favour inarticulate characters that may not say much, or know exactly how to say it in an articulate manner, but that have a hidden 'ocean of experiences' (textual, emotional, imaginary, aspirational) to communicate (Tan, 2011b). He often speaks of how he likes to remove the explanations from his books, leaving gaps so the reader can 'flood in the empty space' with their own experiences and personal associations (Tan, 2011b). Finally, he often emphasizes the importance of embracing ambiguities so that 'we rescue ourselves from an oblivion of closed meanings, a bankrupt literacy' (Tan, 2011a, p. 7). This is precisely what the inquiry set out to do through his wordless narrative: open spaces for the sharing of experiences, emotions and wonder that emerged from the encounter with his images.

Last on board, but most importantly, were the children who participated in the inquiry with us. They came to the project from a wide range of countries, with a variety of different languages, literacy backgrounds and migration experiences. However, whether they came from Peru, Moldavia, Congo or the Philippines, they brought knowledge, insights and enthusiasm, which enriched our investigation and created new forms of intercultural communication. We hope that we have been successful in bringing their voices together and transmitting some of their knowledge, experiences and enthusiasm in this book.

Slippery terms, sensitive issues . . .

For historical and political reasons, the terms used to describe people who leave one country and move to another, such as 'refugees', 'asylum seekers', 'economic migrants' or 'A8 migrants', have had a variety of connotations as well as being incorporated into legal terminology. One of these terms is 'immigrant', often associated with 'illegality' and other negative descriptors. Countries have therefore adopted different policies around the use of the word. Alongside this term are the labels used in referring to students with home languages that are different from the main language used in the society and the education system in which they are inscribed. As Cummins and Early note, 'These terms differ across geographical contexts and over time within geographical contexts. The various terms are loaded with ideological connotations and these have been hotly debated in academic literature' (Cummins and Early, 2011, p. xvi). These authors decide to use a variety of terms to reflect the shifting identity locations of students and their communities, and this reminds the reader of the ways in which identify shifts, and students are positioned by the societal power structures that surround them.

In this book, we have decided to recover the term 'immigrant', partly because it comes from a Latin root common to the main languages used in this inquiry and partly because we feel that it is a historical term that must be rescued from the negative connotations and have some of the positive connotations restored to it as a reflection on the wonderful children who participated in the inquiry. Teachers need to see through the institutional labels that often assume limitations to the potential within each child (Cummins and Early, 2011). The enthusiasm, intelligence, creativity, warmth and playfulness of the students in our inquiry reveal the potential they have to offer any country and their citizens.

The multilingual and multisite nature of the inquiry meant that researchers were working with different terminology to describe similar phenomena, and we have tried to include different terms but provide definitions when necessary to avoid confusion; for example, English language learners (ELL) is often used in the USA, while English as an additional language (EAL) is used in the UK (these are the terms we will use here, although we occasionally use 'bilingual learners' in the same sense). Terms such as 'literary circles' or 'pláticas literarias' are understood differently in each country, as are the histories of much-debated terms such as 'multicultural' or 'intercultural'. Again, we have aimed for clarity rather than a detailed explanation of how these terms are used in each context, although some indication of this is provided in Chapter 2.

Multilinguality also meant that constant translation, for example, from Catalan into Spanish, was necessary, including the final translation into English in this book. However, because we wanted to reflect this multilinguality, we have included the Spanish version, followed by the translation into English, particularly for the children's responses. These responses also required some editing for the sake of readability, but we have also attempted to retain each child's own particular way of using language.

Less sensitive but equally slippery are the terms used to describe the books that are at the centre of the inquiry, particularly *The Arrival*, which has won a variety of international prizes as a picturebook, a graphic novel, a comic and a 'bande dessinée'. This 130-page book, composed of a series of hundreds of 'silent' pencil drawings' (Tan, 2011a, p. 1) is a hybrid, multimodal text that crosses genre boundaries, and Tan himself has noted that it is a text that cannot be 'categorized'. While *Flotsam* can be clearly labelled as a 'picturebook', Tan's visual text is more like a 'picture' album (in Spanish, 'libro álbum'). Some may argue that it is more of a 'graphic novel'; however, what remains central to both books is that they are narratives without words. For the purposes of this book, we will use the term 'wordless picturebook' and 'wordless narrative' interchangeably (along with 'visual text'), and both terms will be discussed further in the chapters that follow.

Chapters and routes

Because this book was a journey in so many ways, it seemed inevitable to draw on this metaphor for organizing the chapters. This section sets out the structure and briefly describes the chapters in order to facilitate the reader's own journey. We are aware that readers approach books with different purposes so we invite them to join us at different stages along the way.

The book is divided into three parts. The first sets the scene for the inquiry, with the first chapter dealing with the overall frameworks that inform the book: migration and education, visual literacy and wordless picturebooks, and the way these intersect to highlight the theories behind the inquiry framework that underpins the choice of methods. The second chapter describes the three international contexts in which the inquiry took place, detailing the responses to the challenges of working with newly arrived, second-language children in each region, as well as the methodology and participants. Although it is not meant to be a comparative study, readers may find it useful to consider the different ways in which research and educational policies in each country have addressed the issue of migration. The third chapter begins with a description of the research design, including the books we used, followed by the process of data analysis. This chapter will perhaps be of more interest to those involved in research, although we feel that it may be of use to anyone working in an international collaboration.

The findings from the inquiry are presented in the four chapters that comprise the second part of the book. This is where we navigate the interpretative process and grapple with the themes that emerged from the oral and visual responses, and therefore the children's voices come through, together with our attempt to illuminate what they signify about the act of reading a wordless picturebook but also about migration and culture through bringing together different theoretical voices and our own engaged reflection. Chapter 4 looks at how the children used their personal experiences to reclaim the migrant experience – often fraught with difficulties – through their empathetic connections to the narrative. Chapter 5 examines a major type of response used by the children as they interpreted the text based on retellings and inferences. Chapter 6 discusses intertextuality and the ways in which the children drew upon different sources as landmarks to make meaning. In the last chapter in this section, Chapter 7, we focus on how the children engaged with the visual affordances of *The Arrival*.

Teachers will perhaps be most interested in the third part of the book, which deals with the aspects of mediation and pedagogy and how we feel they can transform literacy learning and teaching. Chapter 8 looks at the different ways that mediation occurred during the inquiry and how it helped foster a community that supports learning. We believe that the journey of discovery that we made in the process of this study has significant implications for teaching and can be followed in the classroom in a variety of ways; therefore, Chapter 9 addresses these implications and provides guidelines for using the image-based strategies in the classroom to develop a more inclusive pedagogy. It also includes a glimpse of the onward journeys of the research team, which may be of further interest to education professionals.

As we explained above, we were lucky to be joined by Marcella and Giorgia at a later stage in the project and the 'Coda' is a detailed and passionate account of the inquiry experience in Italy, with children in schools in Bologna where they were 'bewildered' but also in awe of what they call a 'silent book'. Finally, in the Conclusion, we tie together some of the most significant results of the inquiry.

Acknowledgements

The Glasgow team would like to thank the following: the UK Literacy Association (UKLA) and the University of Glasgow for providing the funding for this project; the schools and teachers involved in both the pilot and main projects, especially Janey Fellowes and Hagos Sinkie; our librarian friends, Honor Hania from the University of Glasgow and Gordana Nesterovic from the University of Strathclyde, for supplying us with references and recent publications; Osman Coban who helped with final revisions of style; and all our colleagues and students at the University of Glasgow who provided feedback and suggestions. A very special thank you to all the children who participated in this project and taught us so much about reading images and cultures.

The Barcelona team would like to thank the Ministerio de Educación y Ciencia, of the Spanish Government, for providing the funding for this project (I+D: EDU2008-02131/EDUC), and the schools, teachers and students involved in it.

Carmen Martínez-Roldán would like to thank the graduate students who participated during the different phases of the project: Sarah Newcomer, from

Arizona State University, Elisabeth Lúa and Margaux Pierre, from Teachers College, and, finally, Elizabeth Clark, from Teachers College, who helped with the revision of references for the book. Also, her thanks go to Dr Kathy G. Short and colleagues present at the 2012 Literacy Research Association conference who provided feedback and posed important questions that pushed our thinking further. A special thanks to the children who participated in the project and their families who made it possible for them to stay after school to engage in literature discussions.

Although, in the end, we could not include the contribution from Australia, we are grateful to the team there, particularly to Maureen Walsh for her constant support and enthusiasm.

We feel extremely fortunate that Shaun Tan agreed to write the Foreword for this book and thank him for the inspiration that started us all off and for the illuminating words and pictures he has offered us in the process.

Many thanks are also due to our editors and Kasia Figiel at Bloomsbury, Rosie Pattinson, for her patience and constant support, and to Dianne Murdoch for helping us to include the images from *The Arrival* and, finally, to Hachette Australia for giving us permission to publish them.

Part One

Embarking on the Journey

1

The Vessel: Theoretical Frameworks and Intersections

As we said in the Introduction, our aim was to explore how immigrant children from diverse backgrounds construct meaning from complex visual narratives, particularly when those narratives are about immigration issues. We wanted to find out if and how picturebooks could encourage reflection on the personal, social and intercultural issues involved in the immigrant experience. We were also interested in their experiences of visual literacy, particularly when encountering a wordless picturebook, where the images carry the weight of meaning. As we journeyed through the wide-ranging issues and aspects that concern immigrant children and their responses to visual narrative, we needed a vessel with a strong frame in order to reach our destination.

This chapter brings together some of the contextual and theoretical frameworks that helped us to understand the needs of the children but also to identify the strengths they bring to the educational context. We start with a summary review of some of the main issues affecting the literacy of children who have migrated to a new country and must learn a new language and culture. We present a broad view of immigration and how children fit into current contexts and discourses, and then focus on the educational concerns, moving towards aspects of language, literature and literacy in classrooms of increasing diversity. The second section of the chapter considers research on the use of images in education and on the processes of visual literacy. Here we also look at different forms of visual narratives before moving into the third section, where we focus on the particular affordances of wordless picturebooks and consider how previous research with real readers and these texts can inform our inquiry. The frameworks position our collective understandings of migration, visual literacy and picturebooks, and of the ways in which these topics can intersect. These intersections led to the development of our overall research questions and methods of inquiry. These structures also underlie the analytical chapters in Part 2, and will be further explored and strengthened by theories and research evidence as different aspects of the response are discussed within each of the four chapters.

Globalization, migration and education

The phenomenon known as *globalization*, caused by an acceleration of the movement of people, goods or ideas among countries and regions (Coatsworth, 2004; Sherif Trask, 2010), has been much debated but is certainly not new. According to Coatsworth (2004), the most recent cycle of globalization, which still produces large-scale migratory flows, began with the liberalization of international trade after the Second World War. Since then, significant changes have been introduced in the relationships among people as well as among the established links between the diverse communities. One result has been an increasing development of plural societies, characterized by a constant exchange of both goods and people, through the incessant flow of population between countries and continents.

Immigration is a universal experience, part of the human condition and history, and it has even been suggested that there is no nation prior to migration and that cultural cohesion of uniform groups is an imagined notion in any context (historically or geographically) (Vertovec, 2011). Globalization, however, has speeded up and facilitated the process of migration (Sherif Trask, 2010) with the result that, in recent decades, the massive displacement of populations has intensified, raising issues around the crossing of borders, both literal and virtual.[1] Forced migration and migration by those who decide to leave their country to find their place in other societies has been documented in historical records around the world. Winder, for example, looks back at the 'cosmopolitan ancestry' of the British (Winder, 2004, p. x) going back 25,000 years (!) and, although he concedes that migration 'has never been easy', he notes that 'it cannot be conceived of as a single experience' and that it should be seen as 'a form of enrichment and renewal' (Winder, 2004, p. xiii). Despite this, essentialized notions of national cultures have led, in many countries, to the consideration of migration as a threat (Vertovec, 2011).

Ideological perceptions of migrants, reinforced by political and economic messages, continue to influence these policies of reception. These perceptions often ignore that, for the most part, the host country benefits from immigrants both in terms of 'filling labour needs at different levels of the economy and, more important, injecting into society the energies, ambitions, and skills of positively selected groups' (Portes and Rumbaut, 1996, p. 26). Terminology also has an effect, as the word 'immigrant' has become linked to 'illegal' and other criminalized and derogatory terms and these labels can influence the orientation of a society's response to new arrivals. Some scholars prefer the concept of 'diaspora' over 'immigration' because it offers more positive ways of thinking, moving away from expectations of racial and cultural erasure involved in the process and instead creating something new as they reconstruct themselves and their culture.

As a consequence of evolving perspectives and policies, host countries have adopted diverse models of reception. Generally, the first proposals to address this issue were based on the notion of 'assimilation' or 'acculturation', which imply a total identification of the immigrants with the host culture (Portes and Rumbaut, 1996; Rama, 1987). A consequence of such expectations was the 'disappearance' or abandoning of the original culture. As the number of immigrants increased, later models tended towards the process of 'integration' and policies were developed that involved 'assimilation' in the public sphere together with a respect for diversity in the private context. Currently, immigration policies tend to opt for host models of 'accommodation', which affirm and recognize, at a public level, the cultural characteristics of each migrant group (Colomer, 2012). Another model is that of 'transculturation', defined by Bueno as:

> a cultural process that implies transferring cultural content from one culture to another and that involves creatively taking and relating different aspects of different societies and cultures. From this perspective, individuals learn various cultural codes allowing them to build bridges between the many spaces in which they move. (Bueno, 1996, p. 26)

There is now a large body of literature on the topic of migration, which discusses the factors that lead to emigration as well as the implications for those who arrive in a new country – legal, economic, social, cultural and educational, among others. In this section, we can only consider some of the overall factors and implications that have an effect on the contexts in which our inquiry took place, keeping in mind that these contexts all have their differences (and which we will explore in Chapter 2). We will also focus on the impact of migration on children, particularly in the area of education in general, and language and literacy learning in particular.

The causes of migration and the impact on children

The diversity of contemporary migrant populations and situations in terms of origins, contexts of exit, social class background and skills means that 'immigrants' cannot be considered as a single group. There are also many differences in terms of their experiences of adaptation and incorporation even within one host country (Portes and Rumbaut, 1996; Winder, 2004). An example of this diversity is the heterogeneous composition of the most recent groups, which can include labour migrants, professionals and entrepreneurs, as well as refugees and asylum seekers. While most of the causes of migration are either socioeconomic or political, there are differences between those usually considered 'voluntary' and 'forced' migrants.

People become refugees when they feel their home is no longer a safe place and must find an alternative place to live (Haddad, 2008). According to United Nations (2008) estimates, global refugees number around 11.4 million people. Asylum claims between 2008 and 2012 reached 313,540 in the USA, 137,940 in the UK and 16,260 in Spain (UNHCR, 2012). In 2011, claims reflected the conflicts in West Africa and in the Arab world, with rising numbers of asylum seekers from Côte d'Ivoire, Libya and Syria (UNHCR, 2012). The countries of origin of the largest number of claimants were Afghanistan, China and Iraq. Over the years, a great deal has been written about the causes and impact of this phenomenon; however, as Rutter warns, 'being a refugee is a bureaucratic identity' (Rutter, 2006, p. 33) and greater awareness of the implications of such a 'label' is necessary if the responses of host countries are to really meet migrants' needs in terms of welfare and education.

From an economic perspective, poverty or the lack of job opportunities in the country of origin force people to cross borders in search of better salaries and a better quality of life. Individual or familial economic benefits can be obtained through the major flows of money and goods between both origin and host countries; however, these benefits are often accompanied by a process of struggle and frustration due to newcomers' underemployment or social demotion in the host country (Suárez-Orozco and Suárez-Orozco, 2001). The emotional strain is often compounded by immigrants having left their children behind while they settle and find jobs. On the other hand, because people also make the decision to emigrate because others have done so before them, they can often join family, friends and communities, a situation that can provide emotional, economic and social support, as in the case of Hispanics arriving into established communities in the USA.

Whatever the reasons for migration, the decision will have a powerful impact on families and particularly on children. Suárez-Orozco and Suárez-Orozco remind us that 'the story of today's immigrants is also a saga of their children: a fascinating and critical – but too often forgotten – chapter of the immigrant experience' (Suárez-Orozco and Suárez-Orozco, 2001, p. 1). In addition, some researchers argue that 'children fundamentally shape the nature and course of families' migration experiences' (Orellana *et al.*, 2001, p. 587). Children will often undergo long periods of separation from their parents and from their siblings while one or both parents go ahead to try to find jobs or political asylum. Sometimes, the children are sent on their own by desperate parents or attempt to make their own way as they flee from war, gangs or abusive situations; thousands of unaccompanied minors arrive every year to the USA, the UK, Spain, Italy, Australia and other host countries. It is not only the separation or the journey that can affect their physical and emotional wellbeing but also the arrival in a foreign country where they will have to deal with economic, legal and social consequences along with the implications for their ethnic and cultural identities (Salazar Parreñas, 2005; M. Suárez-Orozco, 2001). The support provided for these asylum-seeker children – with or without their families – varies greatly according to the laws and policies of each country. More generally, the ways in which any immigrant child is welcomed will have a crucial role in how they adapt (Suárez-Orozco and Suárez-Orozco, 2001).

In the USA in recent years, family regrouping or reunification has become one of the main reasons for migrating: 80 per cent of immigrant children arrive in a new place in these circumstances (Suárez-Orozco, 2008). However, this process can also be fraught with difficulties and result in the destabilization of the 'old' family roles and norms. As children go through this process, they are often subjected to changes in their carers, distancing from their 'extended family' and situations where parental authority must be renegotiated as cultural references change in the new environment (Suárez-Orozco, 2008). Even very young children may be forced to assume new and onerous roles and responsibilities, such as acting as interpreters and as mediators of the new social and cultural context. Campano observes that 'they feel a sense of responsibility not only to their immediate family, but also to networks of kin that extend beyond the immediate neighbourhood to various diaspora communities around the world' (Campano, 2007, p. 15). The children are also often in charge of keeping the family connected to the country of origin through technology (Orellana *et al.*, 2001).

There are still gaps in the research on the long-term effects of immigration on children's wellbeing and achievement. Referring to studies from both the USA and Europe, Sherif Trask points out that it is difficult to separate the variables given they range from cultural issues to issues of poverty and discrimination (2010, p. 76). However, while the contexts may differ, to some extent, all children will feel the impact of one or more of the following issues highlighted by Rutter (2003, p. 13) in reference to arrivals to the UK:

- having an interrupted education in the country of origin;
- having horrific experiences in their home countries and during their flight to the UK (for a small number, this affects their ability to settle and rebuild their lives);
- living with families who experience a drop in their standard of living and status in society;
- changing care arrangements: losing parents or usual carers;
- having parents who are emotionally absent;
- living with families who do not know their legal and social rights in the UK, including their rights to basic services such as education and healthcare, and who encounter problems securing education, healthcare or benefits; and
- speaking little or no English on arrival.

Implications for education

One of the most important variables that have an effect on immigrant children as individuals as well as on their future contribution as citizens of their new country is education. M. Suárez-Orozco stresses that 'Schooling in the era of globalization, arguably more than ever before, profoundly shapes the current and future well-being of children, as well as their chances and opportunities' (M. Suárez-Orozco, 2001, p. 345) and proposes a new research agenda for the study of immigration and education in this new globalized era, one that is comparative and looks at the key issues of identities and belonging. For example, Rutter (2006) points to an increasing tendency to consider refugee children's needs more holistically, in a way that emphasizes 'resilience' rather than 'trauma' and which leads to better support both inside and outside school with an impact on education overall. However, many of the current practices that appear to look at these issues continue to focus on the challenges that diversity brings to the educational system. Some have resulted in 'ethnic identification' (Bautista, 1988, cited in Suárez-Orozco and Suárez-Orozco, 2001) and further stereotyping, as immigrants are defined and grouped based on their ethnicity and bound to these definitions. The consequences of this social gaze can be the racism, discrimination, physical or 'symbolic' violence often present in school (Bourdieu and Passeron, 1977).

'Multiculturalism', another often-abused term, attempts to deal with the cultural diversity resulting from immigration but has become an empty and contested idea. Too often it is based on a discourse that celebrates difference but does not seek integration, and it ignores the potential of this process for the creation of new cultures. It often leads to diversity being seen as a problem when cultural diversity can, and should, be a resource. Researchers have proposed new terms, such as 'cosmopolitanism', 'critical multiculturalism' or 'interculturalism', among others. For Vertovec, 'super-diversity' considers the emergence of 'post-multicultural perspectives that seek to foster both the recognition of diversity and the maintenance of collective national identities' (Vertovec, 2010, p. 83). Similar concerns have led researchers in the field of education either to reject the concept of multiculturalism altogether or to highlight critical multicultural perspectives, such as Banks and Banks (2001) and Nieto (2000) regarding the education of immigrants and learners from different communities.

Larrosa questions the complacency of those who are responsible for disseminating the discourse of multiculturality and argues that it trivializes the matter of difference when it is based on the limited practice of 'exhibiting' superficial aspects such as food, costume and stories (Larrosa, 2002, p. 74), a practice that Nieto (1995) describes as the 'heroes and holidays' approach. Suárez-Orozco and Suárez-Orozco (2001) also allude to this kind of celebration of 'folklorism', and argue that (in the USA) this ideology leads to the appearance of ethnic categories that respond to stereotypes that can hamper the construction of a personal and autonomous identity. This approach also obscures the real contributions and strengths that immigrant children can bring to the educational system of the host country. One way of bringing these to light is through Nieto's (2009) proposal of a critical view of multiculturalism with a model that engages learners in critical analysis of different perspectives found in texts, in the curriculum and the use of such learning 'to understand and act on the inconsistencies they uncover' (Nieto, 2000, p. 317). For Nieto, affirming diversity needs to be approached as personal, collective and institutional change, and multicultural education needs to be framed within a context of social justice and critical pedagogy.

One practice that reflects this critical perspective is proposed by Campano in his work in schools in the USA. He proposes the 'ethnic/immigrant narrative' (Campano, 2007, p. 13) as a research method for analysing the role that migration stories, narrated by the children themselves, can play not only in the classroom and in the school periphery but also in general educational practice. Although invisible and unrewarded in the educational system, this type of narrative work allowed Campano to discover that

> Storytelling is one way in which students can begin to understand and perhaps gain a degree of control over the past experiences that may not have been fully intelligible at the time of their occurrence [...] Events of the past are given new meanings in new educational contexts. (Campano, 2007, p. 52)

This approach echoes the words Tan has used to contrast the 'official' discourse about immigration with the experience of individuals:

> The subject of immigration is often abstracted by the language of politics, economics and media, its themes generalised as a set of broad causes and consequences. In contrast, the anecdotal stories being told by immigrants themselves do not operate on the level of collective statistics at all. They are a constellation of intimate, human-sized aspirations and dilemmas: how to learn a phrase, where to catch a train, where to buy an item, whom to ask for help and, perhaps most importantly, how to *feel* about everything. (Tan, 2010, p. 10)

The emotional, empathetic aspect highlighted by Tan relates back to Campano's project because it means rethinking the classroom and the school as collaborative, communal spaces where children are offered culturally and linguistically significant materials through the opportunity to design a 'literacy curriculum built around their own experiences' (Campano, 2007, p. 31).

Language, literature and literacies

Just as populations are shaped by social, political and cultural changes, so too are literacy practices. In addressing the educational needs of immigrant children, it is necessary to take account of the links between literacy and language and the role these play in their life, as well as the types of texts they access. However, reading and writing texts is not enough: in order to make value judgements about their intended use and meaning, educators must help children learn to be critical of the texts they encounter (CfE, online; Reedy, 2010). In addition to considering the changes in literacy practices, the United Kingdom Literacy Association (UKLA) calls for a number of ways for educators to move forward with a shared vision of literacy that will allow the promotion of pedagogies and curricula for the future that are locally and globally relevant to all children. This includes clearer links to diverse home language and literacy experiences, where children's previous learning and 'funds of knowledge' (Moll, Amanti, Neff and Gonzalez, 1992) are used and built on appropriately within classrooms. One way of doing this is through children's literature, which can deepen understanding of the self as well as extend the boundaries of the personal experiences. Literature allows children to play with language, try out new voices and identities and come to closer realizations of who they are in the twenty-first century (Reedy, 2010).

For ethnic-minority groups, participation in a specific society, particularly through the community and the school, means interacting with cultural and linguistic issues that transform the identities of both the 'locals' and the 'newcomers'. Language plays a decisive role in this interaction and is, in turn, also transformed (McGonigal and Arizpe, 2007). This is of particular importance in the contexts of this inquiry where nuances of power and appropriateness are already sensitive issues in the interaction of foreign dialects and language choice within public, political and personal discourse – now altered by the addition of minority and community languages, and by new writers and thinkers emerging from such multilingual backgrounds.

There has been an increased awareness that bilingualism is the norm rather than the exception, given that more than half of the world population is bilingual. Knowledge of other languages is increasingly seen as something positive, which should be nurtured and which has the potential not only to increase bilingual children's cognitive abilities (Cummins, 2001) and develop their understanding of new languages, but also to enrich the host culture. It has also been recognized that bilinguality means not just speaking but living in two different languages, so that literacy practices in the context of the 'home' language and of the other school or locality languages are just as important.[2] The recognition of the value of bilinguality also implies that host communities need to stop thinking about immigration in terms of deficit and to begin understanding this reality as an invaluable opportunity for wealth and knowledge (Campano, 2007; Suárez-Orozco and Suárez-Orozco, 2001). This should lead us towards educational practices that take into account the particularities of the children as an interpersonal approach rather than mere 'exoticism'.

A special context designed to support this work is the use of 'multicultural' or 'global' literature in the classroom. Children's literature that reflects cultural diversity has the potential to broaden students' perspectives by introducing them to the lives, language, social practices and ways of thinking of groups different from their own and, in the process, learn to critically consider diverse perspectives

(Botelho and Rudman, 2009). For those children who find themselves and their experiences reflected in the texts, multicultural literature can provide a special context for telling their stories and thus reinventing themselves through their narratives (Martínez-Roldán, 2003; Medina and Martínez-Roldán, 2011). These types of books can also provide opportunities for children to go beyond the 'heroes and holidays' (Nieto, 2003) mentioned above and provide students with deeper insights into other countries and cultures. With appropriate mediation, this literature has great potential to build intercultural understandings leading children both to recognize their common humanity and to value cultural differences (Short and Thomas, 2011).

To further highlight the changes in perceptions of immigration, as the recent conferences of the International Board of Books for Young Children (IBBY) illustrates, the number of books addressing this topic is increasing.[3] While some may still present a romanticized and often assimilationist view of the process of immigration, others offer insights into the complexities of these issues. *The Arrival* has been widely recognized as one of the most important books on the topic so far.

Crossing borders with visual literacy

Visuals have long been used as aids in the teaching of language and other literacy skills; however, many of them, having being created for a specific purpose, have a practical rather than an aesthetic value. Because of the excellent quality of their graphics and the playful yet sophisticated relationship between words and pictures, picturebooks and, more recently, graphic novels have increasingly been adopted as useful teaching aids, not only for language and literacy but also for approaching a raft of topics such as the environment, disability or multiculturalism, as well as for therapeutic purposes. In order to find out how visual narratives can best support immigrant children in both their language development and in reflecting on their own and others' experience of migration, in this section we return to some of the arguments for using images in education, particularly the relationship between looking and thinking in the active processes of visual literacy. We then summarize what we have learned from previous research on response to picturebooks, particularly from studies with ethnic-minority and EAL/ELL readers, before moving on to the final section of this chapter on the particular affordances of wordless picturebooks and children's responses to these visual media forms.

Images and education

The idea of using visual images for teaching children is certainly not a new one. It can be traced back as far as the seventeenth century to the educational reformer Jan Amos Comenius who created his book of labelled pictures, *Orbis sensualium pictus* (1658), with the intention of making learning easier for children. At the same time, in England, Comenius' translator, Charles Hoole, also suggested using pictures to 'entice' children to learn, and the use of prints and pictures as an important didactic device was also encouraged by John Locke and François de Salignac de la Mothe-Fénelon, among other European educationalists. In the eighteenth century, new and cheaper printing technologies brought more pictures into children's hands through battledores, games and books such as those published by John Newbery. Advances in technology in the nineteenth century allowed the reproduction of coloured images, which soon became part of educational books and other materials.

Although pictures have since become a ubiquitous part of books for children, either for decoration, instruction or aesthetic pleasure, research on the visual in books and classrooms has not developed at the same pace. This may be due in part to the idea that once children learn to read there is less 'need' for images. In her review of 'the visual in learning', Jewitt cites Burn and Dixon's argument that English as a subject has 'a long and intimate relationship with the visual' (Burn and Dixon, 2005, cited in Jewitt, 2008, p. 11), but she also points out that 'Where image is acknowledged in educational settings it is often celebrated for its potential to interest and motivate learners and the link between visual forms of knowledge and learning is seldom made' (Jewitt, 2008, p.15).

However, Heath's explanation of how interpreting the visual arts is linked to the construction of narrative provides crucial evidence for the importance of looking at images:

> Vision is our most efficient way of gathering information about the world around us; hence the filling in of gaps – or the fitting together of parts to make a whole – is highly dependent on visual attention (Driver and Baylis 1998). Such visual focus, motivated by intention, enables the viewer to take on agency or to see with the anticipation that creates a narrative of dynamic events. Fluency in aspects of later language development, particularly the use of conditionals to create hypothetical scenarios, comes with increased visual focus and roles that call for an evaluative, interpretive stance. Speakers who feel a real need to communicate the emerging narrative strive for coherence, using metaphors and other verbal means to call up visual images in listeners (Gernsbacher and Givon 1995). (Heath, 2006, p. 144)

Influential art theorists and educators such as Rudolf Arnheim, Ernst Gombrich, Elliot Eisner and W.J.T. Mitchell have also stressed the active and complex thinking that goes on in the viewer's mind when confronted with a work of art and the potential of art to further cultivate these thinking dispositions. Working on Howard Gardner's Project Zero research team, Perkins (1994) argues that the affective impact of a work of art encourages higher cognitive functions as well as inviting personal involvement and the creation of connections to different human experiences.

The argument for the educational value of exposure to and discussion of visual images is now hard to ignore, and the need for a greater understanding of the role of 'visual forms of knowledge and learning' (Jewitt, 2008) is essential for educators working with children and young people in the screen-dominated twenty-first century. It is in the exploration of the visual image and its potential for developing thinking and for connecting with others where the ability or competence that has been defined as 'visual literacy' can provide the tools for educators to understand the meaning-making resources of images as well as the ways in which viewers or readers respond to them.

The active process of visual literacy

The concept of 'visual literacy' has been taken up by a variety of disciplines, from art to digital technology, and therefore is defined differently according to each particular perspective. The International Visual Literacy Association ascribes the coinage of this term to Debes in the late 1960s who defined it as 'a group of vision-competencies', which can help 'discriminate and interpret' the visual in the environment (Debes, 1969, p. 27). Yenawine (1997) defines it as 'the ability to find meaning in imagery', and Sinatra stresses the importance of links to past experiences: 'the active reconstruction of past experiences with incoming visual information to obtain meaning (Sinatra, 1986, p. 5). Allen (1994) believes that any definition of visual literacy should be extended to take account of research into English in education as well as critical, philosophical and art historical discussion. Raney warns against assuming there is a 'fixed' or 'single code' of interpretation, which may happen as a result of boiling visual literacy down to 'visual syntax', and also widens definitions by placing visual literacy in a historical and social context: 'it is the history of thinking about what images and objects mean, how they are put together, how we respond to or interpret them, how they might function as modes of thought, and how they are seated within the societies which gave rise to them' (Raney, 1998, p. 38).

As part of their argument for the importance of images as a central medium of communication, Kress and van Leeuwen (1995, 2001) have developed the influential 'grammar of visual design', which looks at a social semiotic code for pictures, although they are careful to note that ideology will always be present in the construction and interpreting of codes. Also, and along with other scholars involved in 'The New London Group', Kress has highlighted the need for new literacy pedagogy that explores how the changes in technology affect traditional forms of reading and writing, as well as how different modalities interact with each other in the meaning-making process, creating 'multiliteracies' (New London Group, 1996).

In our inquiry, we understood 'visual literacy' as an ongoing, dynamic process that matches the idea of linguistic literacy, and therefore concurred with Crouch's definition of visual literacy as 'an active process that can lead from an awareness of the codes of visual communication to more analytical, critical reading of visual texts' (Crouch, 2008, p. 195). Frey and Fisher's definition expands this idea and links it to reading comprehension and the interaction with text:

> We think of visual literacy as describing the complex act of meaning making using still or moving images. As with reading comprehension, visually literate learners are able to make connections, determine importance, synthesize information, evaluate, and critique. Further, these visual literacies are interwoven with textual ones, so that their interaction forms the basis for a more complete understanding. (Frey and Fisher, 2008, p. 1)

Underlying the Visual Journeys inquiry are the beliefs that, although response to visual stimulus is innate and 'looking' is intrinsically related to 'thinking', visual literacy can be supported and developed in educational contexts not only as a tool in learning language and linguistic literacy, but also as a skill to be developed in itself. Following the parallel with linguistic literacy, however, we do not see visual literacy as a simple 'decoding' skill but as a way of deepening understanding and critical appreciation through the viewer's active engagement in the interpretative process. From the researchers mentioned above, we take the point that images are a result of social, historical and ideological constructs, and our responses are informed by previous experiences, including social and cultural expectations of literacy practices (Heath, 1983) and 'funds of knowledge' (Moll *et al.*, 1992). We also consider Nodelman's argument that, 'As artifacts of our own culture, picture books require and help to construct readers and viewers who will take their place in that culture' (Nodelman, 2000, p. 41).

Picturebooks, graphic novels and diverse readers

With their characteristic blending of exceptional artistic images with narratives that often arouse complex emotions and their invitation to explore the language of the visual, picturebooks and graphic novels invite readers to use their previous knowledge and then to reassess and extend it alongside new ideas and feelings. Through their often ambiguous, ironic and playful nature, they expand the capacity to make meaning through image and to engage with language in an alternative medium that contributes to their understanding of language and communication as a whole. Tan writes that

> What makes art and literature so interesting is that it presents us with unusual things that encourage us to ask questions about what we already know. It's about returning us, especially we older readers, to a state of unfamiliarity, offering an opportunity to rediscover some new insight through things we don't quite recognise. This is perhaps what reading and visual literacy are all about – and what picture books are good for – continuing the playful inquiry that began in childhood. (Tan, 2001)

Within this active process, there is an important role not only for the ideas and previous knowledge of the viewer but also for feelings and emotions. Tan (2012) urges us to look at an image and ask 'How does it make me feel?' and 'What does it make me think about?' Pushing us to go further towards self-reflection, he argues that these questions may lead to an exploration of 'mixed feelings' and a reassessment of existing knowledge, given that the 'answers are therefore not in the work, a story or picture, but in the readers' contemplation of their own reactions' (Tan, 2012, p. 28).

As Tan writes, presenting 'unusual' or unfamiliar things to the viewer or reader – an artistic strategy brought to the fore in the twentieth century and known as 'defamiliarization' (Shklovskij, 2004) – is one way of capturing and maintaining their attention. One particular type of picturebook that relies on this strategy is what has been called the 'postmodern' picturebook and it achieves this through a variety of different techniques, such as presenting multiple and/or fragmented viewpoints, making use of intertextuality and indeterminacy, breaking traditional genre boundaries, crossing borders between fantasy and reality, abandoning linear chronology and complicating the interaction between words and pictures (Anstey and Bull, 2004; Nikola-Lisa, 1994; Pantaleo, 2009). Postmodern picturebooks are now often used in the classroom as a way of helping children to explore the construction of meaning. Despite their complexities, the evidence is that children are able to enjoy and deal with these texts as well as to learn from them (Arizpe, 2009; Arizpe and Styles, 2003, Pantaleo, 2008).

Graphic novels, many of which also present postmodern characteristics, are also being brought into the classroom to stimulate learning in a variety of ways. Along with the features of comics that have engaged children for decades, graphic novels contain aspects that some consider raise them to 'a more ambitious' and 'meaningful' level than comics (Campbell, n.d., cited in Gravett, 2005; Evans, 2013; Tabachnick, 2009). They tend to be used with older children or young adults. Some of the benefits of using them in the classroom, and which also apply to picturebooks, have been highlighted by several scholars including Alvermann and Hagood (2000), Boatright (2010), Lavin (1998), Schwarz (2006), Pantaleo (2011) and Yang (2008): 1) the development of informational, visual and media literacies; 2) the ability to motivate all levels of readers; 3) an increase in student engagement; 4) the opportunity to develop critical literacy; 5) the inclusion of diverse voices within the curriculum; and 6) the possibility for opening discussion around issues of social justice within the classroom.

What concerns us here is the 'inclusion of different voices', not only as a result of global and multicultural themes – in the sense we have discussed these terms above – brought into the classroom through visual narratives, but mainly as the result of the creation of the space and opportunity for diverse readers to engage with these texts. The results of initial studies in the UK on the interaction between picturebooks and ethnic-minority children or EAL learners strongly indicate that engagement with picturebooks benefits language skills (increasing linguistic repertoires and confidence in expressing themselves) and allows them to demonstrate their knowledge and experiences and negotiate cultural understandings (Arizpe, 2009; Bromley, 1996; Coulthard, 2003). More recently, studies in other countries such as Spain (Colomer and Fittipaldi, 2012) and Portugal (Mourão, 2009, 2012) show similar findings. These studies support our premise that working with visual narratives to extend visual literacy contributes positively to the development of a variety of linguistic skills as well as to a better understanding of the complex experience of migration, of both an individual's personal story and that of others.

Wordless picturebooks: Affordances and readers

The collective research of authors working within the sociocultural framework of the New Literacy Studies (Kress and van Leeuwen, 2001; Street, 2003; The

New London Group, 1996) challenges us to consider the multimodality of the texts that our children and youth are using in their daily lives. Wordless narratives serve as prime examples of such multimodality in that they prioritize the reading of images through a process of visual literacy; in other words, they magnify the invitation to readers to consider visual elements such as colour, shading, panel layout and perspective as well as the usual literacy elements of character, setting and plot. In this section, we first discuss some of the theories that help understand how wordless picturebooks work and the affordances of this particular medium and what readers must do in order to make sense of them. We then review some of the reader-response research with wordless picturebooks. Finally, in setting the stage for our inquiry, we note three fundamental points that guided our work within the theoretical frameworks discussed in this chapter.

Wordless picturebooks and their affordances

Since the 1960s, wordless picturebooks have slowly but surely become a recognized genre within the world of literature for children, with Beckett noting that they have become 'a contemporary publishing trend' with some specially created wordless series and some author-illustrators working exclusively in this genre (Beckett, 2012, pp. 83–4). As we mentioned earlier, many famous artists have created wordless picturebooks; however, some parents and teachers still consider these as books for the pre-literate child and express concerns about how to 'read' them with their children and whether children will 'gain' anything from them. On the other hand, some educators and researchers have long been using them to develop language and other skills (Arizpe, 2013a).

It is often pointed out that, even discounting the information about the publication, all picturebooks have at least a few words, usually in the title or as peritext but sometimes also embedded in the images themselves (e.g. the name of a street or a shop), and that these can prove highly significant. This has led to the use of terms such as 'almost wordless', 'nearly wordless' or 'sparse verbal text' but as yet there is no consensus about exactly how many words determine one kind or another (Bosch, in press). Rowe prefers to call them 'sequenced picture texts' (Rowe, 1996, p. 221), and Beckett points out that 'wordless narratives' might be a more accurate description (Beckett, 2012, p. 121). In this book, we understand a 'wordless narrative' (whether picturebook or graphic novel) to be a text where the visual image carries the weight of the meaning and where, as Nières-Chevrel puts it, the absence of words is 'not a simple feat of artistry [instead it is] totally relevant and in keeping with topic' (Nières-Chevrel, 2010, p. 137). In other words, even when there is little or no print, there is a significance in this lack, which contributes to the overall meaning of the narrative.

In the USA, these texts are sometimes known as 'pictorial texts', while, interestingly, in both Spanish and Italian, some of the suggestions for labelling these books emphasize the role of the reader: they are sometimes called 'lectura de imágenes' [reading images] or, in Italy, 'silent books' (they use the English words). This active engagement on the reader's part is also emphasized by the two award-winning illustrators of the wordless picturebooks we worked with in this inquiry who have spoken and written widely about their craft: Wiesner and Tan. Tan (2012) emphasizes the reader's role as a 'co-creator' who needs to 'invest meaning', and Wiesner states that 'the reader is an integral part of the storytelling process' and that

> [wordless picturebooks] require the fullest use of an artist's visual storytelling skills and personal interpretation on the part of the viewer . . . it is the reader's own voice that interprets and recounts the narrative. Readers bring their own personal responses to the book, and they guide themselves through it. Readers are made more active participants in the story. (Wiesner, 1992a, p. vii)

Thus, both illustrators point to the reader's more autonomous role but also to the implications this has for the pace of reading and for the reader's creative narrative skills. Their perspectives reflect the radical change in the expectations of wordless picturebook makers, which, prior to the 1970s, tended to be of a pedagogical nature, given that their main purpose was to 'stimulate exchange' between pre-readers and mediators (Beckett, 2012, p. 81). Beckett quotes other creators of wordless picturebooks such as Quentin Blake who speaks of the need to 'meet' and become 'involved' with the text (Blake, cited in Beckett, 2012, p. 107), while Taniuchi refers to readers 'immersing' themselves and 'inventing' their own story (Taniuchi, cited in Beckett, 2012, p. 102).

Children's literature studies also provide insights into the demands made by wordless picturebooks on the reader and, although seminal scholars such as Nodelman (1988), Nikolajeva and Scott (2001) and D. Lewis (2001) do not explore this genre at length, some of their general insights are helpful. For example, Nodelman's (2000) analysis of the implied viewer of picturebooks identifies the invitations or expectations of the picturebook in general, among others the following assumptions: that the child is the implied reader; knowledge about book conventions, narrative and the world; and the signs imply someone capable of making the expected sense out of them as intended by the creator and about the reality of these signs. In short, they are encouraged to become meaning-makers, 'actively engaged in solving the puzzles' (Nodelman, 2000, p. 37).

The active role of the reader in wordless picturebooks has also been recognized by literary and art critics. Rowe, for example, refers to art history to argue that 'meanings do not reside in the image alone [...] the spectator becomes a participant in the creation of meanings [...] individual interpretations are an amalgam of personal and prior visual experiences [so] each viewing holds the possibility of new meanings' (Rowe, 1996, p. 221). The level of complexity at which the visual features appear (for example, whether pictures are in a temporal order, more conventional codes of meaning are used or how closely sequenced the pictures are) will determine the level of sophistication required of the reader in their 'co-creating' role. Although the reader's agency is fundamental in reading any type of picturebook, it is the degree to which the reader is expected to actively engage that marks the difference between picturebooks with and without words (Arizpe, 2013a, 2013b). Picturebook theory and reader-response studies help identify more exactly all the skills that this active engagement involves.

Taking what we know generally about picturebooks into consideration and adding more specific understandings detailed by shorter but more specific studies on wordless picturebooks (in particular those by Bosch, 2010, 2013; Nières-Chevrel, 2010; and Rowe, 1996), we now have a better idea of the main meaning-making activities and skills expected of the reader (Arizpe, 2013a, 2013b). Given the absence of words, these activities and skills must be heightened in every way so that they are even more attentive to significant graphic elements, strive harder to link the sequence of images and dig more deeply into their intertextual knowledge, using all of this to make inferences but at the same time being open to constantly revising their interpretations. Even experienced picturebook readers have been observed to assume a more active co-authoring role as they participate in a process of visual literacy 'meta-awareness' by reflecting constantly on the changing expectations and interpretations (Pantaleo, 2005). These activities correspond quite closely to the affordances mentioned above and stress the interaction that is required if any sense is to be made of the wordless texts. They are part of the process of visual literacy where an initial awareness can develop to the extent that an analytical stance also involves a meta-awareness of these affordances or expectations. Some studies of readers responding to wordless picturebooks reflect at least the initial part of this process.

'Real' readers responding to wordless picturebooks

There is now a considerable body of research that has looked at how children respond not only to picturebooks in general but to wordless picturebooks in particular. These studies focus on ways in which readers approach and make meaning from wordless picturebooks and, despite the differences in context, readers, books and methodologies, there is a shared understanding of the act of reading as a 'transaction' between a text and an active reader (Rosenblatt, 1968). Yet investigating readers' responses is not always straightforward (Nodelman, 2010), nor is it an exclusively individual activity. In the case of wordless picturebooks, as Arizpe (2013a) points out, there has been a tendency to ask readers to 'verbalize' the story, resulting in responses that may not reflect what the children really think about the visual narrative. Graham (1998), for example, who carried out individual reading sessions with a selection of wordless picturebooks with children between four and six years of age, notes their 'perplexed' responses and mis-readings, as well as the tendency to provide a running commentary in the present tense, which resulted in restricted, monotonous language rather than fluent stories. As Arizpe argues, what the picturebook demands is an attentiveness to the language of the image that cannot be easily expressed and instead involves visual perception, imaginative play and reflection before it can be put into words. Findings from studies that did not demand a 'retelling' have revealed that when looking at wordless picturebooks readers make use of strategies similar to those for reading texts with a combination of print and image (Crawford and Hade, 2000) but they rely heavily both on their previous visual reading experience and on intertextual and world knowledge (Bosch and Duran, 2009; Crawford and Hade, 2000). The complexity of the reading process is even greater, as readers must engage in all of the activities mentioned in the previous section.

The use of effective comprehension strategies together with the process of reflection are higher order literacy skills that the students apply to their writing (Pantaleo and Bomphray, 2011). As Ghiso and McGuire show, teacher mediation can maximize the affordances of wordless picturebooks and they observed how both teachers and readers responded to 'the key role of illustrations in communicating information'; the potential of the sparse verbal text; grammar relationships such as 'cause and effect'; connections to life experiences and elements that created story cohesion such as structure and recurring patterns (Ghiso and McGuire, 2007, pp. 347–55). They conclude that 'By requiring much of the reader – determining relationships, inferring emotional states, and pulling together episodic plots – picturebooks with sparse verbal text support the development of an active literary response stance which readers can apply to all varieties of texts' (Ghiso and McGuire, 2007, p. 356).

In sum, research on readers' responses confirms that the wordless nature of the picturebooks demands a heightened co-authoring role that requires taking risks with the imagination, activating intertextual and cultural knowledge and trusting in the readers' ability to make sense of the story. The degree to which readers are aware of and are able to respond to the affordances of wordless picturebooks depends mostly on previous experience with picturebooks with and without words. Although there is usually an initial surprise at the lack of words, any anxiety about the absence of written support systems usually quickly disappears (Crawford and Hade, 2000). Readers enjoy the freedom to create their own parallel texts (Goodman, 1996). They also respond more playfully, both bodily and verbally.

Wordless books and graphic novels therefore seem particularly suitable to observe how readers make meaning through multiple strategies, including the creation of such parallel texts. Gaining a better understanding of this process can help teachers support students' comprehension and interpretative work more effectively. In the next chapter, we move into the national contexts of immigration and education and describe particular methodologies, presenting the readers who participated in the inquiry and looking in more depth at the selected wordless picturebooks used in our journey.

Notes

1   According to the United Nations, approximately 191 million individuals (3% of the world population) were living outside of their native countries as of 2005 (United Nations, 2008).

2   In the United States, for example, the percentage of public school students who were English language learners was higher in 2010–11 (4.7 million or 10 %) than in 2002–3 (4.1 million or 9%). In addition, in the 2008–9 school year, it was estimated that 45% of the students were from minority backgrounds, yet 83% of teachers were white (Aud, *et al.*, 2011, 2013).

3   There are now many websites that provide helpful lists of picturebooks on migration, and a list of children's and young adult books on migration in Spanish and Catalan can be found at http://www.literatura.gretel.cat/sites/default/files/dossier_llibres.pdf.

2

The Passengers: International Contexts and Participants

Changes in the patterns of migration as well as government ideologies and educational theories lead to changes in the development of educational policies and programmes by host nations for children of immigrant families. In order to situate the work done by each of the teams that worked with *The Arrival*, in this chapter we describe these changes and developments in three international contexts (the Italian context is described in the final Coda in the book), including some of the historical and contemporary data on migration, as well as the educational policies relevant to immigrant children. Given that different regions, states and even cities often have varying policies, it was the educational jurisdiction in which the participating schools were based that determined the specific context. Although this is not meant to be a comparative account, in order to facilitate reading we have followed a similar structure in each section and mention approaches to both education in general and to language and literacy learning and research.[1]

The differences in educational policies, along with school regulations, account for some of the differences in the data collection; therefore, at the end of each account, we include a brief description of the schools and participants involved in the inquiry and of how the research design was applied in each case (the overall design and methodology will be discussed in Chapter 3). This helps account for the varying number of children in each context, as their circumstances as immigrants often resulted in their leaving the project, the school and even the country unexpectedly, while other new arrivals were incorporated in the sessions. In these cases, it was felt that flexibility and inclusiveness were more important than adhering to an unrealistically strict criteria. The reader should also keep in mind that there are differences in terminology in each country and that some terms have been translated from Spanish and/or Catalan into English, and we have done our best to address any ambiguities.

The context of the inquiry in Glasgow

For several centuries, the UK has been host to successive waves of immigrants, mostly refugees from political, economic and environmental crises and from a variety of cultural backgrounds and ethnicities. Patterns and reasons for migration have changed from those in the past century with more migrants now entering the UK from A8 and Commonwealth countries because of economic incentives. Since the Aliens Act of 1905, there have been periodic attempts to curb numbers, but even the most recent measures have been only partially successful, given European Union (EU) policies that allow migration between member states and the unstable conditions in many countries around the world – many of which were former British colonies. Overall, in the UK, there are about 5 million foreign-born citizens of either EU or non-EU countries, with some 200,000 arriving every year. In the first decade of the twenty-first century, the proportion of children in primary schools in England for whom English was not the mother tongue nearly doubled to roughly half a million, and in 2010 they accounted for slightly more than half the population of primary-school pupils in London. One in seven primary-school pupils do not speak English as a first language, while approximately 240 languages are now spoken by children in their homes.

Although to a lesser extent than England, Scotland has also welcomed its share of immigrants: Italian, Irish, Pakistani, Bosnian and Polish, among others, and, more recently, due to the dispersal programme,[2] asylum seekers from Congo, Turkey (including Turkish Kurds), Somalia, Iran and Pakistan. Since 2000, the net migration to Scotland has reached its highest ever levels, and data on immigration shows that 34 per cent more foreign-born people were living in Scotland in 2001 compared to 1991, making it one of the fastest-growing rates in the UK. However, recent events such as the financial crisis at the end of the last decade, the tightening of migration laws in the United Kingdom and the discontinuation of the dispersal programmes to Glasgow have slowed immigrant population growth. Although recent figures show that 30,000 people left the country in 2005, there were 38,000 new arrivals, including expatriate Scots and new immigrants, and statistics for 2010/2011 show that migration stood around 40,000 (National Statistics Online, asylumscotland.org.uk and Home Office Asylum Statistics).

The profile of children attending Scottish schools is diverse: over 147 languages have been recorded as home languages of children in schools and there are over 28,000 bilingual primary- and secondary-school children.[3] Scotland has always retained governance over its education system, which is different from the English National Curriculum; this means that Scottish schools can be more flexible in meeting some of the challenges of immigration but it also means greater demands on general teaching and specialist staff.

The city of Glasgow

Glasgow historically has received the largest share of immigrants to Scotland and, like all large host cities, the city has been transformed by successive groups of Irish, Jewish, Polish, Lithuanian, Italian and South and East Asian migrants. New groups such as Eastern Europeans, particularly Slovakians, continue to arrive, creating a cosmopolitan and vibrant city, but also creating challenges for services and communities. At the end of the twentieth century, out-migration was causing the city's population to decline, but, since 2000, the decline has been slowing down as the ethnic-minority population increases. At the beginning of the twenty-first century, Glasgow had a residential population of just over 600,000, making it the largest city in Scotland. The city has a higher black and ethnic-minority population than Scotland as a whole, though it is still predominantly 'white' (nearly 95 per cent).

As a result of the dispersal programme (1999–2010), Glasgow became home to the largest number of dispersed asylum seekers in the UK. Although there are no exact statistics for asylum seekers and refugees, 5,640 were receiving accommodation and subsistence in 2005 from the National Asylum Support Service under its dispersal scheme. They comprised just under 1 per cent of the total city population (Lewis, 2006). Culture and religion provide the bond between the new generations being born in Scotland, but there is a scarcity of information on how these new generations deal with their dual identities, languages and cultures. Although there has been an increasing awareness about asylum seekers and refugees, as well as race and ethnic-minority issues, since Devolution,[4] and organizations such as the Scottish Refugee Council have greatly contributed to this awareness (for example, through Refugee Week and government campaigns such as 'One Scotland Many Cultures' and 'Show Racism the Red Card'[5]), there is still a great deal of work to be done in Glasgow in terms of research and education for inclusion.

The language and literacy challenge

Some of the main challenges presented by immigration are encountered within the classroom, where populations of asylum seekers, refugees and also children who are second- or third-generation members of more established ethnic-minority communities are expected to learn alongside 'native Scots'. Around 12.5 per cent of the child population in Glasgow is bilingual, the largest groups being composed of those of Indian or Pakistani descent (Glasgow City Council, 2008). Between 2005 and 2008, approximately 3,000 foreign national children enrolled in Glasgow schools and early years centres, most of whom came from Poland, Slovakia, India, Pakistan and Libya. Added to these are the 2,000–2,400 children and young people from asylum-seeker and refugee families who have been 'dispersed' to Glasgow. Most newly arrived children are placed in their local school (defined by postal address). Asylum seekers and refugees tend to be housed in areas that already have a high incidence of new arrivals and these areas tend to be economically deprived and facing a variety of social problems. Schools, therefore, have to deal not only with unpredictable population changes but also with the consequences of this deprivation.

The main language and literacy challenges are a result of various factors: pupils at various stages of learning English; a variety of different languages and cultures; and, because of disruption in some immigrant pupils' education, different levels of literacy. There are also different attitudes and expectations about education according to background, for example when coming from countries where there is little educational support and even segregation, as in the case of the Roma community in Slovakia. In addition, schools may have to deal with some pupils' traumatic experiences and with their uncertain status and future in the UK. A recent report on the needs of newly arrived children and young people in Scotland notes that, although most schools have developed a positive climate of equality and staff are caring and supportive, teachers are not always fully aware of the potential emotional, social and educational difficulties that newly arrived children and their families may experience in the transition to a new country or school. In 2009, it was reported that teachers also often lacked awareness and training in terms of language needs: 'Authorities recognise that there are areas for improvement in relation to staff development and training and a current lack of capacity within mainstream education to address the needs of bilingual / multilingual learners' (HMIe, 2009, p. v).

It must also be noted that one of the issues in learning English in Scotland is that not only are accents different from Standard English (the language spoken is referred to as Standard Scottish English), but also many speakers use words from the Scots language. Scots is now primarily a spoken language and, although it is currently used by over 1.5 million people in various dialects, it is still seen by some as a language that has 'lower status'. Despite positive moves in the arts, academia and in educational policy to reclaim and revalue this linguistic heritage, in schools Scots is still considered by many pupils and teachers as 'slang', to be spoken only in the playground or outside school. Teachers and parents believe competence in Standard English is more important, and this is particularly the case for immigrant families, but this leads to a further level of complexity for new arrivals, as they have to learn to distinguish the spaces in which to use these different linguistic forms (McGonigal and Arizpe, 2007).

The response to this challenge

In England, the initial response to the education of newly arrived bilingual children was to assimilate them as quickly as possible through developing their English and ignoring their home languages. However, research and innovative projects on home and school literacies revealed the need to take into account literacy in the children's first language(s) (Drury, 2007; Gregory, 1996; Gregory, Long and Volk, 2004; Kenner, 2000), and this was reflected in the policy document the *National Literacy Strategy: Supporting Pupils Learning English as an Additional Language* (DfES, 2002). Although the National Curriculum and the Primary National Strategy set constraints on classroom pedagogy, some innovative teachers have found ways of going beyond these and use strategies that invite home languages and literacy practices into the classroom. Many of these are based on 'multicultural' or multilingual picturebooks but also on poetry, artefacts, popular culture, folktales and film. Nonetheless, in 2010, the UK Literacy Association (UKLA) was still calling for a curriculum and pedagogy 'that seeks to build communities of learners respecting and valuing home literacy experience and cultural backgrounds' (Reedy, 2010).

Scottish research and policy have also progressed in the area of addressing the needs of bilingual children by recognizing the value of bilingualism and home–school literacy links. In 2004, Glasgow City Council commissioned a report to improve education for ethnic-minority pupils, *Effective Teaching and Learning in a Multi-Ethnic Education System* (Cassells, 2006), which emphasized that 'bilingualism is a strength'. In 2005, the Scottish government produced *Learning in 2 (+) Languages*, a document that identifies good practice in supporting children who are accessing the curriculum through EAL (English as an additional language) and stresses the advantages of bilingualism for a greater linguistic and critical awareness. In Glasgow City Council's (2008) *Policy for Supporting Children and Young People with English as an Additional Language in Glasgow*, principles for support include the ability to identify and meet individual needs; a focus on inclusion; engagement with children, families and the wider community; and working with other services for children to develop a holistic approach. Examples of recent best practice with pupils from newly arrived families can be found in the report *Count Us In: Meeting the Needs of Children and Young People Newly Arrived in Scotland* (HMIe, 2009). However, this report noted that there continued to be little input on the topic during initial teacher education or in-service training and observed that 'the same weaknesses exist in supporting the achievements of new arrivals with English as an additional language as have been present for at least the past ten years' (HMIe, 2009, pp. iv, v). More recently, McKinney, McAdam, Arizpe, Crichton and Britton's (2012) report showed that future teacher education programmes need to consider building knowledge across concepts connected to language and literacy acquisition, culturally relevant pedagogy, cultural awareness and pastoral care of the child.

Glasgow City Council's EAL service is available both for new arrivals and for children who have always lived in Glasgow but use a language other than English at home. The EAL service is no longer based in the bilingual units, which were initially set up to support the children of dispersed families. The service now entails a mixture of in-class support and small group withdrawal. There are also peripatetic support staff that move around clusters of schools, which means the support is more sporadic and is primarily used for assessment purposes and teacher professional development.

Scotland's new curriculum, A *Curriculum for Excellence*, was implemented in all Scottish schools beginning in session 2010–11. It seeks to develop 'successful learners, confident individuals, responsible citizens and effective contributors' via a curriculum that places the needs of the learner at its centre. Literacy development is seen as fundamental in shaping this collaborative educational future and, although the new curriculum also recognizes and values cultural diversity and provides resources for EAL teaching, major resource reductions in schools have meant that little has changed overall. There are successful cases where creative pedagogies have been based on the children's needs and on their linguistic and cultural resources (Smyth, 2006), but these remain isolated and there is still a great deal of work to be done in Scotland with teachers in the areas of EAL teaching and learning and in the promotion of inclusive education.

Research in this context

Although there has been less research in Scotland than in England on refugee, asylum-seeker and ethnic-minority literacy and bilingual learning in particular, academic research and government documents have increased over the last few years (see Arshad, Diniz, Kelly, O'Hara, Sharp and Syed, 2005; Candappa, 2007; Netto, Rowena, de Lima, Almeida, MacEwen, Patel and Syed, 2001). Smyth (2003, 2006), for example, looked in depth at bilingualism in the Scottish primary context and found that within the monolingual curriculum there is little space for recognition of bilingual pupils' cognitive and creative potential. The inquiry carried out by McGonigal and Arizpe (2007) was an initial exploration of the intersections of home and school literacies and the experience of immigrants with regard to Scots and Standard English, as well as the sharing of human experience through stories and pictures. These researchers also noted that much was still unknown about the changing literacy and language practices in the home and the community, as well as about practices related to the use of new technologies. Based on these findings, together with those from a follow-up study using picturebooks as a means of understanding ethnic-minority pupils' use of visual literacy skills (Arizpe, 2010), funding was obtained from the University of Glasgow and the UKLA to set up the Visual Journeys inquiry.

The data collection in Glasgow

The research in Glasgow took place in two multi-ethnic schools with groups of eight to ten pupils who were selected, based on the teacher's suggestions, from the upper primary classrooms. The children were between 10 and 12 years old and there was an approximate gender balance. In the first school, half of the research group was Scottish and half recent arrivals to Scotland. In the second school, all the children came from ethnic-minority communities and, with one exception, had recently arrived in Scotland. Most had been in Scotland under three years, but in some cases it was not possible to determine the exact time due to sensitive circumstances. Between the groups in both schools, they spoke a wide range of main home languages: Urdu, Polish, Somali, Kurdish, Pashto, Rwandan, Slavic, French, Italian, Russian and Arabic. Mobility is a common occurrence among children from migrant families and, as a result, several children were unable to complete the full set of sessions, although new ones were invited to join the group.

Researchers and children met once a week at a regular time for 45 to 60-minute sessions, which took place over a period of eight weeks for both *Flotsam* and *The Arrival*. Researchers usually visited the schools or other venues several times before beginning the sessions and once they had ended, for example to introduce the project or to celebrate its end. The sessions usually took place in the classroom reserved for EAL support, during school hours when the children would have been receiving this support. One and sometimes two researchers were present in the sessions with two to five children. The composition of the groups varied depending on attendance, language proficiency and empathy with each other. In both schools, the EAL support teachers (one of them an immigrant from Ethiopia) participated in some of the sessions.

The picturebooks were read over four sessions in the small groups and the visual strategies (detailed in the next chapter) were carried out over the following sessions. Oral data was audio-recorded and transcribed. Data from participant observations and from memos was included in the analysis along with the data from the visual responses. The list of the children who participated in Glasgow can be seen in Table 2.1.

Table 2.1 Participants in Glasgow

Pseudonym	Country	Languages spoken at home
Claude	Congo	French/Lingala
Ruby	Rwanda	Rwandan
Vassily	Siberia	Russian
Sunil	Sri Lanka/Italy	Tamil/Italian
Mazin	Somalia	Somali/Arabic
Nadia	Pakistan/Scotland	Urdu/English
Ladislav	Slovakia	Slavic
Surayya	Pakistan	Urdu
Dina	Pakistan	Urdu, Punjabi
Józef	Poland	Polish
Faisal	Pakistan	Urdu
Ali	Afghanistan	Urdu, Pashto, Punjabi
Sumi	India	Gujarati, Bengali
Hassan	Somalia	Somali
Sara	Kurdistan	Pashto
Sam	Scottish	English/Scots
Andy	Scottish	English/Scots
Morag	Scottish	English/Scots
Lily	Scottish	English/Scots
Jack	English	English

The context of the inquiry in Catalonia[6]

Spain is a multilingual country: the official language throughout the country is Spanish, but in some regions there is a local native language that is also official, namely, Catalan, Basque and Galician. Although Catalan has a written and literary tradition dating back to the Middle Ages, from the eighteenth century onwards, it suffered different periods of official prohibition, resulting in an almost exclusive use of Spanish, the last one being during the Franco dictatorship following the Civil War of 1936–9. During this period, Catalonia received a major wave of immigrants from the rest of Spain, which made its population double, going from 3 to 6 million inhabitants in just a few decades. The combination of official persecution of the Catalan language and the linguistic pressure from Spanish-speaking immigrants placed this language in a marginalized situation. With the restoration of democracy in the late 1970s, schools in Catalonia became the main instrument for linguistic recovery and for the political will to create a single, unified cultural community, with all individuals mastering the two languages, as opposed to those who would have preferred to develop two parallel school systems divided according to the pupils' native language. Today, this language has over 9 million speakers (ranking Catalan ninth among EU languages by number of speakers) within the State of Spain – in Catalonia, the Valencian Country and the Balearic Islands.

This historical process led to early social concern for the topic of languages and a great pedagogical interest in the ways these develop in bilingual contexts; for example, Canadian linguistic educational models were taken into account in fashioning the educational policies of the 1980s and 1990s. Linguistic immersion models were adopted, with Catalan becoming the accepted language for school use, and particular attention was paid to evaluating the results regarding the mastery of both languages at the end of the compulsory education period. After a few decades, the educational outcome seemed unquestionably positive: Catalan students displayed a mastery of Spanish equal to or greater than students in the rest of Spain and knowledge of Catalan had extended to second- and third-generation populations. As a consequence, the model obtained recognition from the EU as a valuable system.

From the 1990s, a new wave of immigration began to arrive in Catalonia, especially from non-EU countries and in particular from Latin America (43.0 per cent), the Maghreb (27.3 per cent), Eastern Europe (10.7 per cent), Asia (7.4 per cent) and Sub-Saharan Africa (4.8 per cent). In only twenty years, the population of new immigrants has risen to 15 per cent of the population of

Catalonia, which now has 7.5 million inhabitants. This new situation has made the previous educational language model obsolete. From a context of two languages in contact, where one was in a situation of historical marginalization and the other had the power granted by official and international status and Spanish migratory pressure, there was a leap to a mosaic of 200 languages and cultures. The situation now is similar to that experienced by many Western countries during the era of globalization and which has led to having to face the common challenge of designing and implementing policies for social cohesion in multilingual and multicultural contexts. Although some of the uncertainty with respect to the future of the Catalan language had been countered by the situation in schools, the rapidity and intensity of the new migratory phenomenon has given rise to even greater uncertainty regarding the cultural and linguistic future of Catalan society.

The challenges of immigration for schools

At present, 13.3 per cent of students in Catalan schools were born outside Spain; this means 153,000 children and young people, half of whom entered school in the space of the last four years. The foremost challenge for integrating the newcomers is to prevent 'immigrant ghettoization' at schools or in specific classes. In Catalonia, there are significant numbers of publicly subsidized private schools, which account for 38 per cent of the student body. Given that 84.3 per cent of the new arrivals were attending public schools and only 15.7 per cent were attending private ones, there was an outcry among practitioners, parents and the media who denounced this unequal distribution. Of course, this overall distribution varies according to the area, so that some schools have a concentration of 30 per cent immigrant students and some reach extremes of 90 per cent. This concentration has been unintentionally fostered by certain school admission criteria, such as giving precedence to proximity of the home or the attendance of other siblings at the school. For this reason, the new 2009 Education Law included the establishment of maximum immigrant quotas at schools, although its application is still uneven.

A second problem is the constant influx of new arrivals through family reunification laws, so that many school-aged adolescents enter school mid-semester. As long as the number of these arrivals remained low, the system's resources seemed sufficient to accommodate the new situation. However, when the numbers began to rocket and when the arrivals were at the secondary-school level – from 12 to 16 years of age – problems increased. The secondary-school organization and the teaching tradition accentuated the difficulty of providing a response adapted to the distinctive needs of each of the newcomers.

The educational response to the challenges

The first response by the Education Department of Catalonia was the creation of TAEs (Tallers d'adaptació escolar i d'aprenentatges instrumentals bàsics). These 'School Adaptation and Instrumental Foundation Workshops' were designed for students entering secondary school once the school year had begun without a mastery of either of the two official languages. The TAEs took place in the morning at one of the schools in a given area. Students enrolled in nearby schools would go to the particular school where the TAEs were held in the morning, while attending classes at their assigned schools in the afternoons. This system soon demonstrated shortcomings as far as pedagogy and socialization in the classroom were concerned, since the general student body perceived their immigrant peers as strangers who only appeared part-time and did not participate in the general classroom dynamics.

In consequence, over the past few years and as the pace of immigration increased, the Education Administration of Catalonia decided to substitute the TAE model with Reception Classes and the Plan for Language, Multiculturalism and Social Cohesion (LIC). The new educational policies, launched in academic year 2003–4 (Education Department of Catalonia, LIC, 2004), were based on the previous principles of attaining a single cultural community and mastery of the two official languages. A significant change was that the LIC was addressed to all students at a school through two lines of action: multilingualism and intercultural education, although, naturally, specific measures were included for foreign students. It also attempted to improve on the previous plan, which was focused on language learning, eliminating the concept that a language had to be learned before integration could take place and placing greater emphasis on aspects relating to emotions, harmonious coexistence, interrelationships and social cohesion directly affecting students' adaptation. Other principles underlying the new policies were relationships with families and the social milieu (Social Environment Plan); the consideration of immigrants' culture of origin; the integration-oriented work carried out by the entire staff (a Reception School); and the assertion of Catalan as an instrument of cohesion in a multilingual framework.

In keeping with these principles, the main aspect of the new organizational model was to provide reception for newly arrived students directly at the school in which they were enrolled. The main tool for this was the so-called 'Aules d'acollida' [Reception Classes], with structures borrowed from Toronto and Quebec and a definition that differentiates them from the concept of 'bridging classes' where students quickly learn the language and integrate afterwards into regular classes. Thus, newly arrived students immediately enter regular classes, but, for a few hours a week or during a certain period of time, they also attend the Reception Class where a specialist teacher attempts to intensify their knowledge of the Catalan language as the main medium at school.[7] These Reception Classes thus represent an intermediate model between the external and segregating TAEs and the fully integrating one of a Reception School, where all classes would be both ordinary and Reception Classes at once. Reception Classes were launched in academic year 2004–5 and were targeted at students who had arrived in the previous two years. They did not include children under eight years of age unless they had arrived directly from another country. A maximum number of 12 students per class, 12 hours per week and two years of duration were established. In academic year 2007–8, 1,150 Reception Classes were operating.

There are still challenges facing the pedagogy in the Reception Classes. One of them is the urgent need to have trained staff as well as specific materials and pedagogical approaches for considering the great variety of languages and cultures that have so suddenly (in less than fifteen years) appeared in schools and in such a numerically significant manner. Another problem is the irregularity of the work done in these classes due to a constantly changing student body. Children have achieved highly varied educational levels before arriving in Catalonia; they enter school at different times in the school year, speak very different languages, often with differing writing systems, participate in the Reception Classes for a variable number of hours per week and stop attending class after having reached a certain level of communication. The model is now being closely evaluated to measure results based on factors such as previous schooling, language knowledge, adaptation to school, the number of hours spent in the Reception Class and the time already spent in Catalonia. These results are expected to lead to more diversified measures in accordance with the different schooling situations and individual needs.

Research in multilingual contexts

Given the different waves of immigration to Catalonia, it is not surprising that the need to attend to newly arrived children's education has polarized pedagogical attention. The impact of the most recent migration has fostered the interest in studies on language in bilingual contexts, which have been developing in Catalonia since the 1980s, manifested in the proliferation of research, training courses, pedagogical material and children's books on the topic. The educational focus, first on bilingualism and then on multilingualism, has been adopted primarily under the hypothesis of the existence of a subjective competence common to bilingual and multilingual individuals, as well as of a distinction between the conversational and academic spheres in the study of language acquisition by immigrant students. This distinction has allowed researchers to demonstrate that newly arrived students can acquire significant fluency in the language predominating in the host society, but that they take five years (or more) in reaching the levels of native-language students in academic uses of the language (Cummins, 2000, p. 50).

The most recent pedagogical research explored the educational implications of the theoretical foundations adopted (Guasch, 2010), and some of the findings are particularly important for the theoretical framework used in the inquiry in Catalonia. One finding is that the variable that best describes the differences in the language knowledge of foreign students in Reception Classes is the level of adaptation to school, which was understood in this context as the manner in which the children become familiar with the school practices and their level of integration within the group and institution. This variable is so powerful for describing results that it mitigates the real effects of other variables, such as the period of time already spent in Catalonia, the weekly number of hours spent in the Reception Class or the student's initial language (Siqués Jofré, 2008). Along the same lines, Vila, Siqués and Roig indicate that the time of acquisition of the host language is predominantly determined by an educational practice primarily concerned with three aspects: meaning, language and educational community (Vila *et al.*, 2006, p. 154). These are detailed as follows:

1. A focus on meaning implies that all learning involves the construction of shared meanings. This calls for the creation of comprehensible input, and, above all, the development of strategies using oral language that foster the meaning of the activity, children's active participation and the reformulation of their knowledge, in the sense of establishing social and cultural agreements on the different content.

2. The focus on language entails fostering activities in which children can develop both knowledge of the school's vehicular language and

metalinguistic and metacognitive awareness and skills, as well as knowledge of the use and formal aspects of the language(s).

3. The focus on community means raising the self-esteem of children and their families through the school's recognition of what they can contribute to a more egalitarian and cohesive society, while also involving families and the social milieu in the task of education. These are important aspects, since in most societies schools tend to reproduce the relations of power that the majority group maintains over minority groups. Hence, society and schools usually do not transmit values or attitudes that would accommodate foreign children in building their own identities from which to negotiate a project of social collaboration in which they can live their differences, while at the same time establishing a common project for the future of all people in the land.

It was in this context of increasing concern that our research group, GRETEL, joined the international Visual Journey project to study the reception possibilities provided by picturebooks. This was an area that had been largely unexplored given that the pedagogical practice, whether in the Reception Classes or in classes with a large proportion of newly arrived students, tended to ignore the role of literature in this process. The inquiry in Catalonia centred on the relevance of adapting to school in the reception process and on the principles of the most adequate educational practice in this field. This meant placing two aspects in the foreground: first, the shared construction of meaning through oral language, collaboration and active participation; and, second, the focus on aspects of text construction by using picturebooks to foster learning narrative comprehension and the interpretation of complex texts, given they facilitate access through the image and allow literature to exercise its possibilities for emotional and cultural representation in the transition from one culture to another.

The overall project 'La interpretación literaria de álbumes en el proceso de acogida de los alumnos inmigrantes' involved 14 classes, primarily 'Reception Classes' at new public schools – four primary and five secondary ones – in six different towns of the Province of Barcelona and involved 108 students ranging in age from 6 to 16 years from 19 countries. Two researchers led the sessions, between four and six sessions depending on the book, usually with small groups of six students and occasionally with the school's entire student body. The small groups were not specifically selected; instead, all students habitually attending Reception Classes were accepted. Seven different picturebooks were used, among them *Flotsam* and *The Arrival*. In the interventions with these two books, the research design for Visual Journey was followed, whereas, in the use of other books, variants were introduced according to a wider spectrum of objectives ranging from priority attention to linguistic development, intertextual work or dramatization (these results can be found in Colomer and Fittipaldi, 2012).

For the part of the research that followed the design of the international project, eight sessions were held in one school with twelve children: six from Catalonia and six from abroad, all them between 11 and 12 years old. One child left after only two sessions because his mother was deported for not having the necessary immigration documents. Another child took his place and one child from the pilot study was also included in the final analysis which is why there are 14 children overall in Table 2.2. Spanish was used as the language of mediation in all of these sessions. These children were selected to participate with the help of their tutors in order to fit in with the criteria described for the inquiry. Some sessions involved only immigrants or only Catalans, while some involved mixed groups. Table 2.2 lists the participating children.

Table 2.3 includes the children who also looked at *The Arrival* but within the context of the project that used other picturebooks, not all of which were wordless.

Audio-recorded data was transcribed and used for the analysis. Although most of the examples in the chapters that follow are based on these sessions,

Table 2.2 Participants in Barcelona (1)

Pseudonym	Country	Language
Paola	Peru	Spanish
Alan	Ecuador	Spanish
Beatriz	Bolivia	Spanish
Gisela	Bolivia	Spanish
Adrián	Bolivia	Spanish
Cristina	Peru	Spanish
Calin	Romania	Romanian
Naima	Morocco	Arabic/French
Carles	Catalonia	Catalan/Spanish
Emma	Catalonia	Catalan/Spanish
Hilda	Catalonia	Catalan/Spanish
Xavier	Catalonia	Catalan/Spanish
Andreu	Catalonia	Catalan/Spanish
Carolina	Catalonia	Catalan/Spanish

Table 2.3 Participants in Barcelona (2)

Pseudonym	Country	Language
Rodrigo	Peru	Spanish
Denis	Bolivia	Spanish
An You	Catalonia/China	Chinese/Catalan
Antonio	Spain (Málaga)	Spanish
Tania	Catalonia	Catalan/Spanish
Ana	Catalonia	Catalan/Spanish

there are occasional examples from some of the other sessions involving *The Arrival* (some of which were carried out in Catalan). An explanatory note will be included when this is the case.

The context of the inquiry in Arizona

Immigration is a salient and much-debated topic in the USA. Currently, there are an estimated 40.4 million immigrants or foreign-born people living in the USA, representing 13 per cent of the US population and an increase of 30 per cent since 2000.[8] While different waves of immigration have contributed to that number, 65 per cent of the total immigrant population in the USA arrived before 1999. The six main regions supplying immigrants to the USA, according to the 2011 US Census Bureau, are Mexico (29.0 per cent), South and East Asia (25.2 per cent), the Caribbean (9.3 per cent), Central America (7.6 per cent), South America (6.7 per cent) and the Middle East (3.7 per cent). Patterns of immigration have changed during the last decade in that the number of immigrants from Central America, South and East Asia and South America experienced a major increase since 2000.

Nearly 12 million of the immigrants living in the USA today are Mexicans, and they are living in California (36.4 per cent), Texas (21.6 per cent), Illinois (6.1 per cent) and Arizona (4.4 per cent): additionally, 22.3 million individuals born in the USA self-identify as 'Hispanic of Mexican origin', from a total of 33.7 million. This makes Mexicans the largest Hispanic population in the USA, accounting for nearly 64 per cent of the US Hispanic or Latino population in 2012.[9] Nevertheless, the arrival of new Mexican immigrants has slowed in the last decade.[10] [11]

The state of Arizona

Originally inhabited by diverse Native American groups, the borderland that would later be officially named Arizona became part of Mexico during European expansion. Afterwards, it was transferred to the USA as a result of the 1946 conflict between the USA and Mexico that ended with the Treaty of Hidalgo in 1948. Thus, Arizona has been and is the home of diverse cultures where a variety of Native American languages, along with Spanish and English, are spoken. The relationship between Native American communities, communities of Mexican origin and Anglo communities in Arizona has been and continues to be characterized by power struggles, efforts to assimilate and erase differences, resistance to assimilation, resilience, survival and alliances.

Currently, of the 13.4 per cent of the Arizona population that is comprised of immigrants, 59.0 per cent are of Mexican origin. While Hispanics represent nearly 17 per cent of the US population, they represent 30 per cent of Arizona's population. Given Arizona's history as a borderland state and its relationship with Mexico, it is not surprising that 70 per cent of the Hispanic population in Arizona are native born and 30 per cent are foreign born.

Education

The diversity and multiculturalism of the USA is reflected in its school population. Among the student population (ages five to seventeen) enrolled in private or public schools in the USA, 21 per cent are foreign-born or native-born students living in households with foreign-born heads. That means that one-fifth of five- to seventeen-year-olds enrolled in US schools is made up of immigrant children or children of immigrants (or children living in households with immigrant heads). Just taking into account the public school system, 23.9 per cent of pre-K to 12th graders were Hispanic in 2011.[12] In Arizona, on the other hand, Hispanics represent 43 per cent of all K–12 students.

Language practices in the USA have been characterized by a long trajectory of multilingualism. Colonial languages, the languages of involuntary minorities, such as Native Americans, African slaves brought to USA and conquered groups such as Mexicans and Puerto Ricans (Gibson and Ogbu, 1991), as well as languages brought by immigrants throughout the country's history, have all contributed to the US linguistic landscape. More recently, within the foreign population of minors who arrived in the USA in 2006 and later, 86.5 per cent use more than one language at home. If we consider the number of immigrants and native-born population younger than 18 that speak more than one language at home, a continuum of bilingual proficiencies can be expected (Hornberger, 2003), from almost monolingual speakers to fluent speakers of more than one language. Historically, there have been different educational and political responses to such linguistic and cultural diversity, as described in the following section.

Immigration and bilingual education

After initial efforts to systematically attempt to erase the languages of Native American communities (McCarty and Watahomigie, 2004) and Latinos, including Puerto Ricans (Negrón de Montilla, 1970), usually through punishment, different policies and educational alternatives were created. Torres-Guzmán and de Jong (in press) explore how the conceptual construction of multilingualism in K–12 schools from post-Second World War to the present has evolved in very dynamic ways, and they identify four historical periods. Each period has its own metaphor to describe research, political action and ideologies involved in the field of bi/multilingualism, but the periods overlap in many ways. These periods offer a useful way to organize the following overview of multilingualism in the USA.

Torres-Guzmán and de Jong name the first period 'From the "Sink or Swim" to the Dawn of a New Era'. Children who spoke languages other than English were placed in English-only contexts, where they received no bilingual support and their linguistic differences were unrecognized. The 'sink or swim' metaphor refers to the way some children survived such instruction, while others ended up failing or dropping out of school. This strategy lost its prominence after the Second World War when, with the USSR's launching of the *Sputnik* into space in 1957, the US national defence felt the need to develop foreign languages in order to compete globally. However, at the same time, during this period, assimilation through giving up the language of one's home country was seen as the ideal. In an attempt to preserve their cultural integrity while receiving the equitable public education they were entitled to, Mexican American/Latino communities and African Americans brought their concerns about racial segregation and assimilation to court.

The second period is named 'Rights to Language and Culture'. A major event in this period was the abolishment of the quota system that had privileged Western and Northern European immigrants since 1924. A significant increase in immigrants, particularly from Latin America and Asia, took place as a result of The Immigration Act of 1968, which opened US borders for entry to people from around the world. Meanwhile, the Civil Rights movement mobilized groups of workers and citizens on a community level to continue fighting discrimination. One of these fights pertained to the way the educational system was failing minority students. The 1974 Supreme Court Case *Lau v. Nichols* resulted in the US Office of Civil Rights developing the Lau Remedies, which required states to offer bilingual education options at the elementary level. It was a period of innovation in the field of bilingual education and English language instruction. The most common form bilingual education took was 'transitional bilingual education', with its goal of transitioning children into English and 'exiting' them from the programme as soon as possible into English-only instruction. In practice, the 'sink or swim' programme and the transitional programme were substractive programmes. Alternatively, a few additive or maintenance-oriented bilingual programmes emerged, using the students' first language as a tool for learning, while adding a second language.

The third period is characterized by 'Language Separation and Academic Rigour'. During this period, the immigrant population, especially minoritized[13] groups, experienced great diversification. The Latino population, for instance, previously comprised mostly of people of Mexican, Puerto Rican and Cuban descent, now had representation from 21 Spanish-speaking countries. Newcomers started settling in areas that had never experienced large numbers of immigrants. Within the educative field, there was a strong debate around 'English-only' movements versus bilingual education. Dual-language education programmes emerged as an alternative that addressed the language and academic needs of minoritized students by offering education in two languages, while also attracting children from mainstream groups whose parents wished them to be bilingual (Lindholm-Leary, 2005). Schools employed different structures to allocate the languages of instruction, but generally maintained a strict separation between the two languages to avoid arbitrary code-switching from teachers who did not reflect communities' sociolinguistic practices, and to protect the minority language from the threat of English hegemony. The dual-language models promoted and used the metaphor of 'language and culture as a resource' (Ruiz, 1984). At the same time that dual-language programmes were gaining strength in some districts, there was a reactionary conservative anti-bilingual and anti-immigrant movement that promoted English-only education for minoritized children, presenting a hegemonized English educational approach as key to students' success. This movement, still active, restricted and virtually eliminated bilingual education as a viable alternative in several states, including Arizona.

The fourth historical period, which Torres-Guzmán and de Jong call 'Language and Culture Identities Re-imagined Future', is marked by globalization, privatization, the digital turn and the 'post-turn' that began in the 1980s (postmodernism, post-structuralism and post-colonialism). These orientations influenced conceptualizations of language, identity and culture. Educationally, different models of language learning coexist in the USA depending on the state, from the earlier 'sink or swim' method to a variety of English language learning programmes, transitional bilingual programmes and dual-language programmes. As communities become more multilingual, children become more adept at negotiating languages, identities and affiliations. Paradoxically, the educational system is responding to such diversity with an increase in testing and standardization practices. In addition, it is important to notice that, in spite of the proliferation of bilingual programmes over time, most English language learners in the USA historically have not had access to bilingual education. The 'sink or swim' model has always been present and English 'pull-out programmes' have been the most common approach to support students' learning of only English.

Research in this context

Each of the historical periods mentioned above produced research that reflected the historical context and educational debates of their time. The first period dealt with the effects of pre-Second World War studies of the relationship between bilingualism and cognitive function, which led bilingualism to be treated as a handicap and an explanation for poor performance in intelligence tests. This argument was used to justify restrictive immigration policies in the early 1900s (Hakuta, 1985, cited in Torres-Guzmán and de Jong, in press). Code-switching was regarded as a sign of the lack of maturation of both systems, and children who used code-switching were often seen as cognitively delayed. An important contribution to this US debate was Peal and Lambert's (1962) study in Canada showing the cognitive benefits of bilingualism.

During the second period, the cognitive benefits of bilingualism were acknowledged: 'concept formation (Liedkte and Nelson, 1968), metalinguistic awareness (Cummins, 1979), mental flexibility (Balkan, 1970), and the use of more analytic strategies towards language (Ben-Zeev, 1977)' (Torres-Guzmán and de Jong, in press). Cummins (2001) proposed a tri-part framework to explain school failure for bilingual children: the BICS/CALP distinction (which was challenged in subsequent periods), the Interdependence Hypothesis (or, the

Common Underlying Proficiency) and the Threshold Hypothesis. Code-switching started to be seen in a new light, not as the result of confusion, but because of a rule-governed system that involved choices on the part of its users (Hernández-Chávez, Cohen and Beltramo, 1975; Poplack, 1980; Sankoff and Poplack, 1981); however, code-switching arbitrarily determined by individual teachers and not anchored in communities' sociolinguistic practices was criticized. In terms of literacy, reading and writing started to be examined and approached based on what real readers and writers do, rather than on isolated and decontextualized skills (Goodman, 1969, 1978; Graves, 1983).

During the third period, the research aimed to identify features of effective bilingual programmes. Referring to work done by Garcia (1988), Mace-Matluck (1990), Miramontes, Nadeau and Commins (1997), González, Huerta-Macías and Tinajero (1998), Brisk and Harrington (2006) and Howard, Sugarman, Christian, Lindholm-Leary and Rogers (2007), among others, Torres-Guzmán and de Jong refer to these features as including:

> building language programs that are integrated in the school, providing and ensuring strong and knowledgeable leadership; sharing responsibility among school staff for reaching sociocultural, linguistic, and academic goals for all learners; establishing a sense of community, within the school as well as with the home and wider community; ensuring sufficient material resources in both languages to implement the program (e.g., textbooks); ensuring a highly qualified bilingual staff proficient in the language or languages of instruction and knowledgeable about bilingualism, second language acquisition, and their implications for teaching; articulating the program clearly, that is, that curricular grade level expectations and language use expectations for both languages are made explicit and provide a continuous experience for students' language and cognitive development; encouraging teacher collaboration (within and across languages); maintaining high expectations, that is, the school does not use limited English proficiency as an excuse for lowering standards, ensuring the use of current approaches to teaching that builds on students' native and second language resources; implementing a curriculum that reflects and builds on students' cultural experiences; and using culturally and linguistically responsive instructional practices. (Torres-Guzmán and de Jong, in press)

During this period, there was also a shift from research that focused exclusively on decontextualized cognitive strategies and processes to a consideration of the social contexts and practices in which languages and literacy are used, partly influenced by the New Literacy Studies. Research on households' funds of knowledge (González, Moll and Amanti, 2005; Mercado and Moll, 1997), which highlighted the range of bodies of knowledge that minoritized families and communities exchange, became important in challenging deficit views of communities and learners, and for decoupling language, culture and class. Issues of power and ideology emerged as mediating language learning and identity (New Literacy Studies; Martínez-Roldán and Malavé, 2004). In the same way that English-only movements were challenging bilingual education, there was also a return to old literacy approaches from the first period, privileging the primacy of the learning of isolated skills such as phonics and decoding over meaning-making, challenging more meaning-centred and holistic approaches.

During the fourth period, multilingualism and plurilingualism have become the focus of much research, as they began to be much more common in schools, particularly in urban areas (Pennycock, 2010). Hybridity and performativity on learners' use of language and literacy practices have also become focal areas of study (Gutiérrez, Baquedano-López and Tejeda, 1999). More attention is being given in the field of literacy research to the variety of literacy practices children and young people engage in their daily lives, particularly digital literacies, visual literacies and students' reading and responding to different kinds of texts. The New Literacy Studies that had started influencing research in the previous period have taken a hold in many studies as a broader definition of what 'text' means, allowing room for examining the multiple literacy practices and range of texts students are exposed to today at a time when prescriptive programmes and testing still drive much of the instruction offered to bilingual learners.

The data collection in Arizona

The study was conducted in Desert Breeze (pseudonym), a bilingual pre-K–8th-grade arts-enriched public elementary school, serving approximately 740 students at the time of the research. It is an urban school with a student population of almost 90 per cent Latino students, with 65 per cent classified by the school as English language learners (ELLs). The principal researcher had conducted other studies at the school and knew most of the staff working with ELLs. During the recruitment process, it was evident that most of the ten- and eleven-year-old children were second-generation immigrants or, although recent immigrants, had not had schooling experience in their countries of origin, and therefore did not meet this criterion for the study. The project took place as an after-school reading activity. A total of 12 discussions on *The Arrival* were

Table 2.4 Participants in Arizona

Pseudonym	Country	Language
Almah	Iraq	English/Arabic
Janice	Mexico	Spanish
Juan	Mexico	Spanish/English
Ryan	Mexico	Spanish
Toni	Mexico	Spanish/English
Viviana	Mexico	Spanish/English

held, each 35 to 50 minutes long, over two months, plus four additional discussions on *Flotsam*. The main mediator was the researcher, although a graduate student participated in some of the sessions as well. A small number of students who met both the target age and the criterion of having their schooling experience in their countries of origin interrupted by their journey to the USA, and, more importantly, who were interested in participating in the literature discussions in an after-school context, joined the study. The group consisted of six students: three boys and two girls from Mexico and one girl from Iraq; their names and home languages can be seen in Table 2.4.

Differences and similarities

Bringing together details of each of the three main contexts highlights the similarities and differences not only between the general profile of migration in each of the regions involved but also between the responses of the educational authorities and the resulting practices. Overall, despite different populations and policies, there are many similarities in terms of the issues and challenges raised within educational institutions and also in the various attempts to tackle these. The main language and literacy challenges are a result of various factors: pupils at various stages of learning English; a variety of different languages and cultures; and, because of disruption in some immigrant pupils' education, different levels of literacy. In response, there is an increasing wealth of research in all contexts, although the American context had a lead in this area and has therefore been more influential, particularly in the field of language learning.

However, as situations continue to change, different responses have emerged and it is important that educational policies and practices remain flexible enough to accommodate changes, such as new waves of migrant populations and having to take on board the global economic climate. Some models have been proven to be more effective than others but these will need to be continually revised and, indeed, have changed as this book was being written.

It is clear that what are crucial in this area are meaning, language and educational community (Vila *et al.*, 2006), and the use of pedagogy that responds to a real need, one that emerges from the ground up, rather than from ideological policies, and that relies on the expertise and knowledge of those who work in education and in schools. This is where the collaboration of researchers and teachers has the potential to identify the gaps and also the ways forward. This chapter shows how complex the issues are in each case and how bland generalizations cannot be applied. However, they also suggest a ground that is rich in possibilities for language learning (and not only of English or the main language of the region) and for genuine intercultural exchange. The differences in context also provide an explanation for the variations in the methodology, which will be described in the next chapter.

Notes

1   The policies and statistics we refer to in this chapter were valid at the time the inquiry was conducted but it is likely that changes have occurred since then.

2   In 1999, the UK government created a dispersal programme to move people seeking asylum away from London; one of the cities to which asylum seekers were sent was Glasgow.

3   There is no accurate data on the number of asylum-seeking and refugee children in schools because disclosure of immigration status is voluntary and official demographic data is often based on different information.

4   In 1999, the UK government transferred various powers, including education and training, to the newly created Scottish Parliament. This is known as Devolution.

5   http://www.scotland.gov.uk/News/Releases/2007/01/26113250 and http://theredcardscotland.org/.

6   The information and statistics in this section were taken from the website of the Department d'Ensenyament, Generalitat de Catalunya (Department of Education, Government of Catalonia): http://www.xtec.es/lic.

7   It is understood that intensifying knowledge of Spanish is unnecessary for students from Latin America, whereas all the others learn Spanish in the regular Spanish classes and can benefit from the presence of this language in society and in the media.

8   Based on Pew Hispanic Centre tabulations of the US Census Bureau's 2011 American Community Survey (ACS) as discussed in 'Statistical Portrait of the

Foreign-Born Population in the United States, 2011' by Seth Motel and Eileen Patten (2013). Puerto Ricans and persons born in other outlying US territories who are living in one of the fifty states or the District of Columbia are included in the native-born population. http://www.pewhispanic.org/2013/01/29/statistical-portrait-of-the-foreign-born-population-in-the-united-states-2011/.

9 Pew Hispanic Center Statistical Profile: 'A Demographic Portrait of Mexican-Origin Hispanics in the United States' by Ana Gonzalez-Barrera and Mark Hugo Lopez (2013).

10 Of the Mexican foreign born, it is estimated that 18% are unauthorized immigrants, representing 55% of the 11.1 million immigrants who are in the country undocumented. Since 2007, unauthorized immigration has started to slow down, from 12.0% of the total immigrant population in 2007 to 11.1%.

11 Nearly 17% of the US population self-identify as Hispanics.

12 Pew Research Hispanic Trends Project: 'Hispanic Student Enrollments Reach New Highs in 2011' by Richard Fry and Mark Hugo Lopez (2012). http://www.pewhispanic.org/2012/08/20/hispanic-student-enrollments-reach-new-highs-in-2011/.

13 McCarty (2002) proposed that the word 'minoritized' would be more accurate than 'minority' because it better reflects the numeric realities of the schools and communities and more accurately implies how power relations serve to marginalize certain peoples.

3

The Voyage: The Course of the Inquiry

In this chapter, we describe the route of our inquiry: setting out the initial research design; presenting the wordless narratives; and describing the process of data collection and analysis. We provide an account of the image-based research tools and how they were used within a context of responsible research in terms of ethics and pedagogy, and we explain how the analytical framework was initially envisaged and how it evolved. We believe this evolution was one of the strengths of the inquiry, as it reflects a process of cross-national, collaborative dialogue and negotiation based on a shared commitment to understand the intricacies involved in making meaning from visual narratives.

Research design

The research design and methodology responded to the main objective of the inquiry:

To explore the responses of immigrant pupils from different backgrounds to wordless picturebooks in order to understand how they construct meaning from visual images in complex narratives about immigration, journeys and the visual image itself with the intention of creating strategies that can develop their literacy skills, as well as help them reflect on their own or others' experience of migration.

This objective was further defined and widened through the following aims:

1. Considering the role of picturebooks in encouraging reflection on the personal, social and intercultural issues involved in the immigrant experience.

2. Creating a 'safe' and stimulating space for these reflections where awareness and understanding can be fostered.
3. Using image-based research tools to obtain responses, which can then be adapted in the classroom as strategies to develop visual, linguistic and intercultural skills.
4. Initiating a cross-national, collaborative research agenda through the creation of a network of inquiry and practice with university-based research teams sharing experiences and learning on reader-response, picturebooks and immigration.

We know that reading literature and looking at art can have a profound influence on the ways in which individuals construct their social worlds and their identities. As Kozulin (1998) asserts, literature is a psychological tool with the potential to mediate the human experience as well as cognitive change. On the other hand, readers construct and mediate the fictional worlds they encounter in literature through their social and identity contexts (Medina, 2010). Therefore, in order to document and understand the ways in which meaning was constructed by the children, we based our inquiry on a 'qualitative interpretive approach' (Erickson, 1986), drawing on research on literary reading and response in multilingual literacy contexts and which was rooted in culturally responsive pedagogical approaches. Reception theory (Iser, 1978) and reader-response theory, particularly that of Rosenblatt (1978, 1995), on the one hand, and New Literacy Studies, on the other (The New London Group, 1996; Kress and van Leeuwen, 2006; Street, 2003), provided the foundation that allowed us to examine and understand the various reading events that constituted the inquiry. Although these reading events involved only a relatively small number of participants in each setting, all reading events can be productive sites for inquiry (Sumara, 2000) and, taken together, can reveal similarities and differences that add to our knowledge of what goes on in the act of making sense of text – whether it be verbal or visual.

Given the previous experience of some of the researchers, the design and methods built on those used successfully in previous studies (e.g. Arizpe and Styles, 2003; Martínez-Roldán, 2003, 2005; Silva-Díaz, 2005;[1] McGonigal and Arizpe, 2007), but incorporated new methodological ideas to suit the international contexts. A pilot study in Glasgow was carried out to trial the design and methods and to provide initial data for the development of the analytical framework. Previous studies on small-group literature discussions (Short, 1997; Martínez-Roldán, 2003, 2005) also influenced the ways the discussions were organized in Arizona, and, in Barcelona, the team built on their research expertise on 'lectura literaria' [literary reading in school] (Colomer, 1998, 2005) and 'discusiones literarias' [literary conversations] (Colomer, 2002; Silva-Díaz and Manresa, 2005).[2] We also drew on some of the work of Walsh, our partner in Australia (Walsh, 2000, 2003).

The contexts described in the previous chapter set the scene for the inquiry. The variables in each country along with the different backgrounds of the immigrant children involved meant that a strict comparative study would have been contrived and artificial. The teams therefore agreed on a research design that was adaptable enough to take into account the differences in the overall educational contexts and the specific approaches to the induction and education of immigrant children, while retaining a basic structure that was similar enough to allow for cross-national analysis of the responses.

The variations within the design also allowed each team to accommodate specific circumstances. We were aware that working cooperatively would entail discussion and negotiation about which research methods to use and flexibility about how they would be applied. Overall research time and the use of particular methods, for example, had to do with accountability to different funding bodies and the lines of inquiry that each team were already committed to. This meant the Barcelona team worked with the wordless picturebooks within a larger research project that included other types of picturebooks. Unlike Arizona, the Barcelona and Glasgow teams included non-immigrant children in some of the sessions and both were able to work with a larger number of participants thanks to their funding.

The design also had to take account of the language contexts. In Barcelona, the researchers and many of the children shared Spanish as a common language, with Catalan as the second language for the immigrant children (as well as for some researchers). In Arizona, the majority of the children and the researcher could understand each other in both English and Spanish. In Glasgow, the common language had to be English given that the researchers had little or no knowledge of the first language(s) of the participants. These circumstances obviously affected the data collection because, despite mediator support, it limited some of the comments from the children who had to use their newly learned English to communicate what were often quite complex ideas.

The teams agreed on general criteria for the selection of the six to eight immigrant children who would participate in the inquiry. As we have mentioned in the previous chapter, in Glasgow and Barcelona, the teacher's help was enlisted in selecting the children, while, in Arizona, children from different classrooms were invited to participate in an after-school literacy context. The selection of the groups of children adhered as much as possible to a purposive sample (Merriam, 2009), which included:

1. Children who had their primary education interrupted by a 'journey' (or 'journeys') from their country of origin to the country in which they were living at the time of their participation in the study.
2. Age *circa* ten to twelve years old (upper two years in primary school or first year in secondary school depending on the education systems in each country).
3. Time spent in the host country (usually no more than three years).
4. Diversity of countries of origin (as possible).
5. Gender balance (as possible).
6. Attitude towards the project and willingness to participate in the literature discussions either during or after school (no one was forced to join and it was made clear they could withdraw at any point).

The composition of the groups varied slightly depending on the circumstances; the main exceptions occurred when teachers suggested that certain children who did not strictly fit this criteria (e.g. who had been in the host country over three years) be allowed to participate for particular reasons or when a child actively asked to be part of the group (in Arizona, this occurred with a child from Iraq). As mentioned above, in both Barcelona and Glasgow, several non-immigrant children also participated in order to provide further contrast between readings and so that the immigrant children did not feel negatively 'singled out'. As we have also mentioned, the size of the groups also varied, as children had to leave the project for different reasons, such as moving house or city or, in cases in Glasgow and Barcelona, deportation. It must be noted that none of the children who withdrew did so of their own accord. The realities of school research also meant that the schedule had to accommodate a variety of circumstances, such as unexpected absences or school events on the days designated for the sessions. As we have said above, the researchers in every country were above all concerned with creating a space in which the children were happy to participate, felt comfortable in expressing their views and did not feel in any way that this was an assessment-oriented activity. Researchers explained the project to the children, and ethics guidelines regarding consent were followed according to each context. All the selected children were eager to participate and were excited about being part of a project that involved children in other countries.

As well as the children's general wellbeing, at the forefront of the inquiry at all times was the consideration of the pluralities we were working with: the multilingual and multicultural context of the response to the multimodal, multilayered wordless narratives. The complexity of the reading act demanded that we looked further than oral data from interviews. We wanted to use methods that would allow us to go beyond the views of individual participants, given that we were working within socially shared and culturally defined frames. We were thus concerned with providing texts and research spaces that were as open as possible to multiple interpretations. Our choice of methodologies therefore included how to find not only creative ways of inviting the children to share their responses with us and with their peers but also creative ways of understanding these responses through other modes of representation, which could at the same time act as a form of triangulation (Atkinson and Delamont, 2005). We hoped that the findings would lead us to new insights on reading wordless picturebooks and on texts that reflected the migrant experience and interculturality, and to new pedagogical strategies that could develop skills to enhance readers' understanding and awareness of these experiences.

Developing image-based research tools

In what follows, we describe how our research methodology combined elements of the two main approaches to visual research: using images to elicit responses from children and analysing images made by children (Thomson, 2008). It will be detailed in three parts based on the use of: 1) wordless visual narratives; 2) image-based oral responses; and 3) visual responses. We combined these methods with observation and/or interviews in order to ensure the solidity of our approach (Christensen and James, 2000) but our focus was on meaning-making and our main concern was that the sessions would also prove to be interesting and enjoyable for the children.

We will also draw attention to the variations between contexts in terms of how these methodologies were implemented. As researchers working with vulnerable groups of children, we were very conscious of the ethics involved in the inquiry and we highlight some of the issues. Finally, we provide a short account of the way in which the methodology was used with *Flotsam* and how this led to the sessions with *The Arrival*.

Selection and description of the wordless narratives

As we have noted, wordless picturebooks seemed the best option to have as a common literary *corpus*, not just because they remove the barriers that reading words can present to English as an additional language (EAL) learners, but also because of the aesthetically sophisticated, powerful images that many of them offer readers. In the case of *Flotsam* and *The Arrival*, these images invite the reader to create complex narratives about immigration, journeys and the visual image itself. The affordances discussed in Chapter 1 mean that an active stance and contribution of personal and cultural experiences is required, together with an understanding of elements of visual grammar, in order to make sense of the images. We also felt that the effect of surprise and attraction of the visual narrative for children less used to reading and talking about picturebooks could lead to discussions where the visual and literary elements could be identified.

We mentioned in the Introduction that it was Tan's then recently published book *The Arrival* that provided the inspiration for the project; however, because of its length and complexity, it was felt that it would be best to introduce wordless picturebooks through a shorter and more 'colourful' picturebook that would lead to discussion not only about the absence of words but also about artistic features and the idea of 'looking'. We were already familiar with Wiesner's previous sparsely worded picturebooks, such as the metafictional Caldecott winner *The Three Pigs* (2001), so, given *Flotsam*'s theme of a visual journey, the crossing into strange new worlds and the connections between children of different times and places, it seemed the ideal book to start with (it was also published the same year as *The Arrival* – 2006).

Because *Flotsam* did turn out to be an equally excellent choice, the amount of data obtained meant we could not do justice to the children's responses to both books; therefore, reluctantly, we decided to leave the responses and findings about *Flotsam* out of this book and to focus exclusively on *The Arrival*.[3] We have still included a brief description of *Flotsam* in this chapter and a section on how the research methods were applied to the sessions with *Flotsam*, given that they formed part of the children's overall experience in the inquiry, and throughout the rest of this book we occasionally refer to this experience. Additionally, despite their many differences, the highly detailed images of both books created a sense of continuity in the reading of pictures and the sessions prepared the ground for those on *The Arrival*. The *Flotsam* data analysis also contributed to the data analysis process and served to provide contrast and confirmation for some of our findings.

Flotsam

Wiesner is an American children's book author and illustrator, whose picturebooks *Tuesday* (1992b) and *The Three Pigs* (2001) had already gained him

Figure 3.1 Cover *Flotsam*

two Caldecott Medals before he was awarded yet another one for *Flotsam* in 2006. The picturebook begins with a young boy collecting flotsam on the beach who is presented with a barnacle-encrusted underwater camera by a large wave. As the camera does not seem to belong to anyone, the boy takes the reel of film he finds inside to be developed and is astonished at what is revealed in the photographs: an octopus family reading in an underwater sitting room; tiny cities on the shells of live turtles; puffer fish on an air balloon ride. The last photograph is even more surprising when it reveals a young girl holding a photograph of another child holding a photograph of another child and so on going back in time. Like the other children around the world who have shared the camera's secrets, the boy takes a photograph of himself holding the last photograph and hurls the camera back into the ocean. We glimpse the camera's fantastic onward journey and its arrival on a faraway beach with palm trees and another child reaching for it.

Wiesner has always been attracted to the idea of creating a narrative without words; he writes that this task

requires the fullest use of an artist's visual storytelling skills and personal interpretation on the part of the viewer . . . it is the reader's own voice that

interprets and recounts the narrative. Readers bring their own personal
responses to the book, and they guide themselves through it. Readers are
made more active participants in the story. (Wiesner, 1992a, p. vii)

This co-creating role is brought to the fore in a book like *Flotsam*. Without
'guiding' words, readers must look carefully not only if they are to find clues that
help construct the story but also if they are to enjoy the jokes and intertextual
references scattered throughout the book. They must make fuller use of the
connections with their own life and text experiences in order to empathize with
the character and construct his story in their own words, whether or not these
are actually verbalized.

The references to cameras and photography and the images themselves all
point to a key theme behind Wiesner's picturebook: the importance of looking.
As the boy looks through a magnifying glass, a microscope and the camera lens,
the reader looks at and with him. The illustrator plays with the metaphor of the
'eye' of the camera and the eyes of the sea creatures that encounter it during its
underwater journey: 'Characters, or eyes, look out to the reader towards, or
through, something else, and challenge us to notice not just what is depicted
but the very notion of seeing itself' (Smith, 2009, p. 87). The illustrator uses a
variety of strategies to slow down the pace of reading and invite the reader to
look more closely. In particular, the changes in the number and size of the frames
and the layout of the panels contribute to the rhythm and emotional impact
(Pantaleo, 2008). The images draw on the qualities of other visual media: cinema,
photography, comics and picturebooks (including intertextual references to
Wiesner's other picturebooks) and this intermediality encourages the crossing
of borders between different modes. The readers add to the narrative potential
as, together with the character, they cross the lines between reality and fantasy.
As Smith (2009) suggests, it is the boy's ability to actively look beyond the frames
of the real and the surreal that allow him to discover and access the camera's
secrets.

The Arrival

Since its publication in 2006, *The Arrival* has received numerous awards[4] and has
been the subject of various studies and articles,[5] not least by Tan himself (2010,
2011a, 2012). In *Sketches from a Nameless Land* (2010), he writes about the
inspiration and the references behind the story and the artwork, including how
he created images derived from the Ellis Island photographic archive of migrants;
incorporated bits and pieces of his father's own migrant experience; and used

Figure 3.2 Cover *The Arrival*

himself, his wife and friends as models for the characters. Thus, Tan combines his own personal 'story' with moments in global history, bringing them together into a fantasy that attempts to speak to readers of all cultures. The ways in which it invites readers to share their own experiences of migration will be shown in Chapter 4.

The hybrid nature of this book raises many questions, as Lassén-Seger notes:

> The work is also interesting in the way that it transcends traditional genre boundaries and categories of readership. Is *The Arrival* a picture book, a graphic novel or a comic strip? Is it for children, young people or adults? In fact, the book's strength lies in its hybrid nature and the fact that, like many of Tan's other picture books, it is aimed at a broad age range. What makes Tan a fearless picture book artist is, without doubt, his ability to stretch the limits of the picture book medium and his refusal to confine his work within a particular age category. (Lassén-Seger, 2013, p. 3)

In an article where Tan describes himself as an 'accidental' graphic novelist, he explains how this work started as a picturebook and ended as a graphic novel: 'an arrangement of words and/or pictures on consecutive panels on a printed page' (Tan, 2011a, p. 2). He adds that it has the experimental, playful nature of the graphic novel as well as irreverence towards rules, form and style.[6] However, most importantly, he points out that it was the 'best way' to tell this particular story. While we agree that it is definitely longer than most picturebooks, it still fits into Bader's well-known definition of a picturebook (in this case, without the words):

> A picture book is a text, illustrations, total design; an item of manufacture and a commercial product; a social, cultural, historical document; and foremost an experience for a child. As an art form it hinges on the interdependence of pictures and words, on the simultaneous display of two facing pages, and on the drama of the turning page. (Bader, 1976, p. 1)

Tan has designed the book in a way that is reminiscent of a photograph album: the quarto size; the hardcover that looks and almost feels like worn leather; the 'embossed photograph' on the cover; the ornamental borders in the title page and the ribbon marker. Although the character is almost always on the move, the individual images are more like still photographs as they do not contain any motion lines or implied sound effects which are a feature of graphic novels and comics; they are separated by wide, slightly blurred gutters and they make sense on their own even when they form part of a sequence. As we said in the Introduction, the book is very much a 'picture' album ('libro álbum').

The narrative in *The Arrival* has been described by many reviewers and scholars; however, it is probably best to leave this to Tan himself who begins by calling it 'a migrant story':

> A man leaves his wife and child in an impoverished town, seeking better prospects in an unknown country on the other side of a vast ocean. He eventually finds himself in a bewildering city of foreign customs, peculiar animals, curious floating objects and indecipherable languages. With nothing more than a suitcase and a handful of currency, the immigrant must find a place to live, food to eat and some kind of gainful employment. He is helped along the way by sympathetic strangers, each carrying their own unspoken history: stories of struggle and survival in a world of incomprehensible violence, upheaval and hope. (Tan, n.d., para. 1)

By the end, the man is settled enough to bring his wife and daughter to live with him in their adopted country.

Tan carefully balances the negative side of the migrant experience with the solidarity and hope offered by strangers and other migrants. Although the protagonist has experienced poverty, fear and uncertainty before his arrival, and later bewilderment, objectification and discrimination in the early days in the new country, in the end he is able to achieve his goal of finding security for his family thanks to the help and kindness of others. Readers are invited to 'listen' to the inset stories told to the main character by other migrants: stories of escape from (child) slavery, from war and what may be a literal ethnic 'cleansing'. Readers are also invited to share the intertextual references, such as allusions to the history of migration to the USA or to the *Titanic*.[7] Fittipaldi (2008) has pointed out the similarities of the scene where the flying boat goes past large advertisement boards with a scene from Ridley Scott's *Bladerunner*, and Tan has spoken of the influence of other filmmakers such as Stanley Kubrick, Terry Gilliam and Tim Burton. The book thus reveals its 'cosmopolitan' or 'transnational' (Bradford, 2011) character because it combines and blends 'elements from different cultures' and resists 'unitary readings which fail to take these diverse elements into account' (Bradford, 2011, pp. 31–2). The effect of this intertextuality on the children's responses will be discussed in Chapter 6.

The title is the only word that appears in the book that can be read (apart from the words in the peritext – the document fragments on the title pages, the publishing information and the blurb). The translation of the title is an interesting example of how a book's title can 'guide' the reader from the very start. In Spanish, *Emigrantes* places the focus on the people who leave and suggests the plurality of the situation, while in French, *Là Ou Vont Nos Pères* suggests a distant location and journey and invites the reader to identify with the younger generation. (In Italian, the title is a straightforward translation from the English: *L'approdo*.) It would be incorrect to say that, with the exception of the peritext, words have no role in the book because the absence of words is as significant as their presence would have been. Tan has spoken of how words can sometimes become a boundary and restrict the possibilities of meaning-making through images (Tan, 2012), so the lack of them implies an invitation to explore without limitations. The inferences made by the children from the images – analysed in Chapter 5 – are an example of this exploration. Unlike comics or graphic novels, there are no speech or thought bubbles and the 'silent' or 'voiceless' characters (Tan, 2011a) are a reflection on the challenges of communicating in a new language. However, *The Arrival* is not completely wordless in that it does depict words from the fictional language of the new country. It is an effective strategy for sharing the migrant experience of confronting and having to make sense of a foreign language:

> the use of incomprehensible language places us, as readers, in the mind of the protagonist. We are the new arrival, only able to decipher meaning and value from visual images, object relationships and human gestures, and then only by making creative associations. Imagination here is more useful than any knowledge. (Tan, 2010, p. 31)

A discussion of the children's responses to this invented language will be found in Chapters 6 and 7.

Oral response to the visual text

Introductory 'walkthrough'

Each team introduced themselves and the books in different ways but with the aim of generating an interest in the book and in reading and, therefore, encouraging the children to participate. Researchers explained what the project was about and what it would involve. In Glasgow, these served as 'warm-up' discussions where the children and adults began the process of getting to know and trust each other. In Arizona, the researcher also gave each child a copy of the text (during the first four discussions, it was a copy of *Flotsam* and later a copy of *The Arrival*, which was used for the next 12 sessions), which they could take home if they wished. After a brief introduction of the book to the small group, the children in Arizona were invited to browse the book for several minutes in silence, and starting with the book cover they were prompted to share their thoughts about the book. The group stayed on the same page as long as they had thoughts to share and then moved to the next page until the book was finished after 12 meetings. Predictions about what might happen next and connections to personal experiences were encouraged.

In Glasgow and Barcelona, copies of the books were also handed out and introduced to the whole group of children participating in the project. Researchers invited open discussion about any emerging topics, usually centred around the narrative based on a quick first look at the book and title or at least at the peritext, such as covers, book jackets and endpapers. Speculation about the author, the main characters, what seemed to be happening and what the book might be about was encouraged. Another central topic was the wordless nature of the books and this led to talk about the role of words and pictures in narrative. Some questions used at this stage by all the teams were the following:

> What do you think this book is going to be about?
> What does the front cover make you think of? Does it make you feel like reading it?
> How do you read a picture? Can you describe how it is different from reading words?
> Why do you think the author didn't put any words in his book?

The researchers also used prompts about language, culture, food, dress and education in different countries to encourage discussion about the cultural backgrounds of the children. Researchers spoke of their own experience of coming from different countries or of speaking different languages, when this was the case. These helped set the scene for the topic of journeys and migration.

Semi-structured interviews/literary discussions

In order to encourage talk and discussion, we used a combination of group configurations: small- and large-group discussions and interviews, paired interviews and sometimes even one-to-one interviews to follow up on the group discussion or to help a child who had missed a session. While each context used slightly different configurations for discussions, the research teams strove to create a special space, away from the usual school routine and the pressures of assessment. Although we developed some prompt questions to mediate the discussions, as will be exemplified later, an effort was made to formulate them with enough inbuilt flexibility to follow the lead of the children's comments and replies and, at the same time, support them in moving beyond that simple 'enumeration' towards drawing inferences (Bednall, Cranston and Bearne, 2008; Serafini, 2010). Researchers in all three contexts did not completely refrain from expressing their own opinions, although this was kept to a minimum; the questions attempted to be open-ended and flexible, and it was stressed from the beginning that there were no 'wrong' or 'right' answers.

In all three contexts, prompt questions were used to delve more deeply into particular images and themes and extend the literary discussions. Sometimes these were simply 'tell me' (Chambers, 1993) or 'what do you see/think/wonder' (Richards and Anderson, 2003) prompts, and sometimes they were more detailed questions, such as the following, adapted from Arizpe and Styles (2003):

> What is going through your head when you see this picture?
> Why do you think the author decided to draw his pictures in this way? Does it remind you of anything you've seen before?
> What do you notice that is special about the way the author uses colours and light in his drawings? Do you notice anything else that's interesting about the way he draws?

As well as questions related to the narrative and the use of images, the interview schedules included questions about specific visual elements (e.g. colour, perspective, layout), the illustrator's intentions and the themes of journeys and migration. The flexible structure of these sessions meant that discussion could follow directions suggested by the children. It also meant that the process of reading could be done at the pace dictated by the length of the sessions and of the inquiry as a whole. In other words, some images or sections could be 'read' without much discussion, while others could be dwelled on more fully. This was particularly important in the case of *The Arrival*, as it would have taken far too long to discuss every single spread in detail. The flexibility of the schedule meant that each team could include questions that they thought would be fruitful with their particular groups, according to the time available, to the makeup of the groups and other circumstances.

For some images, more specific questions were formulated, but were only used according to the way the discussion progressed; for example, these were designed for the full spread of the town with 'dragon tails':[8]

> What can you see in the shadows? I wonder what it means? What do you think it means?
> What do you think will happen?
> What are those dragon tails? Do you think this is why the man is leaving his family?

Where do you think the characters are going?

I wonder/How do you think the characters are feeling?

Is there anything special about the way the artist uses colour and light here?

Why are there scratches on the picture?

Does this scene remind you of anything?

The following questions helped understand the first inset story told by the young woman the protagonist meets:

I wonder why the colours change suddenly?

Who is telling this story?

What kind of book do you think it is?

I wonder/Where do you think she's escaping to?

In Arizona, instead of semi-structured interviews, the discussions began to unfold from the beginning following the format of small-group literature discussions or literature circles (Martínez-Roldán, 2005; Short, 1997; Short and Pierce, 1998). The organization of the discussions as literature circles implied that the goal was to support dialogue among the children, keeping the focus on the co-construction of meaning and supporting the children as thinkers who could consider different perspectives (Peterson and Eeds, 1990; Short, 1997). This reading engagement invites students to listen carefully and think deeply with other group members to create understandings that go beyond those of individual members (Short, 1997), a goal that all teams had in mind. Some of the questions developed for the semi-structured interviews were also integrated within the discussions.

Annotation of images

The annotations were carried out in Glasgow and Barcelona after at least five or six discussion sessions. The idea for the annotated spread task came from a project carried out by Bednall *et al.* (2008), which was designed to include multimodal texts, including picturebooks, in the reading and writing repertoires of bilingual children (see also Bearne, 2009). Colour photocopies of a range of spreads from the picturebooks were offered to the children who then pasted them on to wider sheets of paper, which framed the images and allowed them a margin to write on. Children were invited to draw lines or arrows across the image and write notes about what they saw, what they thought and any questions the image might raise. They were also invited to draw speech or thought bubbles for the characters appearing in the images. This strategy forces the reader to slow down and look carefully at individual images, allowing time for the discovery of details and for questions or observations to emerge. Researchers were interested in comments arising from the visual features of the image but also the connections and interpretations the readers were making to create the narrative, for example, by commenting on gestures or expressions. In a sense, the annotations became a kind of palimpsest where the children's readings were mapped on to the original image.

Depending on the context, the children were asked to work individually or in pairs but could talk to each other or ask for help with writing from the researchers, teachers or peers. In some cases, scripting by the adult was necessary. When the annotations were done in pairs around a single image, different-coloured pens were provided for later identification of an individual's comments. To finish off the task, the children were asked to share their annotations with the other participants and, if the same image was selected by more than one child, there was further talk based on comparison of comments and questions. In Glasgow, children were asked to do two annotations, one of an image they selected and another of an image that was selected for all of them by the researcher. This meant there would be discussion around the comparison of one common image as well as allowing for comparative analyses. In Barcelona, the children carried out individual annotations based on general guidelines provided by the mediator, which included questions such as 'What do you observe in the picture? What does it suggest to you? What does it remind you of or what can you relate it to?' After this, the children also shared their annotations and talked about some of the specific aspects of their selected images.

Visual responses

The third research method involved the creation of visual artefacts inspired by the picturebooks through drawing and photography. These types of qualitative multimodal visual research methods have proved effective in research for inclusion, although it has been observed that these tools are underused in educational inquiry (Prosser and Loxley, 2007). They have also proved helpful in social science research when working with children who for a variety of reasons struggle to express themselves through words (Fransecky, 1969; Moss, Deppeler, Astley and Pattison, 2007; Young and Barrett, 2001).

Visual methods can also help children choose alternative ways to represent their experiences and views, and in this sense can redress some of the power imbalances between researcher and participant as the inquiry process becomes more active and child-centred. Finally, some of the interpretative processes involved in visual research, which are summarized by Mitchell (2011, p. 11), are particularly relevant to working with wordless picturebooks, such as the use of 'close-reading strategies' and the importance of 'situating one's self in the research texts', which is critical to engaging in the meaning-making process for both researchers and participants.

We felt that eliciting visual responses would allow the children to respond more creatively in consonance with the visual medium of the picturebooks and provide them with further time and space for expanding on their response generally (Colomer, 2000). These methods could help sidestep the challenges of working across different languages, build rapport and encourage more engagement and discussion. They were also designed to look at specific thematic or compositional elements in the narrative.

Photographs

Photography has been a common feature of ethnographic research for many years and 'informant-produced images' allow researchers access to parts of worlds in which they cannot participate themselves (Pink, 2007, p. 88) and are therefore a potentially useful tool in some studies with children. In a large European study with 180 children from 5 countries, researchers concluded that 'children's photographs are not just their "view of the world" but are also a construction of their identity in relation to their parents and their peers' (Sharples, Davison, Thomas and Rudman, 2003, p. 324). Another study showed how children from an immigrant community took photos that suggest their participation 'in a bicultural world' that reflected their immigrant community, as they took portraits to remember people who were migrating to other countries or back to their country of origin (Orellana, 1999).

In Glasgow and Barcelona, following the annotation sessions with *Flotsam*, children were given disposable cameras and asked to take pictures of people, objects and events that were important to them in their new country and which they would like to share with children in other countries (following the idea of the travelling camera in *Flotsam*). This task was only carried out for *Flotsam* as it related directly to the theme of photography in the book. Children's greater use of mobile phone cameras means that photography is a familiar activity and a way of sharing objects and events in their lives, so we felt this task would appeal to them. In addition, for many migrants, photographs can be a way not only of maintaining contact with relatives in their country of origin, but also for sharing their previous life with others in their new countries.

This activity therefore also became the link to the next book, *The Arrival*, which, as we have noted, suggests a photograph album and contains photographic-like images. Tan writes that

> Photo albums are actually perfect examples of how illustrated narrative works most effectively, their power is not so much in documenting particulars, but triggering memory and imagination, urging us to fill the empty space around frozen snapshots, to build on fragments and constantly revisit our own storyline, a kind of visual literacy we all understand intuitively. (Tan, 2009, p. 10)

Having taken the photographs, the children composed them into a linear sequence or in any other configuration (e.g. their favourite ones) in order to present them to their peers, thus revisiting their own storylines, triggering memories and also filling in some of the gaps in their knowledge of their classmates through the visuals. After their sharing, they were asked, 'What would a child from another country who finds your photo in a camera (as the child in *Flotsam*) learn about you?' The presentation sessions where they spoke about the photographs were essential because, as Pink points out, photographic images do not hold 'intrinsic meanings'; they are only made meaningful 'when participants [speak] about *why* and *how* they took the pictures, as well as about what [is] depicted *in* the pictures (Pink, 2007, p. 89).[9]

An issue raised by using photography as a visual research tool is ethics, particularly the sharing of images with people. Given the sensitivity required when discussing experiences of travel and migration, we were very careful when dealing with the photographs. On the one hand, we were concerned about having images of people and did not want to cause anxiety by asking the families for permission to make the photographs public; on the other, we felt it would be limiting if the children could not take any pictures of people. In the end, the children were encouraged to take photographs of anyone and anything they wanted and these were shared only during the classroom presentations.[10]

Graphic strips and drawings

In Arizona, the children drew their predictions based on an image selected by the researcher. The image was of the ship carrying the immigrants reaching the shore and the children were asked to imagine what was going to happen once the ship arrived. In a different session, they drew and wrote about their favourite image and they also wrote fictional and real stories of people travelling, but not about their own journeys. In Glasgow and Barcelona, either during or after the sessions reading *The Arrival*, the children were invited to draw a 'graphic strip' or sequence of pictures that visually narrated a journey. The thinking behind this was that it would be a way of reflecting on the meaning of a journey and the different stages involved (leaving, travelling, arriving) that are common to all journeys and which could be shared. It was stressed that it did not have to be their own journeys to the host country; it could be a different journey or the journey of someone they knew. The sharing could therefore be at a level at which each child was comfortable, but also which encouraged discussion about common experiences. Using a visual medium meant they could use their knowledge and recent work on the compositional aspects of *The Arrival* to 'frame' each of the journey stages or moments. It also meant they could write as many words as they wanted, either as captions or in thought or speech bubbles, features they had already been adding to the annotations.

In Glasgow, photocopied layouts were provided but the children were told they could design their own if they preferred. They were reminded that they could add speech and/or thought bubbles and/or captions. The graphic strips were done individually but within a group session and then shared. The researchers were available to assist with organizing ideas or with writing.

Using the image-based research tools with *Flotsam*

Although we will not discuss the analysis of the responses to *Flotsam*, we felt it would be important to include a brief description of the research methods used because it prepared the children for reading *The Arrival*. Given its length, it was possible to cover the whole book in two to four sessions, leaving the rest for the annotation and photography tasks. Because the literary discussion approach was new to the readers, the prompt questions were formulated to help them focus their attention on the importance of looking carefully, for example:

[full spread of boy looking at crab on beach surrounded by objects]
What do you notice about the things the boy has on the beach (magnifying glass, microscope, binoculars) – I wonder why the author included them?

[boy looking at fantastic photographs]
What do you think the boy thought/felt when he looked at those photographs? Have you ever felt like that when you looked at a photograph or a picture of a strange place?

[full spread of children's photographs in black and white]
Tell me about these pictures. Why are they round? Why do they change colour? What do these numbers mean? Who are these children?

[spread of boy taking self-photograph]
What is the boy doing now? Who is looking at him through the camera? I wonder what he'll do next?
What do you think will happen to the camera?

[final spread]
Where do you think the camera has come to? What do you think this girl will see in the photographs?

In Glasgow and Barcelona, two annotations were done in the session after the literary discussions; in the cases where these were done in pairs, children were encouraged to help each other look, think and write. In Glasgow, non-immigrant children were paired with immigrant children so they could provide some language support.

To introduce the photograph task, the researchers reminded the children that the camera had travelled from one place to another or one country to another and that the children had taken their own pictures to share with other children. The children were then given simple digital or disposable cameras and asked to take photographs of the things, places and people that were important to them in their life in the new country and which they would like to show to a child, a relative in their country of origin or someone they did not know, in another country.

In Glasgow and Arizona, they kept the cameras for approximately a week and there was a session in which they presented the photographs to the researchers and other children in the project. In Glasgow, they chose two photographs, which the researchers had printed for them. In Barcelona, the researchers created a cardboard-box imitation of the old-fashioned camera in the book and the children were able to actually put their photographs into it.

For this task, the Glasgow researchers concluded that

For this group of children the photography task became a way of controlling the way they wanted to see and be seen by others, moving away from stereotypes and sharing their wider communities with each other. At the same time the photographs encouraged them to reflect on the idea of looking carefully, increase their understanding of the visual image and to think about artistically complex texts. (Arizpe and McAdam, 2011, p. 242)

The last set of photographs of the children in *Flotsam* who shared the camera, which are in black and white, worked as a link to Tan's sepia images. The photographs of people and objects taken by the children also linked to the images on the first page of *The Arrival* where the series of objects appear in individual frames and are an indication of the narrative's context and characters. The theme of journeys across the sea was another link, suggested in the unknown language and the fragmented documents that appear on the edges of the first 'title page'.

Responsible research: Ethics and pedagogy

In putting together the research design and methods, we had two main concerns: first, that these were ethically constructed in a way that took into account the sensitivities of working with immigrant children; and, second, that the inquiry tools were supporting the children in their learning (Banks, 2001). The power inequalities between the adult researchers or mediators and the participating children could not be entirely avoided. We were aware that children often construct responses that they believe will please the researchers or that researchers could easily guide responses without meaning to. However, we attempted to address these issues through constant reflection as well as through taking what we learned from the children in this inquiry to construct a more culturally responsive pedagogy that could have positive consequences for other children.

Throughout the project, we were aware of the need for care when discussing experiences of travel and migration, and even more so in dealing with photographs (Leitch, 2008). As mentioned above, the use of visual methods does imply serious consideration of a range of ethical issues, and in particular when working with potentially vulnerable children, although guidelines developed by various international organizations can help deal with these issues (Mitchell, 2011), and throughout the research process we were particularly cautious when working with photographs and the graphic strips that included personal information. Research involving children representing social issues and/or personal experiences through visual media requires an awareness of the potential hazards and the need for safe, child-centred practices (Leitch, 2008). While being aware of these issues, it is also the case that photographs and other images created by children have become an intrinsic part of using mobile phones and social networking, and, as we have said before, children have a great deal of knowledge about the technology involved in these practices, which could be put to use in the classroom (while not neglecting instructions on safety issues).

Sharing a book that concerns displacement and talking about journeys meant references to personal experiences of migration, which may have been traumatic. Some of the issues in *The Arrival* could relate to unresolved legal status, and we were aware that some children may have been forbidden by parents or carers from talking about certain events related to their journeys or status. Accordingly, the researchers were careful not to question children directly about their experiences, and at all times children were given the opportunity to remain silent about particular issues and not to disclose private information. Guided by the teacher, researchers attempted to provide a space that felt safe and comfortable for talking about the issues raised by the picturebooks if they so wished. In this way, we tried to make sure that their emotional responses were not upsetting to them or to others.

Finally, we were keen to ensure that the tools could also act as effective pedagogical strategies that engaged and assisted children in learning a new language or about a new culture, as well as using their knowledge and experience with visual media to develop their visual literacy. Initially developed as research tools, we found that these strategies provided the children with different pathways for building on and sharing each individual's literacy skills and experiences. Some of the pedagogical implications for the inquiry will be discussed in Chapter 9.

The next section of the chapter details the development of the analytical framework.

Developing an analytical framework

In this section, we describe the process of arriving at the shared analytical framework that gave rise to the findings discussed in the next part of the book. As we sought to explore the responses to wordless picturebooks in order to generate theories that would help understand how immigrant pupils construct meaning from visual narratives, we had to confront several challenging aspects of this inquiry. One of these was the negotiation of this analytical framework across the variations in disciplines (literature, literacy, language education) and the epistemologies that inspired the different research traditions of each team. This negotiation was part of our research 'journey', as we all had to cross invisible borders in order to learn from others, so that, at the end of this particular intercultural exchange, we could create something new that would work for all of us and for our particular data.

The crossing of borders was also necessary to deal with the challenge of capturing the fluid and slippery nature of this data. For a start, the multimodal qualities of the picturebooks we were working with meant that verbal and visual elements merged and interacted with each other to create a quality that was different from what they each were originally. Responses to an aesthetic experience such as this one depend on subjectivities, as well as cultural and social contexts, and can develop in a variety of directions. As we know, observable responses are not equivalent to literature's internal experience (Crago, 1990). Added to this, the responses were mostly in a language that was new to most of the participants so the expressed responses may have been less precise than the children desired or intended. The languages used to express the responses were also evolving, partly as a result of the process itself as the children learned new terms and partly as a natural result of language learning, with the connections and disconnections to a new culture implicit in this learning. These challenges help explain why the data resisted division into rigid categories and both the data collection and the analysis processes themselves mirrored the idea of border crossings as one that involves the need to find one's way in the process of going back and forth, either virtually or literally, crossing and re-crossing the landscape afforded by our data. To counter these challenges, we started by designing data collection methods that could help remove some of the linguistic challenges the children might encounter. This also included situating the research methods within the theoretical frameworks that positioned our collective understandings of migration, visual literacy and picturebooks, as described in Chapter 1.

During the first phase of analysis, once we had collected the data, each team consulted earlier analytical models of response to picturebooks in order to establish initial approaches, while following Erickson's interpretive model of qualitative research where 'the basic task of data analysis is to generate assertions that vary in scope and level of inference, largely through induction, and to establish an evidentiary warrant for the assertions one wishes to make' (Erickson, 1986, p. 146). The data was thus analysed inductively and deductively for content, themes, patterns and social meaning within the different analytical models explored by each team to arrive at a set of common categories (described and exemplified in the next section). While these initially proved useful, we found that, as the collective analysis process and dialogue among teams continued, the lines between the categories started to blur and themes began to overlap. The categories initially created became too isolating and narrow and did not seem to capture the reality of the reader-response data, which was multilayered and defied neat boundaries. The data demanded going beyond being 'sorted' and 'classified' to the extent that we realized we needed an approach which corresponded more closely to the fluidity of the responses themselves, to the hybrid characteristics of the inquiry itself: the transnational experience and migration of data between contexts. Therefore, following Atkinson and Delamont (2005), we decided to further explore the multiple coding and structuring principles through which the cultural and social reading experience of this particular group of children was enacted and represented through the different research methods. This led us into the second phase of analysis.

Through iterative multiple readings of the entire data set, particular assertions were confirmed or discarded. The collaborative approach within each team and with the other teams led us to discuss, confirm and revise our analysis and ensured that the evidence was solid enough to describe as findings. In this way, our analytical approach continued the process of discovery whereby 'systematic interactions between data and ideas as well as the emergent properties of research design and data analysis' were in constant dialogue (Atkinson and Delamont, 2005, p. 833).

In the rest of this chapter, we offer a detailed description of both phases of analysis. We describe our attempts to systematize the data by first looking at the contributions of previous analytical frameworks developed from reader-response to picturebooks. We then look at how these influenced the initial approaches and resulting categories from the analysis made by each team and how these led to the first shared model of analysis. Finally, we problematize this model and describe how it evolved into the analytical framework for the findings that we present in the following section of this book.

Phase I: Analytical frameworks for response to picturebooks

In their exploration of children's responses to picturebooks, Arizpe and Styles (2003) examine various analytical models, particularly those proposed by Kiefer (1995) and Madura (1995, 1998), two of the earliest studies in this field. Kiefer adapts M.A.K. Halliday's four semiotic functions of language to describe the different types of verbal response or 'language' used by the children: informative (which includes more descriptive comments or simple comparisons between images or intertextual references); heuristic (which groups speculative comments related to understanding such as inferences about the illustrator's intentions, character motivations and cause–effect); imaginative (through which readers enter the world of the book, often using figurative language, putting words into the characters' mouths or putting themselves in the characters' shoes); and personal (which includes comments that link the readers' experiences with any aspect of the images and text). In turn, Madura builds on Kiefer and Rosenblatt to establish three categories of response: descriptive (retellings and comments about the pictures); interpretive (comments on the narrative and links between the text and personal experiences) and thematic (the appreciation of themes, styles and techniques.

Sipe argues that a weakness of previous studies on responses to picturebooks is that it is difficult to replicate their conditions or to apply their typologies to research in other situations. The strength of his own typology is that it emerges from five research projects involving a specific age range and that it could be applied in similar contexts. His aim was to develop a 'theory of literary understanding that is specific to contemporary young children, and that is grounded in their responses to literature' (Sipe, 2008, p. 9). Based on educational and literary theories and on the extensive research he carried out over at least ten years, he drew up the most detailed typology of response so far. Sipe's five main categories for children's understanding of literary texts are: 1) Analytical; 2) Intertextual; 3) Personal; 4) Transparent; and 5) Performative. The first and widest category, Analytical, is subdivided into another five categories: 1a) making narrative meaning; 1b) the book as made object or cultural product; 1c) the language of the text; 1d) analysis of illustrations and other visual matter; and 1e) relationships between fiction and reality. Sipe distinguishes further subdivisions in these and the other categories and provides clear examples through the children's words as they interact with the teacher, their peers and, in some cases, the researcher. Although there are no categories in his model that refer to the interaction between readers of different cultures to a text, Sipe does note that

> The vast question of how culture shapes, constrains, and enables literary response is an area under active investigation. . . . All of these factors make it important to contextualize children's responses to literature and to seek to understand the ways in which a diversity of response from a diversity of cultures can enrich literary discussion and interpretation. (Sipe, 1999, p. 126)

The teams discussed these previous models and decided each would approach the data in the first instance with them in mind but with the flexibility to bring other perspectives into the analysis. In what follows, the main findings from these initial approaches are described, some of which, after various discussion sessions, fed into the creation of the shared model.

Glasgow

The Glasgow team were keen to use Sipe's detailed framework as a starting point in their data analysis for the oral responses; however, there were several crucial differences between these inquiries: the structure of the sessions; the specific group of immigrant readers; and the wordless picturebooks. In fact, Sipe himself was less certain about how these categories would work with the ten- and eleven-year-old readers we were working with (email correspondence with E. Arizpe[11]). Despite this, the team found most of Sipe's categories as a useful first approach to the data, although, because of the differences in research context, they felt a different framework was required. More specifically, this occurred in relation to the theme of journeys.

Sipe does include 'thematic' statements in the responses within his analytical category. Again, because of the lack of words and multiple layers of *The Arrival* and the particular group of children involved in this inquiry, and perhaps mainly because of their age and circumstances, the Glasgow team considered this topic-related category should be given more prominence. There were many references to travelling and all that is involved in this process, from methods of transport to passports and including the feelings of those who travel and those who are left behind. It was not only the immigrant children who had travelled; the others had also experienced journeys in some way, either by moving house or going on holiday to a foreign country. There were also comments about the reasons for travelling, particularly in relation to the main character leaving his family, such as work, looking for a safe place to live or simply as a holiday. We found that the overlap between this theme and the 'life to text' and 'text to life' connections within Sipe's 'Personal' category required a more in-depth exploration of the migrant experience as reflected in the responses, which we completed during Phase II of the analysis.

Barcelona

In her work within the context of this inquiry and in collaboration with the other members of the GRETEL team, Fittipaldi investigated 'the possible contributions of the reading of picturebooks to the teaching and integration of immigrants' (Fittipaldi, 2008, p. 2) and the value they found in shared reading. Fittipaldi developed categories based on the work of Arizpe and Styles (2003),

Parsons (1987) and Siro (2005) into what she called 'claves de lectura' or 'reading codes'. These are:

1. Mediatic: which alludes to the links made between the children and popular media texts such as television, cinema or music videos; the language influence of these texts and the way the children approached their reading.
2. Realist: which emerges when readers compare their reading to that which they consider 'real' and which is often understood as a reality/fiction or even truth/falsehood dichotomy and is a measure for comparisons and value.
3. Metaphoric: which occurs when readers observe figures they consider symbolic and construct metaphors that 'activate not only knowledge relative to social traditions and cultural conventions but also experiential knowledge, closely related to their life stories' (Fittipaldi, 2008, p. 87).
4. Personal: which includes responses in which the children 'project' (Gombrich; 1979) their experiences into the book, reading their story 'between (or beyond) the lines' (Fittipaldi, 2012, p. 76).

Although this precise terminology was not used in the final framework, these categories further informed the analysis with respect to intertextual, personal and compositional responses.

Arizona

In Arizona, the discussions and the children's written stories were analysed for emergent themes and discourse patterns (Erickson, 1986; Gee, 2005), as well as for the specific strategies used to make meaning. Having used Sipe's (1996) categories for her dissertation study, the researcher entered the 12[12] discussions into NVivo and coded the children's responses using those categories. 'Making Meaning' was the category with the largest number of responses, and Sipe's subcategories under Making Meaning were especially useful to understand and analyse the children's responses. Almost half of the children's responses under Making Meaning were coded under Retelling of the Story (45 per cent) and most have Speculative Hypotheses/Inferences (45 per cent); 9 per cent of children's comments were Clarification Questions and the very few responses (1 per cent) initially coded as Personal Opinions or Evaluative Thematic statements were later merged within the Retelling or the Inference categories as appropriate. In addition, the team examined how the children used language within the groups to make and negotiate meaning among themselves. Informed by a sociocultural perspective on learning (C. Lewis, 2001; Moll, 1990, 1994, 2001; Vygotsky, 1978), they searched for instances of mediation of children's interpretations and responses within the discussions that could lead to an understanding of the social nature of the children's responses.

The following subcategories were identified in the data:

1. Children's comments in which they seemed to use their own or others' experiences with immigration to make sense of the text (Campano, 2007; Moll, 1994).

2. Children's co-construction of their own version of the story or parallel texts (Goodman, 1996).

3. Questions asked by the children or comments with the apparent purpose of engaging others in their own interpretive process: inquiry talk (Lindfors, 1999; Martínez-Roldán, 2005). Lindfors links inquiry acts to communication acts, 'conversational turns that *turn* toward the partners for help' (Lindfors, 1999, p. 51), and she suggests that children have their own culturally learned ways of doing so – ways that can be difficult to hear when they do not sound like our own ways.

4. Different inquiry or response styles showed by the children:
   a) A 'flexible observant' style, by which children engage in multiple interpretations and 'hypotheses', giving various equally plausible scenarios for the group's queries or the images in the book.
   b) Use of storytelling or 'performative narrative' – a kind of storytelling in which they created and 'performed' dialogue by adopting the characters' perspective, imagining their thoughts and words, and sharing them in an animated, almost theatrical or performative way.

5. Borrowing others' strategies to interact with the text: the children incorporated into their own narratives and responses the meaning-making strategies they observed other children in the group using.

6. Language choice (given that the group and the mediators were bilingual).

7. Diagetic border crossing, the 'stepping in and out of the narrated story world for a variety of purposes' (Mackey, 2003, p. 592).

Some of these categories were explored in Martínez-Roldán and Newcomer (2011), which brings the themes together in the format of 'case studies' (see also Martínez-Roldán 2012). Some also influenced the development of Chapter 4 (children's discussions and experiences on immigration), Chapter 5 (making meaning) and Chapter 8 (on mediation).

The initial collective analytical approach

The discussion of the results of each team's approaches led to the formulation of an emergent shared set of analytical categories through which the data was revisited. These are explained briefly below[13] because, although some of them continued to evolve and led to a reorganization of the data, they provided a base for the findings that emerged in the end from the analysis.[14] Also, we consider that describing this process is a more honest reflection of the development of a collaborative inquiry and reflects the challenges of working with data of this kind but also the productive nature of shared methods and reflections.

The initial analytical framework (see Figure 3.3) was based on two interconnected levels:

1. The process of the response based on the codes used to make sense of the narrative. Within this level, four categories were defined:
   a) Personal: responses that reflect a projection of the readers into the visual text based on their real-life experiences as a way of illuminating the narrative;
   b) Referential: responses that refer to the identification and description of the elements in the story (what is happening, to whom, when, where);
   c) Compositional: responses that refer to the visual elements used to construct the narrative (colour, perspective, layout, movement, etc.) including the book as object and its wordless nature; and
   d) Intertextual: responses that refer to either other media texts or relate aspects of the imaginary worlds portrayed in the images to cultural references.

Levels of Response / Processes of Response	Literal statements (identification, description and simple connections)	Inferential statements (elaborate, interpretative and/ or symbolic connections)
Referential	Identification and description of the elements of the narrative and images (the story)	Interpretation of the elements of the narrative and images (the story)
Personal	Simple connections: text to life/life to text	Elaborate connections: text to life/life to text
Compositional	Identification and description of textual categories	Interpretation of textual categories
Intertextual	Simple connections to other texts; media; cultural references	Elaborate connections to other texts; media; cultural references

Figure 3.3 Initial analytical framework

2. The level of elaboration for the responses within each of the previous categories. The two levels were considered as follows:

   a) a literal response that implies a straightforward identification or description, or the establishment of simple connections; or

   b) an inferential response that implies a deeper, more subtle reading and interpretation where the connections are more elaborate and play a more central function in making sense of the text.

Phase II: Beyond categories and borders

At first, it seemed that this model covered the most salient aspects of the data from all the countries involved and organized them in a way that the differences between a more descriptive and a more interpretative response became apparent. However, as the transcriptions were re-examined in more detail, overlaps began to occur, particularly in the case of the Referential category where the identification and description of elements often included compositional or cultural elements. It was also difficult to determine when the reference was to personal experience or general knowledge (e.g. 'in some countries men wear hats like that'). Therefore, a more overlapping format for the main categories was suggested (see Figure 3.4).

This model highlights the overlaps in the following specific areas: elements of the composition with narrative functions; intertextual allusions to explicate the ways of creating the image; and references coming from cultural knowledge based on personal experience. Although this model was more fluid, we still felt that even more complex issues were emerging, which required a different approach. Like Brooks and Browne, we felt that '[i]n practical application, the

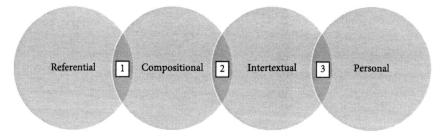

1. Compositional elements with narrative function.
2. Intertextual allusions that explain ways of constructing the image.
3. References originating from a cultural knowledge, based on personal experience.

Figure 3.4 Contact lines between categories

Source: Fittipaldi, 2012, p. 83. (Reproduced and translated with permission from the author.)

participants' interpretations are not so tidy and easily categorized. Rather, the responses are overlapping, transient and often revised, as is consistent with the nature of cultural practices and the fast-paced give and take of discussions' (Brooks and Browne, 2012, p. 83). These researchers, who have furthered Sipe's work, explore the idea of a 'culturally situated reader-response model' where readers assume cultural positions when making sense of what they read.

This overlapping also occurred as we began identifying the different levels of referential responses, some of which were at first described as 'failed' referential responses. In other words, when the readers misinterpreted what seemed to be evident clues as compared to 'explorative' inferences or 'potent' inferences, which supported the joint construction of meaning. The elaboration of this hypothesis was linked in some contexts to the progression of the reading sessions, so it was also difficult to isolate the more 'literal' observations from more elaborate 'inferences'. Many of the hypotheses the readers built referred to the situation, motivation, thoughts and feelings of the characters but these could not be associated clearly with either personal situations or disassociated from the aesthetic features of the images, resulting again in an overlap between the referential, the personal and the compositional.

Despite the simplicity of the responses that were related to the Personal category, we realized that there were more complex issues related to migration and attitudes of distancing. It was felt that it would be important therefore to discuss these aspects together, and this emerged into the findings in Chapter 4, which revolve around the complex aspects of migration addressed by the children and their impact on the children's identities and on themselves as readers.

The Referential category (ideational or analytical talk) also evolved and returned to Sipe's analytical categories, which involved, among other elements, responses in which the children were making meaning of the text, which Sipe further categorized as including retelling, clarifying questions, inferences and hypotheses, personal opinions, and evaluative and thematic statements. This overlap, along with the difficulties in differentiating between a simple retelling and an inference, also seemed too arbitrary, so we found that a more expansive definition of retelling as inference was necessary. Focusing on children's interpretive work through retellings and co-authoring helped to overcome the borders created by the categories, highlighting the ways they used language, personal experiences and local history, and peers to navigate the texts. The findings are discussed in Chapter 5.

The Intertextual category allowed us to categorize the responses that contained intertextual references according to type (text to text, text to life), as well as analysing the elements in the book that triggered these responses. Everyday cultural practices were drawn upon as well as links to popular audiovisual products such as films and videogames. This identification, however, seemed to isolate, rather than to integrate, the links the children were making to the rest of their reading and to the function of these previous links within the social construction of knowledge. Thus, the analysis began to move towards the ways in which the readers located themselves in the book through intertextuality. This is the topic of Chapter 6.

Under the Compositional category, we grouped the responses that referred to any of the visual elements used to construct the narrative, including the consideration of the book as a 'material object'. As in the case of the intertextual references, this listing of responses did not really convey the ways in which the children were engaging with the affordances of the text. This can be seen more clearly in Chapter 7.

It also became apparent that even what we would have considered 'literal'-level responses were often based on having to infer from a variety of visual clues, so that children were constantly building hypotheses, even if it seemed at first to be a simple observation. What we began to realize was how subtle the work behind the responses was, so subtle that it was not always evident to the readers themselves and often it could not be expressed. To use Rosenblatt's metaphor, it was the tip of the 'iceberg' of meaning-making that was visible, while underneath, sometimes more visible than others, were 'the sensations, images, feelings, and ideas that are the residue of past psychological events involving those words and their referents [...] called forth' (Rosenblatt, 1988, p. 5) by the reading but harder to bring to the surface.

Finally, although we were aware of the influence of peer and mediator response, it also became evident that the mediation role of those who were facilitating the discussions and of the children themselves was one of the most crucial factors in exploring and developing understanding. The type of questions and comments and the social interaction in the literary discussions often determined whether these remained at a more literal level or moved towards a consideration of wider aspects. The interaction between the participants, their negotiation of meanings and comments were also a determining factor in the development of the discussion and therefore individual responses must be seen within the context of the interpretive community. The role of the mediator and the formation of the interpretive community will be discussed in more detail in Chapters 8 and 9.

It seemed that the unseen, multiple voices in these multiple settings resisted being driven into clearly delineated and confined spaces. Given the text's visual nature, which defies categories that have been created mostly for texts in which the story is told through both written text and images, the analysis seemed to be demanding a less bounded context; a more holistic description based on the insights obtained from previous frameworks and from a consideration of a wider focus, which we can describe as more permeable. Because of the difficulties of delineating responses by category because of too much crossover, reflecting in part the border-crossing theme of the book as well as its structure, we ended up turning the initial table on its head and taking as a start the idea that all responses were inferential, as we discuss in Chapter 5. However, we felt that, as a result of the complexity of the responses and the collaborative nature of the research, it would serve no purpose to reduce the analysis to a precise model or diagram.

The notion of border crossings seemed to explain the permeability of the categories, as this occurred both between the readers and the book and between the research team members' epistemologies and research experiences. This notion includes the specific reference both to travel across 'borders' (national and cultural) and also to the ability to move across fictional borders (to go through the 'visual journey' of the text) and/or to identify and interpret intertextual and intercultural connections between worlds of origin and arrival. The wordless nature of these books, together with their theme, thus invited these crossings and blending of categories.[15]

Notes on transcription and translation

All the oral data was audio-recorded and fully transcribed by each of the teams. The excerpts that appear in the following chapters have been minimally edited (without giving notice) to exclude false starts, repetitions and 'thinking noises' (Mackey, 2011, p. 37) and facilitate communication. The responses in the original language appear first, followed by a translation. Any non-English words are translated into English in brackets following. In each excerpt, it is made clear which is the voice of the adult through the use of the term 'Mediator'; in the majority of cases, it was the researcher with teachers making the occasional comment. If it is not clear from the context of the quoted excerpt, the children's pseudonyms are followed by that of the host context, and if their country of origin is significant for that response, it is also included. A table of all the children's names, origins and languages can be found in the Appendix for quick reference. From the next section onwards, the three host contexts will be abbreviated as GLW (Glasgow), BCN (Barcelona) and AZ (Arizona).

Notes

1　Silva-Díaz (2005) was one of the researchers involved in the initial idea for this inquiry, although she did not participate directly in the rest of the process.

2　Within the GRETEL research team, 'lectura literaria' [literary reading] is understood as a way of approaching literary texts, which views these as texts open to interpretation and which considers readers as active subjects, capable of constructing meaning and of participating in 'discusiones literarias' [literary conversations], that is, conversations about a collective reading by students and teachers of a particular text.

3　Findings from the work with *Flotsam* in Glasgow can be found in Arizpe and McAdam (2011), and in Sydney in Walsh, Cranitch and Maras (2012).

4　For a full list of awards, see http://en.wikipedia.org/wiki/Shaun_Tan#Awards/.

5　Various studies, such as Bradford (2011), Campano and Ghiso (2011) and Hunter (2011), have noted the positive potential of *The Arrival*; however, the study by Pantaleo (2011) mentioned in Chapter 1 is the only other one that deals with children's responses (there is an article on adult immigrant responses: Kapadia Bodi, 2008). A more negative critique by Saguisag argues that the book 'ultimately naturalizes Western myths about immigration and assimilation' (Saguisag, 2010, p. 20), an assertion that bears some exploration but with which we do not agree, as in many cases this 'myth' is reflected in reality and because Tan's ultimate purpose seems to be to offer hope rather than despair.

6　The differences and similarities between picturebooks and comics have been the subject of recent debates; see, for example, the forthcoming special issue 'Comics, Picturebooks and Childhood' of the *Journal of Graphic Novels and Comics*.

7　We are grateful to the children of another school in Glasgow, St Louise's Primary School, for their discovery that the image of the young news-seller is based on an actual photograph of a news-seller with the headlines for the sinking of the *Titanic*: http://www.gettyimages.co.uk/creative/titanic-stock-photos (#10153771). The children realized that, if read upside down, the unknown language corresponds to the exact shape of the words of the original news headline.

8　There are no page numbers in the book so a description of the spreads was used instead.

9　Moss (2001) echoes this in her conclusions for a study on the gendering of reading, which used photographs of reading activities in the home taken by children. Although the methodology provided Moss with data about this topic, she warns that the images can be deceptive and that it is important to ask questions about what they mean, rather than 'read them at face value', given that photography, like any other medium, 'mediates what it records, and constructs what it wants us to see' (Moss, 2001, p. 289).

10 For the purposes of research dissemination, only persons in public spaces or who could not be recognized have been shown. Memory cards and negatives have been either deleted or disposed of. For a fuller discussion of photography as a methodology in this inquiry in relation to *Flotsam*, see Arizpe and McAdam (2011).

11 Larry Sipe's death during the middle of our inquiry was not only a personal loss for many members of the teams but also a professional loss, as his advice had been invaluable until that time.

12 In Arizona, all children participated in eight discussions but there were 12 discussions in total because there were additional sessions for children who missed out a session, usually conducted with two children and the researcher, so that they could follow the story and the other children's comments when they rejoined the group.

13 A more detailed description of these categories, with examples, can be found in Fittipaldi (2008).

14 The initial approach to the data from the annotated spreads is discussed in Farrell, Arizpe and McAdam (2010).

15 The annotated spreads and the graphic strips or drawings were also examined under these new perspectives and examples from their data have been incorporated into each chapter, providing further support for the themes.

Part Two

Navigating the Interpretive Process

4

Reclaiming the Migrant Experience

The content analysis of the children's discussions of *The Arrival* revealed that much of their discussions revolved, as expected, around immigration issues. They shared knowledge about diverse aspects of this process; however, while they brought knowledge from history books and popular culture, most of the discussions seemed to be anchored in their personal experiences. It was obvious that the children's past histories were 'of considerable importance to them as ways of constructing meaning. It is as if the pictures act as a trigger for a host of memories – each one personal to the child' (Bromley, 2003, cited in Arizpe and Styles, 2003, p. 153).

The children showed an awareness of socioeconomic issues influencing migration and events such as violence and war depending on where they came from, as well as some of the hardships of the immigrant experience. Some of them also used the discussions to position themselves and reclaim a particular identity as emigrants and even to reclaim an expertise on the topic that did not come from the authoritative knowledge of books but from experiential knowledge. In this section, we examine the content of the children's discussions that focus on immigration, not only through their personal stories but also through their empathetic connections with the fictional visual narrative.

What does emigrant mean? Awareness of factors that influence immigration

Mediador: *'Emigrantes', ¿sabéis qué significa?* ['Emigrants', do you know what it means?]

Gabriel: **Nosotros**, *que venimos de Rumanía y entramos en otro país. Es eso,* *'emigrantes'.* [**We**, who come from Romania and arrived to another country. That's it, 'emigrants'.]
(BCN)

The content of the children's discussions about immigration in response to *The Arrival* involved interpretative work full of inferences; however, some of the children often crossed the border between the story in the book and their own lives. While the children brought personal experiences to their interpretations of *The Arrival* in all inquiry contexts, one group of immigrant children in BCN explicitly positioned themselves as 'emigrants'. Perhaps the title of the actual book, *Emigrantes* in Spanish, versus *The Arrival* in English, mediated this positioning, or maybe the political contexts and educational programmes in each country played a role in how the children saw themselves in the host country. Nonetheless, as we will discuss later, even if the GLW and AZ groups of children did not explicitly self-identify as either emigrants or immigrants, through their sharing of personal experiences we learned a great deal about their awareness and understanding of the reasons that may lead or force people to move.

Specifically, the children's discussions revealed their awareness of some of the socioeconomic and sociopolitical factors that force people to leave their countries. In all three research settings, the children entertained several hypotheses for the protagonist leaving his country; however, one common reason was related to the families' or countries' financial situation; in the children's words, the protagonist left to go in search of better job opportunities.

For example, in several discussions, the children in AZ repeated that the immigrant was searching for a job. Moreover, for one of the children, the immigrant was leaving from Mexico and going to AZ for that purpose. In BCN, when the children discussed the full-spread image of the boat arriving at the harbour with the two statues (see Figure 4.1), they also thought that one of the statues represented an immigrant in search of work (in the example that follows, we have highlighted these comments):

Alan: *Estas dos estatuas me parece que éste de aquí es un – es como – está* *representado como un inmigrante*
Mediador: *¿Por qué? ¿por qué piensas eso?*
Alan: *porque tiene una maleta . . . una taza de café y comida*
[. . .]
Naima: *ah – porque aquí vienen las personas*
Mediador: *Podría ser como dice Naima que porque ahí va la gente ¿no?*

Alan: *Viene gente pa – trabajar – pa – mandarle dinero a su familia*
[…]
Mediador: *y a ver Naima, ¿qué piensas?*
Naima: *Que ha venido a trabajar*
Alan: *Puede trabajar dos años – para*
Naima: *para llevar a su familia allí, también: – como ha dicho el Calin.*

[Alan: These two statues, it seems to me that this one is a – is like – he is
represented as an immigrant
Mediator: Why? Why do you think that?
Alan: because he has a suitcase . . . a cup of coffee and food
[…]
Naima: oh – because here the people are coming
Mediator: It could be, as Naima says, because here is where the people
go, no?
Alan: The people come to work, to send money to his family
[…]
Mediator: let's see, Naima, what do you think?
Naima: That he has come to work
Alan: He can work for two years – to
Naima: bring his family there also – as Calin has said.]

Figure 4.1 Boat arriving at the harbour

Alan's response that he may work for two years suggests that maybe the father planned to earn enough money to be able to go back to his country, although Naima proposed that the father was going to bring his family to the new country. Ryan, in AZ, echoed Alan's alternatives as he suggested that the dad was going to work '*para regresar con su familia*' [to go back to his family]. Whether the children believed that the father was going to bring his family after two years or return to his country, their responses were aligned with what Suárez-Orozco and Suárez-Orozco learned about the immigrant parents they interviewed in the USA, in the sense that 'a primary motivation for leaving was to pursue better opportunities for their children in the new country' (Suárez-Orozco and Suárez-Orozco, 2001, p. 22). Although the discourse in GLW was less about leaving to find work, there were various mentions of the protagonist having to find a job and money in another country before being able to bring the rest of his family over too:

> *Well probably he's going to leave that country because he has to pay like a lot of bills and he doesn't have that much money and he doesn't have a job, so he like has to leave the country. And then like go to another place and start a new life, like new kind of year, fresh options.* (Hassan, Somalia)

> *I think the man had to go to a different country to find a job, the wife and the daughter had to stay back, the man had to come first and they had to come after.* (Ruby, Rwanda)

> *The men have to work to get some money and then they come back to their families.* (Claude, Congo)

> *Because maybe there's no jobs for the man, the husband or their daughter's school is not good or something.*[1] (Sara, Iran/Kurdistan)

Moving from the protagonist's story to their own lives, in all three contexts of our study, we had children sharing the idea that, like the protagonist in the story, the reason some of their parents migrated was the search for job opportunities. The children in BCN who had positioned themselves as emigrants explicitly claimed that they had moved across nations to work: '*Porque nosotros venimos a trabajar*' [Because we come to work]. In all three contexts, the children's responses represented immigrants as dignified workers, resulting in a sharp contrast to some of the negative ideological discourses about immigrants that circulate in the children's host countries, such as the belief that they will take people's jobs, go on welfare or that they are criminals (when actually they have very few benefits and are not allowed to work until granted permission to stay).

Although the GLW children mentioned socioeconomic reasons for leaving, their hypothesis about the man's reasons for leaving alternated between these and issues around insecurity. They seemed more aware of immigrants having to escape from violence and war and look for safety and security elsewhere. Ruby (Rwanda) thought the people on the boat were fleeing from war in their countries and mentioned the evacuation of women and children to a safer place. The girls from Pakistan and Kurdistan also mentioned 'danger' as a reason for emigrating (it is interesting to note that, perhaps as a distancing strategy, Sara chooses to refer to 'animals' as doing the killing):

Mediator: *Why is he looking for another country?*
Sara: *Because probably in the old one there, where his wife and daughter lives right now, probably like there was like*
Surayya: *Danger.*
Sara: *Yeah, danger – it's dangerous because there's like animals that could kill people or something.*

Hassan, from Somalia, went further and mentioned torture and extortion as well as the idea of arriving at a place that ensures protection:

like if [refugees] *are tortured in one country and they will want to get out of there or if they've been treated badly, like they're good persons and the bad people keep on asking for money.* [. . .] *I think this is about refugees* [who] *come to this place that's has a wall around to protect people.*

In all the research contexts, there were suggestions from both immigrant and non-immigrant children that emigration could lead to finding a safer place to live. In the case of *The Arrival*, some participants made hopeful comments about how the host country was receiving the passengers; for instance, in BCN, referring to the double-spread pages with the giant statues, Calin (Romania) considered the welcome would be positive: '*porque si no, no harían esas estatuas* . . . [que se ven] *pacíficas*' [because if not, they wouldn't build those statues [that look] peaceful]. In GLW, they attributed positive feelings to the protagonist, saying he felt 'a wee bit happy' or 'excited' because he has arrived in a new place. Nevertheless, the immigrant children in all contexts were clearly aware of the hardships that migration usually implies, both throughout the journey and upon arrival.

Hardships of the immigrant experience: The stress of moving across nations

As we mentioned in Chapter 1, immigration is one of the most stressful situations a family can experience and one of the key sources of stress is separation, whether it is short or long term. In Suárez-Orozco and Suárez-Orozco's (2001) study, only 20 per cent of the children in their sample came to the USA as a family unit, and thus the anxiety prompted by such separation is significant.[2] There were plenty of comments in the different contexts of our study, in which the children focused on the strong emotions and feelings that separation brings to the family. Referring to the first images of the book, the children in AZ commented:

> Toni: *Yo veo que hay mucha tristeza porque hay muchas familias que una persona de sus familias se está yendo para el tren.*
> Juan: *Sí. También como dice Toni, la familia se ve muy triste porque se están separando.*

> [Toni: I see that there is so much sadness because there are many families in which one of their members is taking the train.
> Juan: Yes, as Toni says, the family looks very sad because they are getting separated.]

Such a situation was not an unfamiliar experience for many of the children whose parents travelled first, as Toni's comments throughout the discussions revealed: '*Mi papá, primero se vino de México para cuando nosotros fuéramos con él en unos meses ya pudiéramos entrar en una parte donde vivía*' [My dad he came first from Mexico so that when we were going to join him a couple of months later we could go to the place where he lived]. In AZ, three out of the five children shared the experience of having one of their parents coming first to the USA (two fathers, one mother) but they were later brought over once the parent was able to do so; however, they missed their extended families, as Almah said: '*I miss my family. I mean my mom's family. My grandma, my grandpa, my other grandma and my other grandpa.*'

In BCN, there were also children whose parents migrated first but both these and other immigrants used strong language to describe the anxiety and painful feelings of separation immigrants feel. Calin (Romania) even described the pain of separation as equal to that of bereavement: '*Porque la persona que muere también te deja y tienes que superarlo*' [Because the person who dies also leaves you and you have to overcome it].

In GLW, at least four children had also had the experience of their father coming to the UK first (as we have said before, we did not have the exact information for each case, given the sensitivity of the status of some of the families). They did not mention their own family separations directly but did speak of the sadness and worry of separation. For example, Sunil (Sri Lanka) stressed the 'sadness' the little girl felt when her father was leaving and mentioned the paper bird he gave her as a present to make her feel better. Ruby, from Rwanda, was particularly focused on the images of the family separation, and kept returning to the question of why he had left and reflecting anxiety about the possibility of reunification (it is worth noting that she was living with her father and sister and, with one exception, all the photographs she took for the project were of these two relatives). Dina (Pakistan), Józef (Poland) and Faisal (Pakistan) all spoke of the man's worries about his family because he left them behind, possibly in danger. They also mentioned his sadness when he remembers their parting.

In spite of the protagonist leaving his family behind temporarily, the children characterized him as someone who loved his family deeply, as a person for whom the most important thing was his family. Remarking on how carefully the protagonist protected the photo he took with him when leaving his family, the children in AZ asserted how much it meant to him:

> Toni: *También parece que esta foto significa mucho para él porque lo envolvió y lo agarró bien, lo echó a una caja y esa caja la echó en otra y en otra.*
> Mediador: *Es cierto.*
> Juan: *De seguro es para protegerla porque para él su familia es lo más importante . . . lo más apreciado.*
>
> [Toni: It also seems that this photo means a lot to him because he wrapped it and took it carefully, put it in a box and he put that box within another box and within another.
> Mediator: It's true.
> Juan: Surely it's to protect the photo because, to him, his family is the most important thing . . . the most precious thing.]

Further into the story, as they commented on the image where the immigrant is looking through the window of the ship, the children again focused on the feelings of separation as experienced by the main character. The children in BCN also commented on the character's feelings, imagining his loneliness and expressing empathy towards him; Alan speculates: '*porque si come: ha de comer solo, ¿no? y ahí ha de extrañar a su familia*' [because if he eats, he probably eats alone, right? And there he is probably missing his family]. These expressions of empathy, which are a crucial sign of engagement, emerged throughout the discussions in all contexts; we will return to the concept of empathy later in this chapter and in Chapter 5.

A group of children from BCN contributed another dimension to the discussion on immigration by introducing the topic of forced migration, viewing it as a decision that their parents imposed upon them as minors (although they acknowledged that it was as a result of a decision their parents were also forced to make themselves). Cristina commented: '*A mí me dijeron: te vienes o te vienes*' [They told me: 'you either coming or you come']. With a cracked voice, she explained:

> Cristina: *Aquí mayormente los padres te dicen: 'me voy a otro país', son los que mandan, pues lo tienes que hacer, tampoco puedes quedarte ahí muriéndote de hambre ¿no? porque tienes que acompañar a tus padres, porque tus padres . . . haces lo que te mandan, entonces vienes y tus amigos y tu familia se queda ahí, lástima, mayormente los padres mandan y los hijos tienen que ir.*
> Beatriz: *Es medio lógico.*
> Mediador: *Depende la edad de los hijos también.*
> Cristina: *No, a partir de los dieciocho puedes hacer lo que quieras, pero yo, yo tengo once.*

> [Cristina: Here, for the most part the parents tell you: 'I'm going to another country', they are the ones in charge, so you have to do it, you can't stay there dying of hunger either, right? You have to follow your parents because your parents . . . you do what they tell you, so you come and your friends and your family stay there, sadly, mainly your parents tell you what to do and the children have to go.
> Beatriz: That makes sense.
> Mediator: It depends how old the children are too.
> Cristina: No, after [you are] eighteen you can do what you want, but me, I'm eleven.]

Cristina's comment, '*but me, I'm eleven*', illustrates how powerless she felt in the family decision-making process.

The picture from Dina's graphic strip in GLW illustrates the beginning of her journey from Pakistan to Scotland and her straightforward comments, as well as the expressions on the characters' faces, reveal the emotions involved in this forced parting (see Figure 4.2). Her oral description of this parting also emphasized: '*there's my friends and when we left to airport I was really crying and all my friends and auntie they were all crying and really missing me*'.

In addition to focusing on the experience of the separation, the children's discussions stressed how equally difficult arriving to a new country can be, having to deal with so many different practices. For instance, in GLW, some children's statements referred to how they dealt with the 'foreignness': '*First time I didn't know what was like, the fruit like watermelon, bananas, all that, I didn't*

Figure 4.2 A frame from Dina's graphic strip

know' (Vassily, GLW). Dina heavily annotated the image where the man goes with his pet in search for food. She wrote that they were hungry and wanted bread and milk but could only find fruit and vegetables. She highlighted the difficulty of negotiating both language and food, drawing an arrow pointing to the shop labels and writing: '*The man don't know the language*' (see Figure 4.3). She asked for a new page to continue her writing and added: '*He was tense because he don't know what people says*.'

Moreover, the children went beyond expected feelings of confusion as the result of arriving in a new country to more serious concerns: '*Cuando vienes aquí tienes que superar que ya no estás en tu país, y tú estás aterrorizado*' [When you come here you have to overcome (the fact) that you are not in your country, and you are terrified] (Calin, BCN). Like Calin, many of the children in BCN used strong words to express their emotions upon arriving in a new country. Their use of words such as 'terrified', dreadful', 'totally scared' speaks to the intensity of their fears and some children also suggested that immigrants could be the victims of violence.

The children in AZ mentioned similarly strong emotions in their awareness of the stress of arrival. In describing the page where the passengers disembark in the harbour, Ryan used the word '*desesperados*' [desperate] and repeated it again later when the man is looking at his family photo: '*Está desesperado, triste por no estar con su familia. Aquí toma las fotos. Está triste, está pensando qué va a hacer*' [He is desperate, sad because he is not with his family. Here he takes a photo. He

Figure 4.3 Dina's annotation

is sad, he is thinking about what he's going to do]. Ryan made those comments as part of the discussion of the section in which the immigrant undergoes the health check and finally receives some official-looking documents. Therefore, the children's responses as well as Tan's images speak to how, in addition to the feelings of separation, immigrants have to deal with the burden and stress of the official processes of immigration, bureaucracy that can be dehumanizing and confusing.

To the anxiety and confusion about navigating such bureaucracy, for the children in AZ another layer of stress is added with the notion of being considered 'legal' or 'illegal', a topic they mentioned twice, the first time in their very first discussion:

> Toni: *Como en el aeropuerto si estás tratando de agarrar papeles.*
> Mediador: *¿Cuándo van a viajar? ¿Cuándo van a entrar a otro lugar?*
> Juan: *It's an 'Extension card'?*
> Mediador: *Uh huh. Okay. Así que cuando estás tratando de agarrar papeles ¿para qué?*
> Juan: *Para ser ciudadano.*
> Toni: *Para estar aquí legalmente.*

> [Toni: Like at the airport if you are trying to get [official] documents.
> Mediator: When they are going to travel? When they are going to enter a new country?
> Juan: It's an 'Extension Card'?
> Mediator: Uh huh, OK. So when you are trying to get documents for what?
> Juan: To become a citizen.
> Toni: To be here legally.]

This reference to being in a country 'legally' needs to be situated within ideological discussions in the USA about undocumented immigrants, who are often described as 'illegal', thus criminalizing those who enter without official documentation. The dangers of being taken randomly from the streets by the border patrol, based only on their appearance, to be returned to Mexico is a highly stressful experience for many Latinos living in AZ even if they are citizens.

The children also showed awareness of the stress immigrants may experience upon arriving and undertaking their job search. Some children realized that, as soon as he got to the new country, the protagonist in *The Arrival* was faced with a feeling of disappointment. In AZ, Toni commented that the main character felt '*frustrado*' [frustrated] because he could not find a job. Suárez-Orozco and Suárez-Orozco found that immigrants' optimism and motivation seems to change 'after parents settle in the new country and begin to have a better sense of the formidable task ahead' (Suárez-Orozco and Suárez-Orozco, 2001, p. 22), which for so many includes unemployment and severe social demotion.

Becoming bilingual: Gaining and losing languages

Another situation many immigrants encounter when arriving in a new country relates to the learning of a new language. References to this aspect of immigration, along with observations about language in general and about Tan's invented language in particular, were frequently made throughout the discussions in all contexts (the role of language in the children's understanding will be analysed further in Chapter 6). In AZ, for example, all the children mentioned the protagonist's experience with the new language and Almah imagined his reaction: *'He doesn't know the language and he's like, "Huh? What? What are you saying? I don't understand you." And then he's trying to explain it with hand signs and pictures'.* This led them to talk about personal experiences as bilingual learners or learners of English.

In GLW, the children shared experiences about understanding the Scottish accent and learning some Scots words. Faisal noted that the character would be happy when he learned the new language and that this had happened to Faisal himself when he began to understand and read English. In response to the 'picture dictionary' the man makes for himself, Józef and Faisal talked about using dictionaries or computers to understand new words. Both he and Józef commented that even without knowing the language they could go into shops, like the immigrant did, because *'when you buy, you don't have to talk'* and *'everybody can do maths'.* Dina added an annotation to the sketchbook Tan shows in the protagonist's hand: *'The man don't know the language so he got a book for learning'.* Lily, a native Scot, showed awareness of an immigrant friend's language difficulties:

> When my friend came to this school and she knew a bit of English, but she wasn't that good. But when she went [back] to Turkey she forgot all the English words and [when she came back] I [said], Meltem, I can't understand you, cos you need to end up learning these English words again. And I had to [...] help her again.

Moving across languages and learning a new language and culture is an immense task but the children viewed immigrants as resourceful and exercising some agency. As mentioned above, Józef (Poland/GLW) highlighted that immigrants can use their numeracy skills for some activities. In AZ, when the children saw the main character searching for an apartment and booking one without knowing the language, they imagined the character thinking: *'Let me try to figure out what's that'* (Almah, AZ). In fact, that was exactly Almah's disposition in the bilingual group discussions where sometimes the children used Spanish and she was the only one not knowing Spanish. Every single comment produced in Spanish was not directly translated but she followed the discussions and asked when she did not understand.

For some immigrants, learning a new language, however, also implies language loss, especially in the context where there are no bilingual education programmes available for the children to sustain and develop their home and new languages and in contexts where linguistic diversity is not appreciated much. The children in AZ, after asserting their bilingualism, also commented how some of them or their friends were losing their first language and how they felt about not knowing much about their language. As de la Luz Reyes asserts, many immigrant children and their parents feel that they 'must make the false choice between English and Spanish' (or their home language) especially in contexts where anti-immigrant rhetoric surrounds the discourse on this topic (de la Luz Reyes, 2011, p. xiv). These choices have implications for children's identity development.

Negotiating an immigrant identity: Silence and appropriation

Children across all contexts empathized with the main character's experience leading some of them, such as some children from BCN, to position themselves as emigrants, as mentioned earlier. The children from GLW and AZ shared knowledge of some of the processes involved in immigration, such as passports, border controls, health checks and even some personal experiences related to coming to the USA or the UK, but they did not refer to themselves as immigrants. In the case of the participants in AZ, they self-identified as Mexicans or Mexican Americans or as being originally from Iraq. Maybe the fact that AZ was once part of Mexico and that the population of AZ is 30 per cent Latinos also had an impact on how the children saw themselves, or perhaps the negative connotations of the term when linked to the notion of illegality had an influence on children's responses. In GLW, some of the children did refer to themselves as 'refugees', a specific legal term, which, as we explained in Chapter 2, means that they are no longer 'asylum seekers' (with the connotations this implies) but have been granted permission to stay in the UK (although not necessarily with permanent leave to remain). On the other hand, Józef, an 'economic' immigrant from an A8 country, did not see himself as an immigrant either, probably because he was able to go back and forth to Poland without any problems and because of the increasing population of Poles in GLW (59 per cent of the A8 immigrant children in GLW schools are Polish according to a Glasgow City Council report, 2007).

In the case of the refugee children in GLW, it seemed to the researchers that the children wanted to move on from these difficult experiences. The representation of the difficulties and anxieties of their immigrant experience may be 'too close' to events and memories they may not want to be reminded of or to share with others. There is also the possibility that they were reluctant to disclose any personal feelings to peers or adults they did not know well, particularly within an institutional context. Additionally, given that personal responses to texts in the classroom are often discouraged by teachers, the children may have assumed we did not want to hear this type of comment. A clear example of this distancing can be seen in Ali's insistence that his experience was nothing like the one undergone by the immigrant character: He summarily told us he had come from Afghanistan (via Pakistan) on an aeroplane, was met by his father and went straight 'home'. He denied any difficulties with understanding the 'new' language and insisted his father taught him English immediately.

A different example of distancing was observed by researchers in BCN who interpreted the humour in some of the children's painful narratives as an effort to distance themselves from some of the more painful experiences. In response to the illustration in which the protagonist is leaving his family, Adrián recounted how, in a similar experience, he had been sad and tearful when his mother travelled to Spain for the first time and left him behind in Bolivia. He spoke of being deeply sad but responded to his peers' question '¿*Lloraste?*' [Did you cry?] with a laugh. Although it could be argued that he was adhering to his group's gender expectations for boys who should not cry, it is also plausible to think that he used humour to keep some distance from the painful memory.

For some of the immigrant children in BCN, this potential desire to move away from difficult experiences involved in immigration is best exemplified in the children's comments about relatives who chose not to talk about their experiences. For instance, Hilda recalled her grandparents' experience of immigration and reflected on the many things that are not told in the family, maybe – she wondered – because of lack of time or to avoid the suffering that can come from such memories:

> ... *yo creo que a veces, por ejemplo, si yo le pregunto a mis abuelos cuando emigraron que cómo se sintieron y tal- que a lo mejor no te cuentan – o no todo o sea – que igual te lo resumen rápido pero que en verdad no te lo dicen*

suficientemente bien como para imaginártelo no, pero en un libro siempre te
dicen todo mejor y te queda más claro.

[I think that sometimes, for example, if I ask my grandparents how they felt
when they emigrated and so on, maybe they don't tell you, not everything; in
other words, maybe they summarize it but in reality they don't tell you with
enough clarity that you can imagine it, they don't, but in a book they tell you
things better and it becomes more clear to you.]

The same idea is discussed by Paola, who thought of her own father when she
reflected on the protagonist's life:

Como vino mi papi también, casi la primera parte me ha hecho recordar 'ay, tal
vez mi papá también pasó esto', tal vez porque, no sé, él tampoco me cuenta
mucho de eso, no conversamos así . . . me cuenta, pero no todo, todo, no tan
completo [señalando el libro].

[As my dad came too, the first part has made me think: 'oh, perhaps that also
happened to my dad', maybe because, I don't know, he doesn't tell me much
about it, we don't talk like that . . . He tells me, but not everything, everything,
not as completely [pointing to the book].]

The Arrival seemed to effectively support the immigrant children's sense of
making and negotiating their identities and offered them a channel to make
sense of the many emotions they experienced. Some of the images in particular
offered a platform for the children to understand themselves and their
experiences in a more profound way, as Calin's reflection in BCN suggests:

Si estás un poco así pensando, se parece a tu historia, y puedes entender las
cosas . . . compararla; sí, sí piensas mucho, todas las historias de todos los que
estamos aquí se parecen un poco a esa.

[If you start thinking, it looks similar to your own story, and then you can
understand things . . . compare them; yes, you think a lot, all the stories of all
of us here are similar to that one.]

Reclaiming unique knowledge as immigrants: 'It is not the same to imagine as to feel'

While some children may have chosen not to talk explicitly about their
experiences of migration, other children in BCN who identified strongly with

the protagonist's experience seemed to reclaim their experience as immigrants and established the difference between learning about immigration and experiencing it. It is frequently asserted that in order for a child to engage with a book they must be able to 'connect' or 'find something of themselves' in it. Most of the studies on children's responses to picturebooks mentioned previously highlight the importance of personal response when working with children and have shown that children have strong emotional reactions to the picturebooks, based on personal needs, interests and early memories, all of which are involved in meaning-making. Sipe claims that readers have a 'universal impulse' to 'draw the story to themselves' and this is connected to the pleasure of finding that a story (or parts of it) mirrors their own lives (Sipe, 2008, p. 152).

As the children talked about *The Arrival*, the discussions offered those who felt more culturally proximate (Larsen and László, 1990) a space to make sense and gain insights into their own and their parents' experiences as immigrants. For children native to the host countries who may have felt more culturally distant to the immigrant experience, such as the Catalan children in BCN or the Scottish children in GLW, the discussions provided them with opportunities to develop empathy and to gain insights into their classmates' and other immigrants' experience, inviting them to enter into an intercultural space (which will be the focus of Chapter 6).

Indeed, one of Tan's expectations for his work, including *The Arrival*, is that it will help readers develop empathy:

> when faced with the unexpected, we might respond with either apathy, prejudice or curiosity. Of course the last one offers the only source of genuine hope: curiosity is really a kind of empathy, a will to find 'otherness' actually interesting rather than problematic, whether that be a person from another culture, a political idea, a tentacled creature, or any much smaller day-to-day encounter with the unanticipated. (Tan, 2012, p. 31)

The children's discussions across contexts illustrate how effectively the book helps mediate a feeling of empathy among the children. In BCN, many of the non-immigrant children found themselves relating to their own experiences and emotions during journeys they had undertaken through the links the book allowed them to make. In GLW, the non-immigrant children also related to the images of separation through instances of their own, such as Morag's (Scot) father's frequent absences due to his job or when Nadia (Pakistani/Scot) accompanied her father on a trip to Japan while her mother stayed behind:

[The image of the father alone in the hotel] *makes me kind of feel sad but kind of happy as well, cause it kind of reminds me of my dad who has to go away,* [he's] *always having to go away, cause when he left me he has to travel, it reminds me of that.* (Morag)

Like when I was going to Japan, the stairs were too big, when we climb onto the airplane, the stair was too long [so] *my mum came up with me and then I had to leave her* [...] *then I started crying in the plane, looking out the window trying to see Mummy.* (Nadia)

Books such as *The Arrival* are relevant because of their potential to place the reader in the shoes or 'skin' of others, as Hilda (Catalan), in BCN said: '*te pones en la piel ... del que llega aquí y empieza a vivir*' [You put yourself in the skin ... of the person who comes here and starts living [here]]. Calin, from Romania, followed a similar line of reflection in the final discussion:

Calin: *Sí, a mí sí que me gustó* [el libro].
Mediador: *¿Sí?*
Calin: *Sí, pienso que es algo interesante la vida de un emigrante.*
Mediador: *¿Y por qué lo ves interesante?*
Calin: *Porque, aquí a lo mejor cuando vienes aquí algunos tienen problemas por ser emigrantes y por ser de otra forma, ¿no? Y ... a lo mejor si alguien lo lee se da cuenta cómo se siente esa persona ...*

[Calin: Yes, I liked [the book] a lot.
Mediator: Yes?
Calin: Yes, because I think that the life of an emigrant is something interesting.
Mediator: And why do you see it as interesting?
Calin: Because, here, maybe when you come here some people have problems for being emigrants and for being different, no? And ... maybe if someone reads it they will realize how that person feels ...]

Yet, as the immigrant children in BCN clearly stated: '*No es lo mismo imaginar que sentir*' [It is not the same to imagine as to feel] (Beatriz, BCN). After being invited to reflect on their reading experience in the last discussion, the immigrant children questioned the ability of others to really understand their experiences. Beatriz and Calin claimed that as immigrants they read the book differently from non-immigrants:

Mediador: *¿Y piensan que si ustedes no fueran emigrantes hubieran entendido de la misma manera al libro?*

Beatriz: *Que uno tiene la experiencia de viajar a un país diferente, el que no es tu país, cambias de lenguas, de tradiciones, comidas, muchas cosas de esas y no, como por ejemplo tú vas aquí a un español y no te va a decir: 'ay sí -lo he sentido', no, porque él no es de otro país y él está aquí con su familia y con todo también, nosotros no.*

Calin: *A ver que, yo pienso que no porque, porque por ejemplo si tú estás en el mismo país y alguien viene a la escuela, pues tú no sabes lo que siente esa persona, lo que siente su corazón, lo que hay adentro de su corazón cuando ha dejado a su familia y a sus amigos ahí y tiene que acostumbrarse y no sabe hablar* [el nuevo idioma], *no sabes cómo se siente esa persona, bueno, puedes imaginártelo, pero no muy bien.*

Beatriz: *No es lo mismo imaginar que sentir.*

[Mediator: And do you think that, if you hadn't been emigrants, you would have understood the book in this same way?

Beatriz: One has had the experience of travelling to a different country, one that is not your country, you change your language, your traditions, food, many things like that and no; for example, here you go to a Spanish person here and he won't say to you: 'Oh yes, I have felt the same', no, because he is not from another country and he is here with his family and also with everything else, we are not.

Calin: Let's see, I think not, because, for example, if you are in your own country and someone comes to the school, well, you don't know what that person is feeling, what she feels in her heart, what is in her heart when she has left her family and friends there and she has to get used [to the new place] and she doesn't know how to speak, you don't know how that person feels, well, you can imagine it, but not so well.

Beatriz: It is not the same to imagine as to feel.]

Personal experience then, in the immigrant children's case, is a key element that allows access to a certain way of reading. In this excerpt, Beatriz and Calin highlight the many processes of change that they confronted during their move from one country to another. Some of these processes are visible to others but the internal processes of mourning and the transformations of identity implied by these changes are often not made evident.

In Beatriz's and Calin's words, books like *The Arrival* can invite the sharing of experiences and emotions generated by migration, which often have no place in school. The group discussions and visual strategies in this inquiry offered these children the opportunity to provide teachers, peers and researchers with a small glimpse of their individual odysseys. In our pluralistic societies, school should make sure spaces like these are made available where immigrant children can open up and share their experiences with others. The implications of the intercultural exchange within these safe spaces and the pedagogies that can help create them will be explored further in Chapters 6, 8 and 9.

Notes

1 In this example, the reference to the daughter's schooling may have to do with disadvantages that girls have experienced in the Kurdistan area as a result of both tradition and conflict (Osler and Yahya, 2013).

2 We could not find a comparable statistic from the UK but, to illustrate the other side of the situation, it is worth noting that estimates from the UK Home Office in 2005 were that 6,000 unaccompanied asylum-seeking minors (under 18 years) were being looked after at the time. These children are often sent on their own by desperate parents or are victims of trafficking.

5

Making Meaning through Retellings and Inferences

In Chapter 4, we focused on the content of the children's discussions on issues of immigration. We now shift gears towards a major type of response used by the children as they interpreted the text: the Referential category that involves children's retellings and inferences. Our conceptualization of the Referential category evolved throughout the project. As we mentioned in Chapter 3, from the outset, the analytical frameworks proposed by the work of Kiefer (1995), Madura (1995) and Sipe (1996, 2008) were particularly useful to guide our analysis. Kiefer distinguishes between *Informational* and *Heuristic* responses. The *Informational* category includes, among other things, responses that offer information and describe what is narrated through the illustrations, while, in the responses coded as *Heuristic*, the children make hypotheses, inferences and speculations aimed at supporting their comprehension of the text. Likewise, for Sipe, the *Analytical* category involved, among other things, responses in which the students were making meaning of the text. For Sipe, this meaning-making process was further categorized as including Retelling, Inferences and Hypotheses, Personal Opinions, Clarification Questions, and Evaluative and Thematic Statements.

In an effort to identify referential statements in a more nuanced way, in our initial analysis, we considered two main forms of referential responses: *literal statements* (L.S.) and *inferential statements* (I.S.). With L.S., students generally expressed a basic recognition of simple elements that were overtly present in the text – they identified what they saw. With I.S., students generally engaged in more interpretative work, made inferences and shared connections that they had made between something indicated (but not always overtly presented) by the text with some prior knowledge they had gained. More specifically, in the Literal level, following Madura's (1995) work, we included responses in which the children were identifying and describing aspects of the story, such as the characters: '*No, esa es su esposa*' [No, that is his wife] (Ryan, AZ); the action: '*Like, he's putting his hat, she's putting his scarf, and she's putting his this thing*' (Almah, AZ); the setting: '*Like, I will say, this is like the home of where they live and things that they usually use. Like they use these and I guess a picture of her mom and dad and her*' (Juan, AZ). In sum, these were comments in which the children seemed to respond to the questions 'What?', 'Who?' and 'Where?'

Under I.S., we included responses that seemed to involve more interpretative work, inferences about the characters' motives or actions, such as when Hassan (Somalia/GLW) speculates about the plot: '*I think one of his relatives live here and he's come to stay with them because his house is, the place he lived is being probably like attacked by this kind of dragon tail thing.*' These responses seemed to address the 'Why?' question more than the others.

Given that the Referential category had to do with the telling of the narrative, it was not unexpected to see that the largest number of the children's responses to *The Arrival* were coded under Referential. In AZ, for instance, almost half of the children's responses coded under Referential involved Retelling of the story and almost have Speculative Hypotheses/Inferences, using Sipe's (2008) subcategories for Meaning Making. The categories of Retelling and Speculative Hypotheses/Inferences paralleled the Literal and Interpretive levels we had identified. Comments coded as Retelling represented a more literal description of the story, while the Speculative Hypotheses and inferences represented more complex interpretive work.

The BCN team distinguished between different levels of inferences: *Basic inferences* (almost descriptive), such as Carles' inference about the characters: '*no parece que sean muy ricos, porque tienen una tetera rota*' [it doesn't seem they are rich because they have a broken tea pot]; *Failed inferences*, such as when Hassan, after looking at the train station at the beginning, came to the conclusion that the three family members were going together on a trip (when it was the protagonist who would travel first to bring his family later); *Explorative or Tentative Inferences*, such as when several children in BCN tried to explain the role that animals played in the story; and, finally, *Inferences that powerfully led to the co-construction of meaning*, such as when the children were trying to make sense of the meaning of the dragon-tail shape that appears at the beginning of the story as a shadow over the city. Initially, they suggested it was just a dragon, and as the dialogue moved further they speculated that it represented a problem or a sickness, something that hunted the characters and made them want to leave the city. We also examined the children's inferences for types of responses and identified three major categories that helped us understand the children's interpretive work.

Engaging in inferences

While an 'inference' has been defined as 'a conclusion reached on the basis of evidence and reasoning' (*Oxford English Dictionary*, online), we were excited by some of the historical uses of the term, particularly by the following quote from Aristotle: 'When a child first draws an inference, or perceives the force of an inference drawn by another, we may call this the birth of reason'; and by Mill's (1843) insight: 'To draw inferences has been said to be the great business of life' (*Oxford English Dictionary*, online). The children's reading of *The Arrival* enabled them to participate in this 'great business of life' to which Aristotle attributed 'the birth of reason' and they were not shy about embracing the challenge. As we analysed the children's inferences, we found that the Jett-Simpson Classification System for Verbalized Inferences developed in 1976 was particularly helpful for this purpose (see Figure 5.1). Jett-Simpson (1976) proposed one of the first classification systems to examine children's comprehension and inferences constructed not from a skills list where comprehension questions assessed what the adults believed the children should be able to do but from what children actually do as they read. With this emphasis, Jett-Simpson (1976) analysed the

Categories	Description
Plot Categories • Cause/effect • Elaborated event • Added event	Inferred cause/effect Inferred embellishments of picture facts Totally new event added that fits the context of the picture story
Setting Categories • Place/object • Refinement • Time	Inferred name of object or place Inferred description of environment Inferred simultaneous events and/or standard time referents
Character Categories • Identification • Refinement	Inferred name or role Inferred description of physical qualities or appearance and of internal behavior

Figure 5.1 Representation of the Jett-Simpson Classification System for Verbalized Inferences (1976, Edited)

verbalized inferences of children to a wordless book, and found, as also happened in our work, that character- and plot-based inferences were most frequently used by the children. The children also made setting-based inferences.

Jett-Simpson's (1976) 'Elaborated' and 'Refinement' categories reminded us of our most basic literal responses and the most elaborated inferential responses. She also described subcategories for Character inferences that include aspects of both the external and internal behaviour of the characters. The lines that differentiated between character, plot and setting inferences were blurred at times in her study as they were in ours.

Most inferential statements in all three research contexts tended to focus on details surrounding the main protagonist being in the otherworldly place (plot-based inferences), and how he and his family were feeling about being there (character-analysis-based inferences).

In GLW, while the character-analysis-based inferences generally reflected the students' own emotional experience of the text and of lived events, the plot-based inferences tended to reflect: a) the student's *personal experience* with migration, disorientation and alienation (these responses often contained sophisticated understandings of the diverse causes, dangers and experiences of migration) as previously mentioned in Chapter 4; and/or b) a reference to *something learned within the realm of pop-culture/media* to describe the story, as will be shown in Chapter 6. In what follows, we present examples of the three main categories of inferences.

Plot categories

The six parts into which *The Arrival* is divided provided students with plenty of opportunities to make sense of the plot and subplots. The images that provoked the most discussion, negotiation of meanings and inferences were found in the peritext (e.g. cover, title page and endpapers); in Part I in which the protagonist leaves his country; and in Part II in which the protagonist arrives in the new country.

Part I describes the departure of the protagonist. The children spent quite a lot of time making sense of the plot, understanding and negotiating the reasons for the man leaving his family and place. They contemplated several possibilities. In Arizona, Juan initially thought that maybe he was just going to visit his parents: '*De seguro él se salió del, se fue del trabajo, puede ser que se fue a otra parte a visitar a sus padres . . . I think he's gonna go to a lot of places . . .*' [For sure, he left, he left his job, it may be that he went to another place to visit his parents

...]. Later in the story, he proposed that the man might be a scientist who '*had to go to make science*'; along those lines, Ryan proposed that '*A lo mejor lo mandaron a alguna agencia*' [Maybe an agency sent him]. Finally, they agreed about the economic situation being really bad as the reason for the man leaving, as discussed in Chapter 4.

Setting and tone/mood categories

Setting inferences were the least frequent inferences expressed by the children. The parts of the book that prompted more setting inferences were, as expected, the beginning of the book, the arrival of the protagonist in a foreign city where boats fly, and the stories within the main story, narrated through the inset stories. At the beginning of the book, the children easily ventured their inferences about time and place. The children speculated that the book was '*going probably to be based on a story that happened a long time ago*' (Toni, AZ) because the book looked old.

The children in BCN speculated that the book was about the past but in the future. Alan, for example, commented: '*si lo miras bien puede ser futuro* [...] *pero algunas cosas tienen – tienen* [estilo] *viejo*' [If you take a good look the book can be about the future [...] but some things have an old [style]]. Likewise, Beatriz and Cristina proposed that the book has things relative to both the past and the future:

> Cristina: *porque era antiguo este libro ¿no?*
> Beatriz: *pero a lo mejor hay algo de futuro*
> Mediador: *¿cómo?*
> Beatriz: *... a lo mejor hay algo de futuro porque esto del barco volante como que no es de antes*

> [Cristina: because this book was old, right?
> Beatriz: but perhaps there is something about the future
> Mediator: How?
> Beatriz: ... Maybe there is something about the future because this ship that flies, that is not old.]

Setting inferences were especially challenging for the children when they were trying to read the inset stories. For instance, in AZ, when discussing the inset story told by the food merchant, the children required a great deal of adult mediation to be able to identify characters, time and place and to figure out the subplot.

Character categories

The children contributed many inferences about the characters' roles and about their appearance and feelings. They speculated about the girl's and her family's feelings, as when Viviana (AZ) described the girl's feelings and her father's actions trying to console her:

> [Ella siente/She feels like] *como sadness y furia porque su papá se va a ir y* [and fury because her dad is leaving] *and that's why she is imagining that a lot of bad stuff is happening in the outside world.*
>
> *And here I notice that the girl is getting sad so then the father got her a cat to make her feel happy.*

Viviana's descriptions revealed great insights into the different kinds of feelings people may experience when the family is separated. She was aware that one can be sad, but moreover when you are really sad you may also feel '*fury*'. Fury and sadness can happen at the same time and this young girl is already aware of the complexities of these feelings, especially within the context of family separation. She was also aware that these feelings can be so strong they have to come out and be made visible in some way, in this case through projecting them into the environment through the girl's imagination: '*Yo digo que esto la niña se lo está imaginando porque ella sabe que su papá se va a ir y lo que se siente adentro se está saliendo para afuera*' [I would say that the girl is imagining this because she knows her dad is going to leave and what is felt inside has to come out].

The children's inferences about the protagonist seemed to capture the sense of disorientation he experienced in the new country. Almah from AZ and Ali from GLW had similar expressions referencing the disorientation: '*It's like, "When am I going to get home? I think I'm lost. I don't know where I am"*' (Almah); and '*He gonna be thinking, "What place is this?" "Am I in my dream?" or "Am I sleeping?"*' (Ali).

This power of fiction to engage with the emotions of others and encourage different perspectives is not a new idea but it is important to stress this great potential of fiction to support the development of empathy. Meek reminds us that literature offers the reader the opportunity 'to consider another point of view, and even the prospect of reconciling different viewpoints [...] not only reduce the unfamiliarity but also make what is familiar less stable, more inclusive of difference' (Meek, 2001, p. xvi). Moreover, Nikolajeva's exploration of reader's affective engagement with fiction, based on cognitive theory and recent brain research, suggests that visual or multimedia texts are particularly effective in encouraging empathy. She begins by explaining that 'Cognitive criticism purports that the reason we can engage with fictive characters is because of the connections between the mediated experience of the text and emotional memories stored in the brain' (Nikolajeva, 2012, p. 276). However, she also notes that because emotions are non-verbal, language is limited in conveying complex emotional states, while 'a visual image can potentially evoke a wide range of emotions circumventing the relative precision of words' (Nikolajeva, 2012, p. 278). This argument is of crucial importance in our inquiry because it helps explain how the power of the non-verbal narrative in *The Arrival* extended the emotional experiences of both the immigrant and non-immigrant children – whatever their actual experiences and memories actually were – which supported a better understanding of oneself and others.

While these three main categories for inferences were initially useful for understanding the children's responses, we still had a challenge differentiating between the levels of responses, especially between a literal response and an inference, given the visual nature of the text. It seems that the wordless and complex nature of a text such as *The Arrival* defies categories that have been created mostly for texts in which the story is told through both written text and images. In a sense, the categories focus on the outcomes, not the mediated processes that get the children there. It may therefore be more useful to think in terms of the fluidity of categories that illuminate the reading process. An example of such fluidity in terms of the categories of Retelling and Inferences follows, focusing on the children's retellings in which they created dialogue for the characters.

Interpretive work through the creation of dialogue

One salient response in the children's transactions with *The Arrival* was retelling in which they created dialogue for, or attributed thoughts to, the characters. In all three contexts, children used this type of response. The GLW team usually identified these types of statements as inferential statements and saw them as presenting children with a different avenue to communicate their inferences and perhaps 'make up for' the lack of written text, as the following excerpt from Jack (England/GLW) suggests: '*He* [the immigration officer] *is like "What's this? I can't understand what you are doing in this country." [And] The man is saying "Sorry?" . . . and he's showing that picture, saying, "I've left, I've left them, my wife and my daughter."*'

Perhaps the creation of dialogue and inner thoughts supported the children in similar ways to the way drawings or signs supported the protagonist, by making up for not understanding the new language. In describing the protagonist's efforts to communicate, Faisal (GLW) explained:

> *Here he's saying to him in his language, 'Okay'. Here he's drawing a bed and showing* [Faisal points], *'I need a bedroom. I'm new here.' And* [the other man] *is saying, 'I have a bedroom'. And here he's saying, 'Let's go'.*

The creation of dialogue for the characters enabled the children to explore how they were thinking and feeling and their statements reflect different ways of responding to a new and strange place: Hassan's (GLW) statement suggests an experience filled with curiosity: *'He'd be thinking, "This is a funny town with funny animals that nobody's ever seen". Like this kind snail of thing.'* For Gisela (Bolivia/BCN), the experience is also filled with anxiety: *'Y como aquí, está medio enfadado, porque dice: "qué voy a hacer, estos no me entienden"* [and here, he looks angry because he says: 'What will I do, these people don't understand me'].

Almah's (AZ) comment on the illustration where the newcomers are getting out of the ship suggests knowledge of the fatigue that a long journey can cause:

> *These people that are waiting and waiting they're like: 'Finally; here!' and that man is saying: 'Come on this way, people don't worry, this way, this way' and yelling at them. And then he opens* [the gates] *and they're like: 'Finally!' And they picked up their suitcases and then down the road.*

Almah's use of the words *'Finally, here!'* suggests that it was a long trip and the characters were tired and eager to arrive at their destination. She used similar expressions to describe her own journey from her homeland in the Middle East to the USA. Her description of the man who receives the arrivals as comforting the passengers by telling them *'don't worry'* while at the same time he is *'yelling to them'* seems to be an effort to reconcile what for her was a positive experience of travel with the images of the book in which the man is clearly yelling at the people (she sustained this positive perspective on immigration throughout her participation in the discussions). In her version of the story, the people who receive the immigrants try to communicate confidence and comfort.

In another example, this time from Ryan (AZ), we can appreciate the interpretive work embedded in these retellings that involve dialogue. As he describes the scene when the protagonist befriends the man who sells food with his son, Ryan adds voice to the characters:

> *Porque aquí, donde él le está contando aquí todo esto, él le está diciendo: 'cálmese, a mí también me pasó lo mismo.' Aquí como que se está recordando de todo.*

[Because here, where he is telling [the protagonist] all of this, he is saying: 'calm down, the same thing happened to me.' Here he seems to be remembering everything.]

He then continues retelling the inset story of the seller:

Aquí es cuando llegaron donde el señor y le dijeron: '¿qué le pasa?' 'Nos queremos huir' y 'yo tengo la escalera y tengo un mapa' y aquí le está diciendo, 'pero quiero dinero' y entonces la señora le dice: 'le doy esto para que nos vayamos de todo este problema.' Entonces le da la medalla y ya le da la escalera . . .

[Here is when they arrive where the man was and they said to him: 'What's going on?' 'We want to run away' and 'I have a ladder and a map' and here he is saying, 'but I want money' and then the woman says: 'I give you this so that we can leave this problem behind.' Then, she gives him the medal and then he gives her the ladder . . .]

Ryan's text: *'le doy esto para que nos vayamos de todo este problema'* [I give you this so that we can leave this problem behind] reflects his insights into the hardships the couple were experiencing, a context in which it was definitely more important to part with her jewellery than to risk their lives. This is a complex scene because it is part of an inset story and the children spent some time negotiating what had happened. Some of them thought that the man who asked for the money before giving the ladder to the couple was actually offering them money in an act of kindness. It took a while for them to realize that even in such difficult circumstances someone would want to take advantage of the traumatic situation the couple was experiencing.

Evidence of the amount of inferential work involved in the children's retelling in which they added dialogue was also found in the annotation task, where the children in BCN and GLW were given the option of including speech and thought bubbles. Carolina, a native Catalan, added the following to the image of the strange pipes and objects in the hostel room: *¿Para que servirán? Pensará el protagonista* [What are these for? The protagonist must be thinking].

Various pairs of children in GLW made up these dialogues between them, as Claude (Congo) and Sunil (Sri Lanka) did when they were looking at the same spread mentioned above, the beginning of the second inset story. In fact, even though it is not clear whether the boys had understood that the man is referring to a different context of danger, their comments are very similar to those of Ryan and they did understand that he is trying to reassure the protagonist that he is sympathetic. Like Almah and Ryan, their inferences seem to be influenced by their own experiences; in this case, both boys were asylum seekers and shared the same (Catholic) religion, although they were from very different countries. (It is particularly poignant that Sunil was deported shortly after this session.) As Claude scribed the comments, all of which refer to the man, their dialogue went thus:

> Claude: *That guy he is saying 'trust me, I know all about it, I've seen it'*
> Sunil: *the man what he saw because he was scared of that first of all*
> Claude: *'Trust me I've been through it, I've seen it'*

This kind of response in which the children enacted a dialogue and gave voices to the characters served as a window into their thought processes. As the children listened to themselves and listened to other students' versions of the story, they engaged in a construction and negotiation of meanings that supported, and at the same time revealed, their interpretive and creative processes. Such retelling reminded us of Vygotsky's work on the relationship between thought and language in which language is described as a tool for thinking and also of Vygotsky's interest in understanding the process that 'a thought traverses before it is embodied in words' (Vygotsky, 1986, p. 218). For Vygotsky, 'thought is mediated by signs externally but also it is mediated internally by word meanings' (Vygotsky, 1986, p. 252). He explains:

> The relation of thought to word is not a thing but a process, a continual movement back and forth from thought to word and from word to thought. In that process, the relation of thought to word undergoes changes that themselves may be regarded as development ... Thought is not merely expressed in words; it comes into existence through them ... Every thought moves, grows and develops, fulfills a function, solves a problem [...] (Vygotsky, 1986, p. 218)

From this perspective, as the children used talk and dialogue to interpret the visual images, they seemed to be gaining a new understanding of the story.

There are also examples of the children putting the characters' thoughts into words based particularly on their expressions and gestures. In the following example from GLW, based on the image that shows the protagonist's wife and daughter finally arriving and stepping out of the flying 'box', Claude (Congo) and Morag (Scotland) observed and interpreted their body language and translated these thoughts into words:

> Claude: ... *his wife looks like, 'Wow, this is strange, where are we?'*
> Morag: *It looks like* [the daughter] *is thinking 'I wonder who that is?' then she sees it's the dad.*

The children sometimes made use of expressions and gestures themselves as they created these dialogues. In one clear case, a performance even abandoned words when a group of children in GLW reached the page where the man seems to be trying to answer the questions posed by the immigration officer; Józef (Poland) also began a retelling with dialogue but then jumped up from his seat and exclaimed: '*I can do like what he's doing.*' The mediator said, '*You want to do the faces that he's doing? Okay. Let's see.*' At this point, Józef proceeded to reproduce, one by one, the posture, gestures and facial expressions of the man in each of the frames, his body language, connecting the still images with movement so that the event became a smooth but silent performance. This form of retelling, which clearly was based on inferences, came together to create a mimed performance that put the boy in the position of the man who does not comprehend the language he is hearing and who is forced to express himself through gestures.

The role of this retelling involving dialogue and gestures helped the children to make meaning of the story, leading us to question whether all of the students' comments in response to *The Arrival* should be considered as potential inferences at some level, given the wordless and complex nature of the text. As we continued sharing our analysis across contexts and holding conversations about the children's responses, we approached all the narratives the children created to tell the story, whether they were close to the meaning expected by the mediators or departed from it, and whether they had been coded earlier as literal or inferential, as the children's creation of what Goodman (1996) describes as parallel texts – the text a reader creates and imagines as he/she reads based in his/her background, cultural models and experiences; the reader's own version of a story. We theorize that the wordless nature of *The Arrival* serves as an invitation to readers to become co-authors or 'co-creators', as Tan (2012) intended, and the children embraced this authorship through the creation of parallel texts.

Becoming co-authors with Shaun Tan: The creation of parallel texts

As mentioned earlier, at the outset of the study, most statements in which the children appeared to be describing or simply stating what the story narrated through the images were coded as Retelling, such as when Ryan, in AZ, responding to the first pages, retold the story of the immigrant leaving his country:

Aquí esta historía trata que la niña esta dormida. De repente se levanta, está desayunando. Ella ve la maleta. El papá, mientras, se está alistando. La mamá tambien y la mamá la arregla a ella. Entonces, ya que están listos, ella agarra la maleta y el papá se la pide. Ella se va y entonces ella se va porque vieron esta [inaudible, pointing to the 'dragon tail' shadow].

[This story is about a girl that is sleeping. Suddenly she wakes up, and is eating breakfast. She sees the piece of luggage. The dad, meanwhile, is getting ready. The mom is also and then the mom gets her ready. Then, as they are ready she takes the piece of luggage and dad asks for it. She leaves and then she leaves because they saw this [inaudible, pointing to the 'dragon tail' shadow].]

In this excerpt, Ryan seemed to make a straightforward account of what the images seem to narrate in one of the first pages on Part I; less obvious in this retelling is his inference (like Hassan in GLW) that the whole family is leaving at that moment because there is a danger in the city, as he confirms in a later turn. The rest of the children agreed that only the father was moving at this time because, in Almah's words: '*He's the only one who's carrying a suitcase. I mean all that's one suitcase. Just . . . everything . . .*'

In the excerpt above, Ryan is assuming that the whole family is moving; later, he explicitly comments on the three family members getting dressed and ready to leave. The researcher wondered whether the comment should be left under the literal level and only coded as inference the conversational turn in which he actually expressed his belief that the whole family is moving. Finally coded as Retelling, these kinds of statements revealed the blurred line between the literal and the inferential levels in the children's responses and supported a view of retelling as interpretive or inferential work.

Moreover, because Tan's images are (at times intentionally) ambiguous or made up of unfamiliar objects and events, there is often an intersection between literal remarks about what can be seen on the page and inferential statements about what these elements must represent or indicate. Identifying information in an image, even if it is literal and seemingly basic, often requires the student to consider context (based on previous frames – and based on previous literal observations), and their own personal frames of reference (which might be intertextual in nature, or based on lived experience). When students make seemingly literal comments ('*that's his wife*') based on what they observe directly in the illustration, it is also an inference based on normative understandings or assumptions they hold (in this case: children seemed less likely to assume the woman was his sister, because they might be attuned to mainstream images of the nuclear family). Therefore, in a wordless text, especially a postmodern or 'postmodernesque' (Allan, 2012) text such as *The Arrival*, given that there is no print telling the story, any retelling of the story made by the children was their interpretation of the images and so involved some level of inferential and interpretive work in which the children became co-authors with Tan.

The children's responses are clear examples of Goodman's (1996) notion of reading. He proposes that all readers, as they read and retell a story, construct a parallel text to the one they are reading and, because each person relies on his/her unique background knowledge and experiences, readers reading the same text are constructing different parallel texts. We believe this is especially the case when children are reading and retelling wordless texts, given that such retelling involves in fact a re-creation of a story told in images that requires different levels of inference. In the following excerpt, Hassan (GLW) begins to develop a parallel story based on the map as a treasure map. He had already suggested that the man was going on an 'adventure' to 'find treasure'. The map encouraged him to proceed with this story and he invented the dialogue with the man who was helping the protagonist find his way, or, in this case, to find the treasure. The pet became a helper or companion in this enterprise, perhaps reflecting the traditional figure of the animal helper in fiction. Following Hassan's lead, Ali made a more explicit link to film narratives continuing with this story by going back to the 'dragons' and identifying them as the 'monster' that must be defeated before obtaining the treasure:

> Hassan: *I think he found like this kind of map to like a treasure, and, oh yeah, that's probably like a guy that helps him, and then he says, 'Did you find a map? I think I know where you, I know where that place is, I'll help you'. And then he has this kind of pet thing to help him go where they are going.*
>
> Ali: *And this picture, it shows you a monster* [going back in the book and pointing to the 'dragon tails']. *It's because in every film you see – if you want to go to the treasure – you have to fight a monster.*

The more diverse the children's literacy and life experiences are, the more likely their parallel texts will be diverse as well. For example, in AZ, Almah (Iraq), who had a long trip to get to the USA, staying at different hotels, and Ryan (Mexico), who is knowledgeable about family reunification, created very different parallel texts anticipating what would happen once the passengers arrived in the harbour, as illustrated in their pictures. Almah showed the immigrants arriving in the new country with their suitcases with plans to book into hotels, while Ryan showed the immigrants being greeted by their relatives (Martínez-Roldán and Newcomer, 2011).

Likewise, the children in the three contexts negotiated different parallel texts and interpretations when reading the images of the scene when the passengers arrived in the ship and underwent an examination before being let into the country (see Figure 5.2).

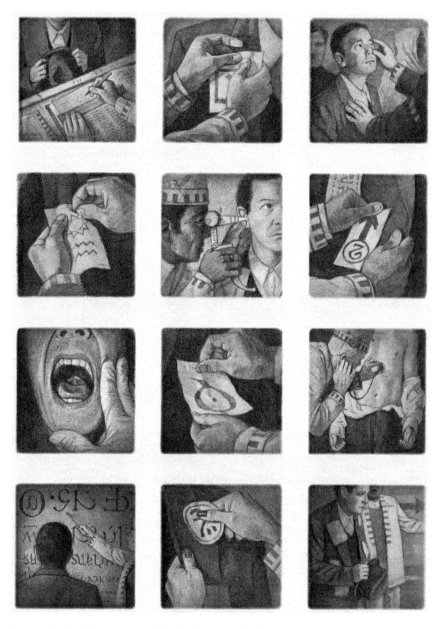

Figure 5.2 Undergoing a health check upon arrival

The children in GLW proposed several hypotheses: Andy interpreted the scene as searching and checking for drugs and pursued his idea of the man being at some sort of global corporation meeting. Nadia brought in the idea of germs, something that Claude also brought up. Sunil used words such as 'register', 'control' and 'national', which is revealing about his own situation as an asylum seeker. Finally, after some discussion about his registration, Naimal speculated that the people checking the protagonist might have thought he was a terrorist. The children's backgrounds clearly had an influence on their parallel texts:

Andy (Scot): *They're checking them.*
Mediator: *They're checking them. What are they checking for?*
Andy: *Drugs maybe.*
Claude (Congo): *Or if you have a sickness in there, they have to like to test you before you come in if you have a sickness. Cos they have to check their eyes, because they've been living in village, they want to check their eye that they can see properly, cos they probably don't see doctors.*
Sunil (Sri Lanka): *I know! I think they're registering for this country because they have the stickers for and controlling. If he have anything wrong.*
Nadia (Pakistani/Scot): *It could be like they're thinking that he's, he's trying to – he's a terrorist, trying to come to another place.*

On the other hand, Jack, who often needed a wheelchair and was probably more familiar with regular health checks, was more specific about what the examination involved:

No, I think it's like a check-up because see if he's like travel from one – if it's like a cold weather, he might got a cold, so probably they're checking like the ears, if he has any ear infection, probably his mouth because he might have any like tooth problems.

Faisal's suggestions may reflect the type of conversations that concern immigrants from Pakistan, while Józef's parallel text is more in line with his interest in science or with reference to film:

Faisal (Pakistan): *I think the people are coming here and when they sit in the room and go to the country, they want to check if they don't have bomb with them to destroy their country [...] And they're checking [because] they can put a gun in there and they can hide drugs in their mouth ...*
Józef (Poland): *No. I think they're checking the DNA.*

While some of the children in AZ also thought that the recent arrivals were being checked by doctors to take care of them after such a long trip, some of them made the historical connection to the medical check-up immigrants were forced to go through when they arrived at Ellis Island to see if they would be allowed into the USA, knowledge that the children most likely acquired through their social studies' curriculum.

Clearly, the context in which the children have been raised, their educational and personal experiences, and their experiences with stories in different media, including TV and movies, all seemed to mediate their interpretations and creations of parallel texts. The discussions provided a safe space where those diverse parallel texts or interpretations could be negotiated.

Supporting students' referential work

The challenge of making inferences from such a complex and ambiguous text as *The Arrival* seemed to excite students and kept them fully involved in looking and talking. There was the noticeable trend within the children in GLW and BCN that, further into the session, students started responding on an increasingly inferential level. It seems that the assembling and articulating of 'evidence' through their more literal statements, along with their predictions, helped students to connect what might at first seem like disparate elements or pieces of information in order to make some sense of the beginning of the story through I.S. For instance, a simple literal observation/statement such as '*that man has a suitcase*', along with literal observations about the protagonist hugging a young girl and woman who appear to be his family, allowed a student to make an inference such as '*he is leaving his home*'. As Meek (1988) asserts, texts teach children to read – an idea that highlights the importance of providing readers time for prolonged engagement with texts. For the children in AZ, the first two discussions prompted more Inferences than Retellings. At the beginning, the children made a great number of predictions; perhaps because they did not have enough contextual background to interpret the text, they tended to hypothesize and infer rather than describe. Later on, it seemed they felt more comfortable retelling the text until they again encountered a complex part (e.g. the inset stories) and the inferences increased – although there was no clear pattern explaining why some discussions prompted more inferences than others.

Making inferences, for the students in the three countries, involved a process of offering possible explanations, hearing feedback from other students, gauging responses from interviewers, looking forward and backward in the book for more clues, and reformulating the inference. This sequence reflected the construction of an interpretative reading community: literal reference plus hypothesis plus 'confrontational' hypothesis plus affirmation or not of the hypothesis by continuing or returning to particular elements in the text. During this process, statements tended to be repetitive as students formulated their understandings/inferences. Even when students posited an inference, they seemed to know it was only a tentative suggestion up for negotiation. This negotiation tended to take a collaborative approach, whereby a comment was offered by one participant, then certain parts of that comment were adopted and built upon by others until it could be confirmed or dismissed. This type of dynamic evidences the social nature of reading and talking about books together. As will be discussed in Chapter 8, a key element of this social process is the role of the mediator or facilitator of the discussions. While a book like *The Arrival* is full of potential to support readers, it is clear that the mediator's questions and follow-up comments have an important part in helping shape the children's responses.

6

Intertextual Journeys into Intercultural Spaces

Józef (Poland/GLW): *I think he got his documents or a gun say in his suitcase.
    And he was from a Mafia family.*
Mediator: *About the Mafia. Where did you see that about the Mafia?*
Józef: *Because I got a* [Xbox] *game Mafia they've got clothes like this.*

The front page of *The Arrival* starts us off on a journey, turning us all into immigrants as we are drawn into a world that looks familiar yet strange. The man and the strange animal on the front cover disorientate readers in time and space, leaving us to draw on our past lives and reading experiences to make meaning out of these visuals. We have been positioned as readers to make intertextual links to the texts of our life (personal and textual) in order to make sense out of what we see. In the opening extract from Józef, it is clear from his reply to the mediator's question that he had to draw upon his previous knowledge of men wearing suits and carrying briefcases from his playing of the electronic Xbox game called *Mafia Wars*.

This process of children making intertextual connections to previous texts (print based, visual or the narratives of life) has been well documented in literature (Brooks and Browne, 2012; Sipe, 2008). Rosenblatt does not use the term 'intertextuality', but she did discuss the way in which readers draw on their experiences with people and the world in order to shape the work they are reading (Rosenblatt, 1982). Pantalco referred to the process as 'cross-fertilisation' (Pantaleo, 2008, p. 29): the process of the reader creating meaning as they bring their own intertextual histories to the text creating an intertextual synergetic relationship. This chapter will focus on intertextuality in three distinct ways: first, we will take a brief look at the ways in which Tan used intertextuality when he drew upon his own background as source material for *The Arrival* and created a text that juxtaposed 'the familiar or *normal* with the exotic or *weird*' (Tan, 2012,

p. 22); followed by a discussion of the ways in which the children drew upon different sources as landmarks to make meaning from the text; and, finally, by looking at how Tan's text positioned the children as readers to make intertextual connections that were drawn from their own cultural repertoires, which in turn led the children to engage in intercultural exchanges and to the beginning of a critical cultural awareness.

Tan's own use of intertextuality

Tan's own background impacted on his attraction and desire to explore the theme of migration, so that the entire text represents 'a distillation of a universal migrant story' (Tan, 2012, p. 25), and, as we have noted, he considers his readers as co-creators who will invest their own meaning into his narratives. Throughout the book, he has created illustrations that play with the boundary between the familiar and the exotic, thus creating opportunities for the children to respond from their own cultural repertoires. The front cover provides an example of the familiar and the exotic, a man wearing dated clothes alongside a strange animal, which Tan says was inspired by his own childhood memories of raising tadpoles in an aquarium (Tan, 2010, p. 35). On opening the book, the endpapers display rows of passport-sized portraits of people; Tan explains they were 'inspired by photographs from the archives of the Ellis Island Museum in New York City' and that they represent 'a key threshold of cultural memory' (Tan, 2010, p. 12). The peritext makes use of textual fragments borrowed from documents that could have belonged to the immigrants in the pictures. Within the peritext, readers also encounter Tan's ingenious creation of a new language script, which he created by cutting up the Roman alphabet and rearranging it into a new script, which we have noted is an effective strategy for sharing the feeling of having to make sense of a foreign language and, according to Tan, is a strategy to make all of us new arrivals. Within the narrative, Tan also draws upon New York City landmarks such as the receiving centre at Ellis Island and embeds this into his illustrations. Even the man, his wife and strange pet have been created to resemble his own family, including pets (Tan, 2012, p. 24). Thus, Tan made abundant use of intertextuality and the children responded to this and added their own.

Sources of intertextuality as textual landmarks

The first stage of our analysis involved identification of all the references where the children made intertextual links; this included specified and unspecified media, textual artefacts (photographs, pictures, art, reference texts from school) from their lives and texts that exemplified stories from their lives. Further analysis helped us notice that, as the children responded to the book, their intertextual comments tended to cluster around specific points or themes in the text, suggesting that Tan's technique of moving from the strange and exotic to the familiar prompted the children to engage in intertextual meaning-making as a way of making sense out of the unfamiliar. Geographically speaking, we all need and use landmarks to orientate ourselves to new landscapes. Mackey (2011) suggests that this is also what readers do when encountering a new text. Readers are drawn to textual landmarks within the texts that resonate with texts from their cultural repertoire. These landmarks act as points of navigation, which aid the children in constructing pathways through the text. We found a pattern emerging where the children would be disorientated by the strangeness of the text, and in order to orientate themselves they would centre on images (landmarks) in *The Arrival* that fitted with their prior experiences or knowledge, which they would then share with each other. Some of those landmarks came from the media.

Media as transnational references

While each child has his/her own 'landmarks', among all the responses in each location was one common connection, a response that mentioned the film *Titanic* by James Cameron, which Fittipaldi (2008) categorizes as a 'transnational reference':

> [El barco] *es muy grande, ¿no? Es, es . . . parecido al* Titanic. [. . .] *Los que son ricos están adentro y los que son pobres adentro pero muy abajo* [. . .] *Sí, en el* Titanic *yo lo he visto. Los ricos arriba y los pobres abajo de todo.* (Gabriel, BCN)

> [[The ship] is very big, isn't it? It's, it's . . . like the *Titanic*. [. . .] The rich ones are inside and the poor ones are inside but much lower [. . .] Yes, in the *Titanic*, I've seen it. The rich above and the poor below everything.]

> *I think it's* Titanic . . . *then it is show three little windows. Then this three are in here, but then it show more, and this three are one, this three. And that is all ship, and this is from one . . . erm . . . window goes to all big ship.* (Józef, GLW)

Que el señor está mirando la foto de su familia que empacó. Fue lo primero que
empacó. Y por eso está poniéndose triste y está viendo afuera de su ventana del
barco y va en un barco . . . el Titanic. (Viviana, AZ)

[The man is looking at the photo he packed of his family. It was the first
thing he packed. And that's why he is getting sad and he is looking out from
the ship's window and he is in a ship . . . the *Titanic*.]

In the example from BCN, the child made the link to help them understand the
social status of the people on the ship, whereas Józef in GLW and Viviana in AZ
made the link when trying to understand the compositional aspects of Tan's
portrayal of the ship from the perspective of zooming out within each frame.
This intertextual meaning-making can be explained by Lemke's (1992) work on
textual analysis. As a social semiotician, he believed 'every text, the discourse of
every occasion, makes its social meanings against the background of other texts
and the discourses of other occasions' (Lemke, 1992, p. 257). Lemke (2004)
developed the concept of Halliday's (1985) 'metafunctions of language' and
presented three terms to describe how readers make meaning from all semiosis:
presentationally when they link to a theme; *orientationally* when they link to a
stance or an ideology; and *organizationally* when they link to the structure or
composition. Lemke's ideas allowed us to make sense of the extracts above,
showing that the children made links to the visual presentation of the ship,
which reminded them of the *Titanic*, but the children from BCN also made
orientational links in terms of identifying with the social status of the passengers,
while Józef was drawn to the idea of the *Titanic* to make sense of the way Tan
had organized the text. This also applies to the opening extract from Józef, as we
could argue that he was making presentational links because the protagonist's
clothing reminded him of the men in the *Mafia Wars* game, but he was also
making organizational links between the aged appearance of the text and the
fact that the Mafia game was set in the 1920s.

Children's intertextual connections to films were not limited to *Titanic*. In
BCN, the children also responded to the visual presentation of the ship and the
sea journey by mentioning other films connected to the sea, such as *Poseidon*,
The Little Mermaid and *Finding Nemo*. Unspecified films were also alluded to
with themes related to tragedies, disasters and monsters. In AZ, the children also
referenced unspecified films to decide whether the 'dragons tails' were dangerous
or not. Toni responded: '*Depende la ocasión y como se vea el dragón porque en*
algunas películas sale una niña con el dragón pero el dragón tiene, ella se lo imagina
asi horroroso pero en realidad es un buen dragón' [It depends on the occasion and

what the dragon looks like because in some films there is a girl with a dragon but the dragon, she imagines it to be horrifying but in fact, it is a good dragon]. Some of the children in GLW also made references to Bollywood films and posters. These links to popular cultural media and in particular *Titanic* were not surprising in a world where the film industry markets its products globally. Even though *Titanic* is not a current film, the use of DVDs and online film channels have made access to film ubiquitous to anyone with an Internet connection. These global trends in film distribution and viewing mean that audiovisual popular media has become an essential element of intertextual interpretive schemes.

The children's intertextual connections to films went beyond connections in terms of the content of the films, such as the presentational intertextual connections shown above. They also made organizational connections referencing techniques used in films as well as in photos. In BCN, the children drew on silent films in response to the aged appearance of the book, and at one point Manga comics were mentioned to explain the strip format. In GLW, Faisal responded to the small photographs on the endpapers and linked these to black and white photographs, while Sara said, '*I've seen these kind of pictures . . . in art gallery.*' The compositional factors of zooming out from the ship allowed Surayya to link this technique to a similar technique used in *Flotsam*: '*See, it look like somebody's in – see the flotsam, the fish, that robot fish he had something in his eye and [. . .] and a man in her eye.*'

While identifying and analysing the way the children made meaning presentationally, orientationally and organizationally, we noticed that these categories overlapped, because the children usually made more than one type of meaning, and that the types of meaning made varied across the geographical locations and between children. Identification of the responses revealed that children drew upon a wide repertoire of media to make meaning, confirming Sipe's (2000) previous work on intertextual links, which found that around 10 per cent of the children's responses were connections to other books, TV programmes, videos and films.

Cultural, social and historical landmarks

While the intertextual connection *Titanic* served as an important landmark, there were other references, such as the image on the double-spread page where there are two gigantic statues at the harbour. In all three contexts, there were mentions of the landscape resembling New York (mostly seen in films rather than reality), but, in AZ, some of the children made direct connections to the Statue of Liberty. For one of the children in AZ, this image served as a landmark that led to culturally and historically relevant connections for her as a Mexican girl. Viviana responded to this image with a double intertextual connection, one to the 'Statue of Liberty' in the USA and another to the 'Mexican Angel of Liberty': '*Como la estatua de la libertad pero para ellos … Como en Mexico tenemos el Angel de la Libertad*' [Like the Statue of Liberty but for them … Like in Mexico we have the Angel of Liberty]. The 'Angel de la Libertad' statue is located in Ciudad Juárez, Chihuahua, and was built to commemorate the 100th anniversary of Mexican Independence. As a bicultural girl, Viviana used these familiar culturally relevant images, one from the USA and one from Mexico, to interpret the strange statues in the text. They served as landmarks that supported her interpretations of the unusual elements Tan was introducing in the story.

History also provided several landmarks for the children as they seemed to draw from what they were learning in school to make sense of the text. For example, the following excerpt from GLW shows that Surayya and Sara were drawn to the aged appearance of the text and the clothes worn by the man and they tried to determine the historical period of the clothes.

> Surayya: *… old-fashioned here. Old-fashioned like*
> Sara: *I think that's a 1970s.*
> Mediator: *It's the 1970s?*
> Sara: *Or the 60s.*

They then began to negotiate when in the past this may have occurred. Later, the class teacher confirmed that the class had been studying a topic on the 1960s. Another example came from the children in AZ. They had speculated during their first discussion that the book was going to be about 'history'. After commenting on the cover's aged appearance and their initial browsing of the first pages, they proposed that the book was going to be about something that happened 'long ago'. Although they later adjusted their expectations because of the fantastic elements in the text, references to history and historical events to interpret the story were strong in their first discussion. One hypothesis two of the children proposed for the first page in which the protagonist is leaving was that his daughter was being sent to an orphanage:

> Juan: *Maybe she's going to orphanage or to new place because right here it is like a …*
> Toni: *… like a suitcase.*

Juan: *Suitcase!*
Toni: *Of old times.*
[...]
Mediator: *You said you thought that the girl was going to go to an orphanage?*
Juan: *Yeah.*
Mediator: *What made you think that?*
Juan: *By the picture in the middle.*
Mediator: *The one, this one?*
Juan: *Yeah.*
Toni: *It looks like they're a happy family, right there.*
Juan: *Maybe that's what the girl wish to have.*

Later in that same discussion, the children made connections to a historical period of the USA, the Great Depression, which had seemed to act as background for their initial hypothesis of the girl being sent to an orphanage:

Toni: *Yo veo que hay mucha tristeza porque hay muchas familias que una persona de sus familias se está yendo para el tren.* [I see that there is so much sadness because there are many families in which one of their members is taking the train.]

Juan: *Sí. También como dice Toni, la familia se ve muy triste porque se están separando.* [Yes, as Toni says, the family looks very sad because they are getting separated.]

Viviana: *During the Great Depression.*

Mediator: *Hmm.*

Juan: *Y se ve que es muy triste.* [And it can be seen that it is sad.]

Mediator: *What happened during the Great Depression?*

Viviana: *Um, the economy was bad and there was war so then a lot of people were getting separated. Children were sent to foster care and stuff like that . . . to different countries.*

Toni: *And a lot of* [inaudible] *started to move to like AZ and California.*

Their knowledge of this historical time suggests that they learned this content as part of their social studies' curriculum and had it available as a source to interpret the text. While this background led them to miss momentarily that it was the protagonist who was leaving, it was a historical landmark that helped the children make meaning of the general situation of poverty that may have led the protagonist to migrate.

As in AZ, content learning at school also mediated children's transactions with the text in GLW and BCN. In GLW, while discussing the front cover, Hassan

(Somalia) was drawn to the strange animal and speculated on how this could provide more information about the role being played by the main protagonist: '*man is going to take care of animal because becoming extinct like the Bangladesh tigers*'. The class teacher confirmed that *Bangladeshi tigers* had been discussed previously on a topic about endangered species. References to previous schoolwork were also made in BCN when the children alluded to '*the Greeks*', '*the eighteenth century*', '*the Second World War in Poland*' and '*Christopher Columbus*'.

The children have drawn upon a diverse range of textual sources to make sense of the disorientating points in the text, but the sources come from the cultural practices of the children's daily lives, with an emphasis on media and texts encountered during school. Ivanič (2004) terms this practice 'habitual intertextuality', and it is important for educators to acknowledge and identify these habitual references because allowing children the time and space to use them means they can draw upon their own 'funds of knowledge' (Moll, Amanti, Neff and Gonzalez 1992) and begin the process of opening up about their cultural identity. In the process, they also affirm their own general and specific knowledge.

Cultural location: Mirrors and windows

The sections above all discuss the ways in which the children were able to orientate themselves socially, culturally and historically using intertextual references in response to the landmarks within the text. Tan alluded to this when he explained that 'through strangeness we arrive at a kind of clarity' (Tan, 2012, p. 26), as each reader begins a journey of locating themselves in the book. Tan's text disorientates through the front cover but, on opening the book, his creative use of the images of people's faces from all around the world in the endpapers meant that readers from around the world are invited to locate themselves or identify others within these textual mirrors and windows (Botelho and Rudman, 2009). In doing so, the children began to share examples of how the images related to their own lives, while other children were able to acknowledge that these represented diversity.

There were three examples from GLW where the children related the pictures to examples of popular media, artefacts or people they had encountered in their own lives. Surayya from Pakistan said they reminded her of her gran. She then speculated that her gran could have been alive '*probably 1960, I think they were born in 1970 ... like before the Pakistan made them live in India, my granny, my uncle, my dad, big sister and big brother lived there*'. Sara from Kurdistan continued the dialogue by suggesting she had seen pictures like these '*in a magazine, a museum and an art gallery*'. The boys were drawn to the sepia tones and made thematic links to black and white photographs and films; they also interpreted the author's intentions of thinking about the past and cited examples of photographs of grandfathers and uncles. Surayya and Sara speculated on who these people could be. Surayya offered the suggestion that '*these people are movie superstars from India, Scotland and Pakistan*'. Sara built on her hypothesis and offered: '*I think they are from China, it's probably about cultures*', which allowed Surayya to speculate on the ethnic origins of the people in the photographs: '*these two look like they are English people*'. These ideas were echoed by the immigrant children in BCN who speculated that these were '*gente de diferentes países*' [people from different countries].

Likewise, during the first day, the children in AZ speculated about the people in the endpapers, but they did not seem to relate much to them; instead, the discussion served to place the story within the frame of diversity:

Juan: *Maybe they're his, the people that used to live in the town.*

Janice: *De los de antes.* [People from earlier times.]

Viviana: *People that are in the story.*

Toni: *Los gobernadores de todo el tiempo de ese pueblo* [The governors of all times in that town]

[...]

Juan: *Because it might be that his family* [inaudible] *so he's showing how they look in different places of the world.*

Janice: *Y como se miran y como se visten* [and how they looked like and how they dress]

Juan: *Porque se miran diferente. Mira como ve cada* [inaudible] *tiene su estilo de vestirse.* [Because they look different. Look how each [inaudible] has their own dress style.]

The second day, Almah was in the group for the first time and she commented on how the women in her country used scarves, showing how differently the images spoke to the Mexican children and to the child from Iraq.

As the children continued to discuss the pictures in the endpapers, the dialogue moved beyond making intertextual connections as the children began to discuss what the pictures could represent. The following examples, first from BCN and then from GLW, show how the children moved beyond speculation and identification of ethnic origin to begin socially constructing ideas connected to culture and diversity:

Mediador: . . . *y esta página de los rostros que – que nos sugerirá?*
Emma: *diferente gente*
Hilda: *gente de diferentes culturas – países . . .*
Emma: *también diversidad*

[Mediator: . . . and this page of the faces – what would it suggest to us?
Emma: different people
Hilda: people from different cultures – countries . . .
Emma: also diversity]

Józef: *people like that are from other countries that are helping Shaun Tan.*
   Like this kind of Indian, Arabic . . . Jamaican, Japanese . . .
Hassan: *It's like there's a lot of people from different cultures, different religions*
   and different skin colour, hair or anything. It just shows like a lot of people
   are different.

Józef used his available language competences to ascribe a nationality to the
people in the portraits, while Hassan mediated the response and built on Józef's
observation by offering an overview of diversity. He went on to draw upon his
own 'cultural proximity' to the men and women in the illustrations to explain
cultural information from his own life:

Hassan: *I think they're Muslims cos the traditional Muslim is the boys, when*
   they go to Mosque like wear the headwear for the pulpit and the girls wear
   a scarf over their hair, so the boys don't see the hair. It's kinda like a tradition
   or something.

We have already mentioned that Almah in AZ shared similar information, and
Sara and Surayya also drew conclusions about the pictures representing different
cultures and agreed that most Muslim women wore scarves:

Surayya: *It look like somebody's different. Maybe it's different cultures. Some*
   they got different costumes.
Sara: *Most Muslim people wear scarves.*
Surayya: *Uhuh.*
Sara: *Like that lady there.*

In BCN, the Catalans were also drawn to discussing cultural diversity as shown
by the clothing in the pictures, when Carolina picked up on the different
headwear, hats and '*turbantes*' [turbans], and Emma mentioned '*los rasgos de la
cara*' [facial features].

   In these extracts, the children have responded to Tan's juxtapositioning of the
strange with the familiar by making intertextual links, but they have then moved

beyond these links to speculate on what these passport pictures represent and, in doing so, begin to establish a collaborative community that values diversity and creates equity amongst its members (Short, 1992). Tan's endpapers have acted as a cultural mirror and window for readers to either locate themselves within the text or begin to see and hear about others. The intertextual responses were doing more than allowing the children to make meaning; they were also allowing the children to enter an intercultural space.

From intertextuality to intercultural competence

This process from intertextuality to intercultural competence links to the work of Sipe (2000, 2008) and Bloome and Egan-Robertson (2004) who all view intertextuality as being socially constructed. Bloome and Egan-Robertson talk about the process where 'readers act and react together to make meanings, relationships and take social action' (Bloome and Egan-Robertson, 2004, p. 17). Tan's carefully crafted text has created that cultural milieu, in the way that it continually positions readers as if they were immigrants who need to orientate themselves within their new environment. The children have done this by making intertextual links and the social constructivist nature of their dialogue within the literature circles takes them to a safe space where they begin to share intercultural knowledge and arrive at greater intercultural understandings.

Intercultural competence is defined as the ability of children to function at the borders between several languages/dialects, manoeuvring and negotiating cultural understanding and misunderstanding (Kramsch, 1998, p. 27). Byram's (1987) work on language learning showed that learning another language was about more than linguistic mastery, it was also linked to culture and understanding of one's own identity as a socially and culturally constructed entity. As learners developed language, they also developed intercultural competences. Through empirical work, Byram (2008, p. 69) noted that successful learners tended to:

- show willingness to suspend beliefs about one's own culture and other culture; this led to developing positive attitudes, curiosity and open-mindedness;
- develop knowledge of other social groups, their artefacts, values and cultural practices;
- interpret and form links between cultural practices (documents, artefacts, events) in one culture to another;

- develop critical cultural awareness; and
- apply all of these competences in real-time settings.

Examples of how the children were developing these competences could be found in the extracts. One of the main sources that supported the children's development of intercultural competence was Tan's focus on language.

Language

While *The Arrival* is a predominantly visual text, Tan created an alphabet, which is first encountered on the pages of the peritext. The process of disorientation and orientation discussed above occurs again at this point in the book, exemplified when Toni from AZ pointed out that the title page was '*like the cover* [of a book] *but in another place in the world*', making an organizational intertextual link. This page produced a cluster of responses that show the children's awareness of languages across the world. The following example from GLW showed that the children were intrigued by the new language created by Tan, and made intertextual links to decipher the code when first encountering the new script.

> *This language is actual real cos it's ancient Egyptian language. Or in ancient Egyptian you have these sundials. A sundial thing, symbol like that or a pyramid, then you have to like, figure out the code or something.* (Hassan)

In BCN, the group of immigrant children read the strange alphabet on the title page and Adrián declared, '*aquí no dice nada*' [It says nothing here]. However, together with the mediator, Beatriz and Naima worked together to decipher it and finally declared it was '*como en otro idioma*' [like another language]. The Catalan children also echoed this discussion, working out that the new alphabet spelled out 'Shaun Tan' and the name of the book.

The children in AZ recognized the title page and also speculated about its language, suggesting that it could be Russian or Chinese, languages none of them spoke:

> Mediator: *Toni, you said a language a few seconds ago. I don't know if everyone heard.*
> Toni: *Russian?*
> Mediator: *Ah! Russian. You anticipate that it will be Russian. Hmm?*
> Juan: *By looking at it, it doesn't look like Chinese.*
> Toni: *I've seen Russian letters.*

Juan: *That doesn't look like Chinese.*
Mediator: *Okay.*
Juan: *Because Chinese use like*
Toni: *little symbols . . .*

The children naturally began to speculate about the origins of the new script and in the process showed their awareness and knowledge of other language groups and how their scripts work. Further on in the book, discussing one of the adverts, Surayya from Pakistan decided it could be based on a Hindi script, but, more importantly, she drew upon her own cultural knowledge of how this script worked and began to share this with the group.

> *It says in Urdu, English and Hindi, but it got different writing than that bit, that one. And they don't got this writing in India. Every word in India they got a line at the top of it. Even for writing, make a line. This is can be India, but they like here, it's different.* (Surayya)

Within the peritext, Tan embeds textual fragments from documents that may have belonged to the immigrants shown in the portraits from the endpapers. These textual fragments also act like mirrors, and invite the children to first of all identify the fragments, but, more importantly, they allow some children to identify scripts from their own home languages. As we have mentioned, in GLW, Józef was thrilled to find that one of the documents was a Polish birth certificate, which he translated for the group. The extract below showed the children were working together to decipher the fragments, while using their own experience of stamps in passports to make meaning.

> Sara: *That's in, that man's country, because the language different. The writing's different. And I think*
> Surayya: *Uhuh. It look like something Bangladeshi, India or like that . . . See that stamp, it's in, in my passport . . . I got a stamp and it's in Urdu. It's like Urdu writing on it.*

Some children in BCN tried to read textual fragments in relation to the story images, for example, Alan read the name on the passport at the beginning of the book and speculated that this was the main character's name.

Tan has echoed the dislocation process created by his visual text by using a new script that invites diverse readers to find examples of their own language embedded in the textual fragments. Tan has created the conditions to develop positive attitudes, curiosity and open-mindedness, which was evidenced in

GLW when one of the sessions began with a discussion prompted by the children about the diverse languages spoken by each participant including the mediators.

> Surayya: *Oh, my brother tell me you were Spanish.*
> Mediator: *Ah, that I was from Mexico and I speak Spanish.*
> Sara: *'Hola'.* [Laughs]
> Evelyn: *'Hola'. 'Hola'. Yes, that's Spanish.*
> [...]
> Sara: *I remember the Mexico book last week* [referring to the Spanish edition of *The Arrival*].
> [...]
> Mediator: [I speak] *English, Spanish and French.*
> Surayya: *Urdu, Punjabi, French and English.*
> Sara: *Kurdish, Arabic, French and English.*

The children moved on to discussing the languages they spoke (Urdu, Punjabi, French, English, Kurdish, Arabic, French, Somali, Spanish and Pashto); the languages they shared; their levels of competence; and the different scripts used across language groups. For the children in AZ, this focus on language enabled them to expand their definitions about bilingualism. They seemed to assume that a bilingual person speaks Spanish and English. They were surprised to learn, first, that Almah who didn't speak Spanish was also bilingual and, second, that a non-Latino person can speak Spanish, such as Sarah, the graduate student who participated in some of the discussions and who is a white English-native speaker. The discussion on language supported the development of intercultural competence as they learned about each other's languages and cultural practices.

Critical cultural awareness

The above extracts show that the children responded to the embedded mirrors and windows and shared and developed their knowledge of other cultures, but, as they grew in confidence, supported by the mediators and encouraged by their peers, some of them also began to show evidence of developing critical cultural awareness. In BCN, for example, after discussions about the faces in the endpapers, with prompting from the mediator, Xavier and Carolina moved from recognizing diversity to considering sameness:

> Mediador: *. . . y por qué dicen que se nos querrá mostrar eso de la diversidad que plantean, ¿cuál será el objetivo?*

Carolina: *para mostrarnos que*
Xavier: *que todos somos iguales pero diferentes.*

[Mediator: ... and why do you say that he wanted to show us these things
   about diversity that you are proposing, what would be the aim?
Carolina: to show us that
Xavier: that we are all the same but different.]

Earlier in the chapter, there was a discussion of how the children in AZ responded
to the double-page harbour scene recognizing the symbolism of the statues by
relating them to the Statue of Liberty. In GLW, this scene was the subject of a
long conversation that led to the idea that these statues welcomed the new
arrivals to the city. However, some children reached this idea before others, and
it was the group interaction that eventually moved all the children in that group
towards an awareness of what the presence of the statues in this scene meant.
Surayya (Pakistan) and Sara (Kurdistan) were the first to note their symbolic
welcoming of diversity. Surayya began this particular exchange by saying that
'*these two big statues show us the people, we care about other people's culture*',
although she then moved on to suggest that these statues were of famous
religious people that she had seen in a book at home. Sara also picked up on the
theme of tolerance and suggested that the statues represented an anti-racist
message: '*don't be like racist to other people and stuff*'. Then Hassan (Somalia)
interjected a completely different interpretation based on the characters in the
boat: '*They go to this kind of place here and they're looking for this kind of treasure.*'
He quickly followed up with suggestions that everyone was going on an adventure
and that all the events were set in the future, again building on his knowledge of
film genre and narrative. Eriksen (2001) would have described Hassan as living
his life in 'fast time', meaning he juxtaposed information from multiple sources
and moved very quickly from one source to another. Thus, the conversation
continued in this fragmented manner, with ongoing intervention from the
mediator, until Ali challenged Hassan's hypothesis by making an intratextual
reference to the blurb on the back cover of the book:

Mediator: *So why do you think that these people have come to this place?*
Ali: *It's because nobody has like wars and things over here, and at the back of
   the book it says* [reading] '*what drives so many, to leave everything behind
   and journey alone to a mysterious country, a place without family or
   friends, where everything is nameless, and the future is unknown ...
   A tribute to all those who have made the journey*'.

Hassan: *I agree with Ali cos this book's made for like refugees, so they could come to a country, and like they're tortured in one country* [or] *the bad people keep on asking for money . . . Because, I think . . . this place that has a wall around to protect people. Like the Great Wall of China.*

Sara: *. . . probably all these people in this, in the boat, are all refugees. They've came to this country, and probably this country lets refugees come . . .*

Mediator: *So this country you think is welcoming. Welcoming the refugees.*

Sara: *Mm. Yeah. And I think that man's left the child and the wife there until he checks if this country's okay. Then brings his child and wife.*

Making an intertextual link to films with an adventure genre was a starting point for Hassan, and, while it may be pedagogically expedient to allow children space to make these links, what was pedagogically crucial was the social mediation that took place, which allowed Hassan's schema to be challenged and reconstructed. Hassan relocated his interpretations beyond intertextual references to make meaning based on intercultural knowledge. He then returned his focus to the idea of culture, revisited an earlier point made about Muslim girls wearing headscarves and moved on to deconstructing the statues in terms of dress:

. . . this statues here of the bird on his back I think it's from Africa cos in Africa they carried this kind of bottle things on their head, and it kinda looks like that and he's wearing a kind of a hat, a rich hat from like a people that are rich in Africa. They wear these kind of pointy hat things. And they wear this kind of thing kind of like a dress, but it's not a dress kind of like for boys, men. And it's not a dress kind of look. But it just covers the whole bit of the body.

He focused on the elements of the right-hand statue and related the pot at the feet of the statue to the types of pots carried by people on their heads. He not only describes the dress but also begins to display skills of critical cultural awareness and intercultural interpretation (Byram, 1997) when he offered the perspective that hats of this type were worn by rich people in Africa.

Emerging from this chapter is a clear sense that the children were disorientated by Tan's text and that, in order to make sense out of the intertextual references, they focused upon landmarks within Tan's text that resonated with the texts of their own life. Many of these texts were drawn from popular cultural media. The use of popular cultural media in pedagogical contexts remains ambiguous (Carrington and Marsh, 2009), but these findings show that the children making reference to global cultural phenomena begin the process of collectively identifying shared points of cultural reference. Bloome and Egan-Robertson

(2004) refer to this process when they describe intertextuality as an heuristic device to make and share meanings related to identity and culture, a device that should be encouraged by mediators working with children on textual response.

Botelho and Rudman (2009) develop the metaphor of mirrors and windows further and suggest that narrative can also act as a doorway, allowing children to play with boundaries and cross the threshold in order to locate themselves within the safe space of the text. Medina (2010) expands on this idea in her discussion of the way in which children identify with texts to make sense out of the multiple spaces, people and timeframes they navigate. Within the text, children feel secure and can begin to explore aspects of self and others through their responses, resulting in clearer expressions of their own identity as immigrants and a shared understanding of what this could mean for others globally and locally. Bhaba (1994) would describe this as a third space; Medina describes it as a 'translocal space for cultural production' (Medina, 2010, p. 40), but this space only comes into being around Tan's carefully crafted text when this is coupled with collaborative pedagogies that favour social constructivist approaches (detailed in Chapter 9) to reading. In this case, the children respond intertextually to the gaps, mirrors and windows created by Tan and, in doing so, journey into a safe space where they develop knowledge of self and the other and move towards developing critical cultural awareness.

7

Engaging with the Visual Affordances of
The Arrival

Both the disorientation and the new spaces that *The Arrival* affords the reader are generated by the way in which the visual elements have been composed. Tan employs a variety of complex artistic techniques and aspects of sequential art narrative to provide a network of wordless cues for readers to make meaning and put together a coherent story; this encourages them to consider the book itself as a medium for visual storytelling. Thus, the book invites response as both a material and an aesthetic object. These techniques include, among others, format and layout design, choice of media and colour, lighting and perspective (or angle of vision).

In order to understand what readers must do to respond to the visual invitation of *The Arrival*, it is also helpful to remember that reading pictures is unlike reading text in that it is not a linear exercise determined by temporality but a spatial exercise determined by juxtaposition:

> When reading pictures, our eyes scan the surface, constructing temporal and meaningful sequences. As the picture remains static while the text flows past, our eyes are more or less free to roam, and thus the picture exists in a magical world in which time is not a line but a complex loop, in which everything can acquire a temporal and causal connection to everything else [...] thus pictures are not simply frozen events but rather complex circumstances. (Berninger, Ecke and Haberkorn, 2010, p. 2)

Describing the art of *The Arrival*, Hunter notes that Tan 'invites the viewer to look at everything in the picture' and compares this to:

> the feeling of sensual overload experienced by the main character who cannot know where to look next or what to give most attention to, and so must attend to every nuance of facial expression or gesture until he can

learn to make distinctions and look for the details that matter. (Hunter, 2011, p. 15)

The reader also has to learn to distinguish which of the connections are most meaningful. Given that verbal language is absent, the reader must rely on the tools provided by the only available sign system to deal with these 'complex circumstances'. This means attending to the elements that provide connotative meaning in the language of sequential art selected by Tan, such as frames, closure and transitions between the image panels. Tan himself admits he was experimenting with elements of 'sequential art' that were new to him, such as continuity, panel shape and narrative pace (he refers the reader to McCloud's classic 1993 text on comics).[1] It also means attending to elements of picturebook art (Nodelman, 1988) and, in this case, to the demands that a wordless picturebook places on readers, some of which have been discussed in Chapter 1. In different ways, this attention to the construction of meaningful sequences involves sophisticated activity on the part of both the artist and the reader as they elaborate and revise hypotheses about how they are connected.

In this chapter, we look at how the visual affordances of the text mediated the readers' responses; in other words, how the children made meaning from the sequence of wordless images and how they responded to some of the effects produced by these techniques (regardless of whether they were able to identify or name them).

Our initial analytical category 'compositional responses', divided into 'literal' and 'inferential' levels, was found to be problematic when we began to look in more detail at the data and realized that, given the complexity of the visual text, a level of inference was present in all their responses (see Chapter 5). In other words, even what seemed to be 'literal' descriptions involved a level of inference, even as the thought was put into words, and these became more 'elaborate' (Jett-Simpson, 1976) as hypotheses were put forth and then revised, in some cases becoming retellings or parallel texts. There were also noticeable overlaps between the 'compositional' and the 'intertextual' responses as the children would often hypothesize on how visual structures served as means of representation by making links to familiar illustrations, photographs or films (as discussed in Chapter 6).

A first look at the responses that referred explicitly to visual techniques revealed that these were less frequent and spontaneous than other types of comments and it became evident that the longer and more detailed conversations that did occur were significantly mediated by the adults. This was due to the fact that some of the researchers, particularly in BCN, were keen to encourage a deeper reading of the compositional elements. They began by focusing the children's attention on *how* the work was produced, asking about some of the more obvious visual elements (e.g. colour, frames, perspective and layout) and their functions, and moved to asking about the author's intention and the ways in which the composition 'speaks' to the implied reader. So what the initial analysis also showed was that expert mediation turned out to be particularly important for encouraging and supporting these types of responses (further discussion about the significance of this and other types of mediation will be detailed in the next chapter).

After further analysis and discussion, we decided that the findings around the compositional aspects would be best grouped into: a) those that were more directly related to particular affordances of *The Arrival* in terms of the materiality of the book; its wordless nature (and what this means for 'reading'); and b) the visual and verbal peritext; the basic visual elements; and the complex combination of reality and fantasy.

The absence of words

As we noted in Chapter 1, readers initially tend to be confused by the absence of words because, in most picturebooks or graphic novels, there are usually some, even if the written language is minimal. This surprise was evident in readers in all the research contexts. Tan provides his explanation for not including any words:

> The absence of any written description in *The Arrival* seemed to place the reader more firmly in the shoes of an anonymous protagonist. There is no guidance as to how the images might be interpreted, which can be quite a liberating thing. Words have a remarkable gravitational pull on our attention, and how we interpret attendant images, like captions under a press photo. Without words, an image can invite much more attention from a reader who might otherwise reach for the nearest sentence, and let that rule their imagination. (Tan, 2009, p. 10)

The children quite quickly responded to this invitation as they realized that the information would have to come from the images and, in consequence, began to pore over them more carefully; as Sunil (GLW) said during the second session, '*when* [we looked at it] *first time I couldn't understand what they are saying, but when I look at the pictures of the book* [now] *I understand it'*. The task of interpreting without words highlights an important tension between the way in which the reading of image is perceived as opposed to the reading of words. Confirming Tan's words, the children in AZ insisted that the lack of written text allows the reader more freedom and permits a more 'open' reading. When they were discussing the last page of the book, the mediator asked, '*Why do you guys think Shaun Tan chose this to be the last picture of the book?'* Viviana responded: '*To let us make up the rest of the story'*, and Toni: '*To give us, like, more ideas than with the words. Cause with the words, the words actually tell you what, um, they're doing, but, right here we could picture a lot of different things.'* Likewise, when the mediator asked the children in BCN why the book is comprised only of images, Denis affirmed that it's '*so we can think'*: the words 'guessing' and 'thinking' were frequently used by the children in all contexts. There were several mentions of the need to look carefully and to take time to think about the images. The idea of 'making your own words or your own story' also reflected a perception of the active stance required of the reader. '*Imagining'* was another word frequently used; however, the conversation between Rodrigo, An You and Denis showed that they were aware that, even as the reader returns to the book and notices different things, the story is still tied '*Con lo que ves allí, no puedes sólo imaginar una historia* [diferente]*'* [with what you see there, you can't just imagine [a different] story] (Denis).

The children generally agreed that words helped to complement and to clarify the ambiguities of the image and that a written narrative '*se entiende mejor'* [is more understandable]. Antonio, in BCN, makes explicit this idea of the informative possibilities of text and image when he points out that

> *Si tuviera palabras, cuando envía la familia la carta entonces ya sabrá que la familia viene. Hasta entonces no sabía quién venía, pero no sabía... en cambio con palabras diría 'viene mi familia' y entonces ya se sabría cómo acaba.*
>
> [If it had words, when the family sends the letter then he would know that the family is coming. Until then he did not know who would come but, instead, with words he would say 'my family is coming' and then it would be known how it ends.]

This perception leads to what seems to be a deep-rooted idea that the written text establishes the 'real' and 'unequivocal' meaning. This perception of words as holding the 'correct' interpretation was echoed by other children, including host children such as Lily (GLW) who said, '*I think it was quite difficult to read because there was no words to read from, so you would have to guess and there was no right or wrong answers.*' For historical reasons to do with literacy and power, usually reproduced in the classroom, the word is considered to have more weight and more authority than the image. As Tan himself says, the disorientation produced by his invented script 'reminds us of our dependence on the written word for security and authority when it comes to meaning' (Tan, 2010, p. 31). One of the most telling incidents in the project occurred in Glasgow after reading *The Arrival*, when Claude (GLW) asked the researchers if they could now show him '*the book with the words*' in order to verify the group's reading of the images.

Responses revealed that the image made them feel that they had a wider interpretative margin and that the responsibility and narrative 'voice' had been passed to the reader. Echoing the children in other countries, Hassan (GLW) noted, '*it's trying to like get you to think for yourself like, what the words should be*'. Other revealing comments were made when discussing the intended readership of wordless picturebooks. The children in GLW stressed that these books could be understood by '*anyone*', and Lily (GLW) even argued that wordless books are for '*babies*'. Others suggested they could be used as learning resources for those who did not understand a particular language, such as English (in the case of Scotland):

> Claude (Congo): *cos you can understand in different languages, you don't just understand in English.*
>
> Sara (Kurdistan): *Like a different person that comes here and doesn't know English, they could give these books instead of written books, like we get reading books in our class. And they could give them that. They could understand it their self what the book is about. So they could learn from that too.*

Later, during a discussion in Glasgow about the language and communication, the children noted that the man had himself used pictures to communicate because he did not yet know the language (see Figure 7.1).

The process of reading images

In their discussion about the lack of words, some of the children also speculated about the process of reading images. In GLW, Ali said that pictures '*go straight to your brain*', and that this was a quicker process than having to put ideas into words or to reading words, both of which could be '*boring*' and '*tiring*'. In the excerpt below, also from GLW, Claude was able to express the process in more

Figure 7.1 Communicating with a helpful stranger

detail as he perceived it, but both Sam and Vassily also noted the need to find cues such as the character's expressions:

> Mediator: *How can you read a picture? What else can you get in pictures that tell you what they're about?*

Claude: *The things in the background that makes you think where they are.
[...] I think like the pictures are alive. That's what I always think in my head
[...] like see how I look in a picture, I always think what is happening at
that time, what is happening. Something was moved into that direction or
that direction.*
Sam: *Some things are hiding in the pictures, that you have to look at.*
Vassily: [...] *like expressions in their faces, I would see like if they are surprised.*

Nodelman has suggested that wordless picturebooks create a 'distance' rather
than encouraging involvement between the characters and the reader, given that
thought and emotion are not easily represented in visual terms (Nodelman,
1998, pp. 188–90); however, Bellorín and Silva-Díaz argue that this is not the
case in *The Arrival* because of the more realistic style employed by Tan:

Resorting to the characters' body language is only one of the strategies that
graphic artists can use to express emotions. Other means of representation
can be used for depiction, such as the character's surroundings expressing
his inner emotions, or the development of sub-plots that function as
symbolic co-narratives that express the character's feelings. (Bellorín and
Silva-Díaz, 2011, pp. 222–3)

This was stressed by Hilda, in BCN, when her group saw the book for the first
time:

Emma: *Pues un libro con dibujos.*
Mediador: *Bueno, un libro con dibujos ...*
Carles: *Sin letra.*
Hilda: *Que expresa muchas emociones. Es muy emocional porque: cualquier
gesto, cualquier cosa, ya te está diciendo lo que siente.*

[Emma: A book of drawings.
Mediator: Okay, a book of drawings ...
Carles: Without letters/words.[2]
Hilda: That expresses many emotions. It's very emotional because any
gesture, anything, is already telling you what he feels.]

However, some children insisted on the limitations of visual language for
revealing the inner side of characters, such as Alan (BCN) who pointed out that,
'*En las ilustraciones se puede ver cómo los personajes son por fuera, pero las
palabras nos dicen cómo cada uno es adentro*' [In the illustrations you can see
how characters are on the outside, but words tell us how each one is on the

inside]. Interestingly, while the children may still privilege the power of words to convey information about the characters' internal states, many of the children (as shown in Chapter 5) made character inferences that referred to their feelings or thoughts while relying only on the images, as when Almah (AZ) commented: '*Because in this picture it's like he's sad and he looks down at his picture, family picture, and then he looked outside and he's wondering what's happening with his family right now*' or when Viviana (AZ) explained her interpretation of the dragon-tail shapes: '*Yo digo que esto la niña se lo está imaginando porque ella sabe que su papá se va a ir y lo que se siente adentro se está saliendo para afuera*' [I would say that the girl is imagining this because she knows her dad is going to leave and what it is felt inside has to come out]. Moreover, their creation of parallel texts and their engagement when they added voice to the characters revealed the power of the image alone to support children's interpretations.

The verbal and visual peritext

As in many carefully designed picturebooks, the compositional elements in *The Arrival* begin to carry out narrative functions even before the story technically begins. The peritext, composed of elements such as cover, blurb, endpapers and title page, among others, plays an important role in the book, so readers must be able to make connections between these elements and those that compose the narrative – as well as understanding how it is relevant to the book as a whole. In Tan's book, the written text is restricted to the peritext and, with the exception of the endpapers, words appear on every printed peritextual page as well as the cover and back cover. Publisher and copyright information appears at the beginning and an artist's note appears at the end of the book. The children used this limited amount of print as they started developing a sense of the story and predicting what the story was going to be about. Juan (AZ) noticed Tan's dedication to his parents: '*And it says that "for my parents". Maybe the author is writing this book special and it is for his parents, he is sending them a message.*' Minutes later, also based on this dedication, Toni proposed that the book was going to be about the author's life: '*And you can tell the author maybe he's actually writing about what he lived cause he dedicated it to his parents.*' While the children adjusted their predictions as they gauged more information, the written peritext helped them to enter into the world of the story.

In all three contexts, it seemed that the exploration of the peritext through the shared sensual activity of touch provoked a need to understand the book as an object and to communicate these ideas. The children assessed the quality and texture of the paper (thickness and colour) and argued whether or not it was an old book. For some, exploring the book with their fingertips, stroking the smooth surfaces and verifying the authenticity of the aged binding, seemed almost as important as the close observation of the images. It is not difficult to understand why, given that the book is an unusual size, thickness and weight for either a picturebook or graphic novel. It is also a hardback and the glossy embedded photographic-looking images on both front and back covers create a sense of depth, as noted by these girls in GLW:

Surayya: *It's smooth.*
Sara: *Slimy and it's like – it looks like a 3-D.*
Mediator: *Why do you think they've done that?*
Sara: *To make it interesting.*
Mediator: *Does it remind you of anything?*
Sara: *Probably that's a photo.*

The dark colours and the aged or 'distressed' look are also unusual in a book for children. There were many comments in all research contexts about the book looking 'old' not only because of the colours but also because of the 'scratches' and 'wrinkled paper'. Some said the book reminded them of old photograph albums.

It was evident that the children were familiar with aspects to do with the social circulation of books, such as when two of them looked up *The Arrival* on the Internet on their own initiative. One of them, in BCN, informed the others of the price of the book and the other, in GLW, also noted the price tag on the back of the English edition and said that, if it was really 'old', it would not have that price or the price would have been 'written over' [the old one] (Hassan). Another example of this familiarity was the specialized discussion in BCN about aspects of printing, which occurred when Carles explained why it had to be 'new' based on the knowledge he had gained through his brother who worked in editorial design. Other explanations for Tan's compositional choices were that it made the book look 'old-fashioned' or from 'the old days' because it was 'black and white and a bit brown'. This made the book more interesting for some readers and, together, these features created a coherent look:

Mediador: *¿Por qué piensan que* [Tan] *habrá elegido estos colores?*
Emma (BCN): *Porque si quiere que se vea el libro viejo – pues tendrá todo eso que concordar un poco. No puede ser que el libro sea viejo y las fotografías a color.*

[Mediator: Why did [Tan] pick these colours?

Emma: Because if you want the book to look old, then everything should match a bit. You can't pretend the book is old and have colour photographs.]

Some of the participants commented on the ribbon bookmark, which is also unusual in a children's book. In GLW, they said it reminded them of '*the Priest's book*' or '*The Bible in church*'. Taken together, these features give the book a particular seriousness, formality and 'authority', and, although only one child expressed this directly, saying it looked like an '*important*' book, in general their handling of the book reflected a respect for it as an object. This may also have to do with the knowledge that it was expensive and had been brought in for the special project, or perhaps because of the respect accorded to old family photos or albums, which children are usually taught to handle with care.

In GLW, the children began to scrutinize the assorted bits and pieces of paper that appear in the peritext in detail, looking for clues as to what the book was going to be about (the English bits remain in English in the Spanish edition). The presence of Polish words, which were proudly identified and translated by Józef, also turned the children's minds to thinking of identity cards and passports, so the expectations about a journey were already being formulated, along with the idea of '*many languages*' and places (they also noted the publisher was Australian).

Basic visual elements

For this section, we have only selected the visual elements most referred to by the children and the adults: colour; panels and frames; perspective and angle of vision; and symbolism.

Colour

Colour tends to be one of the visual elements that children pay most attention to and, because of the order in which we looked at the picturebooks, it was particularly highlighted, given the contrast between the subtle shades of brown, grey and mauve in Tan's pencil drawings and the rich, vibrant watercolours used by Wiesner in *Flotsam*. Although most of the children at this stage were unfamiliar with the vocabulary (at least in their new language) to express how the choice of certain colours is used to convey emotional tone, they were very much aware of their impact. In the case of *The Arrival*, the more frequent and predictable responses had to do with the dark and muddied colours representing the aged quality of the book or with the relationship between hue and mood (i.e. dark meaning sadness). However, there were also responses that indicated an awareness of the function of the colours in the borders that frame the inset stories and/or indicate time shifts. This can be seen in the following example from the children in AZ who are discussing an image from the first inset story. After much discussion to clarify the plot, characters and setting, the mediator called the students' attention to the cues to identify the inset stories and Viviana then immediately responds, correctly identifying it has to do with the change of colour:

> Mediator: *Entonces este bote, ¿de donde sale este?* [Then, this boat, where does it come from?]
>
> Janice: *Del señor este que está aquí. De estos.* [From this man here, from these.]
>
> Mediator: *¿Del que le está haciendo la historia? Okay . . . ¿Como sabemos . . .* [Of the man who is telling the story? How do we know?] *What cue does the illustrator give us to know that we are going back to the original story here? There is something different on these pages and these pages. What is it?*
>
> Viviana: *He changed like the background . . . the colour.*

Panels and frames

In GLW, the children were asked why Tan might have decided to use so many and different panels. Underlying their answers was the understanding of the way the panels provide a sense of sequence and context to events on the page, and, therefore, that panels were a fitting choice to organize and present such a detailed narrative, such as in the following comment, which refers to the man's flight in the white booth: 'I think he does little pictures cos he wants like tell us more information, how he get, how he go up and down' (Hassan). The boys in one of the GLW groups agreed that one picture would not be enough to show all the character's actions, while the girls thought that it made the man's story stand out. Józef also suggested that one reason for putting so many panels on a page was that otherwise Tan would have ended up with a much longer book!

In the following excerpt from BCN, from a discussion on the narrative functions of the panels, these were not only understood as an indication of movement but also led them to build on their knowledge of movement in film and of film genres.

> Gisela: *Para que así veamos cada cuántos segundos se va moviendo el personaje.*
> Naima: *Por ejemplo aquí vamos viendo tu-tu-tu* [Hace sonidos que representan los movimientos del protagonista]
> Beatriz: *Lo más rápido, y ver lo que está haciendo, ¿no?*
> Mediadora: *Bien, sí.*
> Calin: *Cómo lo hace, ¿no? Es como si fuera una película.*
> Mediadora: *Es como si fuera una película, dice Calin.*
> Calin: *Pero sin hablar.*
> Alan: *yo voy a mirar más.*
> Mediadora: *Pero sin hablar. Bien.*
> Alan: *Eso me recuerda unos . . .*
> Mediadora: *Sí, dilo. ¿A qué te recuerda?*
> Alan: *Es que esto . . . es como las películas de antes, no hablaban pero se veía.*
> Beatriz: *El cine mudo.*

> [Gisela: So that we can see the character's movement in few seconds.
> Naima: For example, here we are seeing tu-tu-tu [makes sounds representing the movement of the protagonist].
> Beatriz: The fastest . . . and see what he is doing, right?
> Mediator: Good, yes.
> Calin: The way he does it is as if it were a movie.
> Mediator: It's as if it were a movie, Calin says.
> Calin: But without talking.
> Alan: Mmm – I'm going to look some more.
> Mediator: But without dialogue. Good.
> Alan: This reminds me of some . . .
> Mediator: Yes, say it. What does it remind you of?
> Alan: It's just that this is like the old movies, where they didn't talk but they were seen.
> Beatriz: Silent film.]

Perspective and angle of vision

The children in AZ had learned about the technique of zooming in their discussions of *Flotsam*, and, while they did not name the technique, they recognized it in some of the images in *The Arrival*, such as when the train is leaving and in the image focusing on the ship's windows:

Mediator: *Esta página?* [This page] *What does this page tell us?*

Ryan: *Cuando bajan el barco, las ventanillas de abajo.* [When they go down [to the lower floors] of the ship, the little window in the lower level.]

Almah: *A ship.*

Juan: *Maybe* [inaudible] *está tomando la foto como* Flotsam.

Ryan: *como lo hizo desde el puente* [like he did it from the bridge]

Mediator: *He's taking . . .*

Juan: *Like the Flotsam, he's making the pictures look bigger, bigger, smaller, smaller, smaller, smaller and extra smaller.*

Mediator: *Okay.*

Janice: *Como lo hizo en el tren.* [As he – the author – did it in the train]

Mediator: *Okay, like the train. It's perspective. So here is the most close up and then it's like the artist is moving away.*

Juan: *Mmhm.*

Mediator: *Is that what you mean?*

Almah: *moving and moving and moving*

Mediator: *Okay. Okay. So that was a cool connection Janice. It reminded you of the train picture and you said it reminded you of* Flotsam.

In BCN, the children revealed some understanding of how perspective is represented in a two-dimensional space, hinting at how depth and distance are conveyed in images. They also noted how this positioned them as implied readers and made them gaze into the visual landscapes. In GLW, the groups also reflected on the viewpoint and, in the next example, Faisal's comment makes clear that he has understood the focalization:

Mediator: *So, if he's not in the picture . . .*

Faisal: *He was! He was just standing and seeing people. He's standing there and we can't see* [him] [points outside the panel]

Mediator: *So . . .*

Faisal: *He's looking at people.*

Mediator: *So, this is what he's seeing?*

Faisal: *Yes.*

Symbolism

Learning that compositional elements add meaning to the story was a revelation that enhanced the children's view of the complexity of the story and storytelling. In particular, they began to realize that the elements that appeared in the book were not there gratuitously, but they often 'represented' something else, such as the dragon-tail shapes discussed by the children. This interest in the symbolic use of the visual elements emerged, for example, in a discussion among the BCN group when they spoke about the relationship between the landscape and the moods of the character; in this specific example, they are referring to Tan's use of cloudscapes:

> *Eso, que se va alternando y es como el cambio del estado* [de ánimo] *del hombre . . . normal, que no pasa para no poner la cara de cada uno, de cada una de las imágenes, pues hace al hombre . . . cuando hay muchas nubes está depresivo y cuando no, pues se anima y así va.* (Emma)

> [That, it's alternating and it shows the changes in the man's mood . . . normal, doesn't put a face in each image, he makes that the man . . . when there are lots of clouds he is depressed and when there are none he's excited and so on.]

In this type of symbolization, the children revealed as Bellorín and Silva-Díaz have noted,

> that they are in front of a different kind of narrative, which relates differently to reality, and must be read accordingly. They learn that images establish a different relationship to external referents; that the viewer, the beholder, must make some adjustments in his or her internal view of the world. (Bellorín and Silva-Díaz, 2011, p. 224)

They were aware that retelling in words what they had read through images required some kind of translation. Using the '*es como si*' [as if] clause or saying '*it's like*' became a way of giving voice to the characters and verbally expressing that they were taking that licence, given that there is no written text to corroborate what they have hypothesized.

Interestingly, host and immigrant children in BCN would frequently give a different connotation to the same element or episode in the book, indicating perhaps that this inner adjustment of symbolic meaning is strongly related to the reader's own experience:

> when questioned what a figure represented, the children would give different answers. While the Catalan children would allude to 'evil', 'war', 'fear' or 'problems' in general, immigrant children did not think about the war or evil in an abstract manner; they would be very concrete about what the characters felt about 'war' or 'evil'. For instance, they would talk about how the mother

and the daughter in *The Arrival* felt 'sadness' and 'fear' because they were alone. (Fittipaldi, 2008, p. 84, author's translation)

Reality and fiction

As Colomer (2012) notes in her discussion of some of the findings of the research team from BCN, the consideration of the 'truth' or 'reality' of narratives was a common concern of readers and was used as a value criterion in their assessment of a text. In general, the children in all countries were eager to identify which elements were real and which were fantastic. The comments were based on their knowledge of genre, and in GLW, for example, there was a long debate on whether the book was 'fiction' or 'non-fiction'. In AZ, the children raised this question at the beginning of their first discussion. They had asked if the book was new and then speculated that it was going to be a history book based on its colour and aged look. Then they moved on to discussing genre:

> Viviana: *Is it fiction or non-fiction?*
> Toni: *I think it's non-fiction.*
> Juan: *Yeah.*
> Toni: *'Cause of right here the dragon. It looks like a huge old dragon.*

However, by the end of the session, they had changed their assessment and, when asked if they believed it was non-fiction, Toni referred to the peritext:

> *Yo no porque si fuera de animales usualmente los libros en la primera página tienen – like – describe de lo que el libro se va tratar . . . Como aqui en las fotos* [endpapers] *tuviera, así como en lugar de tener así las* [inaudible], *esto tuviera cosas de animales.*

> [Not me because if it was about animals, usually the books have in their first page – like – they describe what the book will be about . . . Like here in the photos it would have, instead of having the [inaudible], this would have things about animals.]

Many of the comments regarding the text were attempts to identify and describe some of the fantastic elements. Regarding the dragon, the children in AZ offered different hypotheses. They started considering the possibility that the book was about animals but as the discussion unfolded they began to interpret the dragon-tail shapes differently. Juan commented: '*I think that in the middle he's going to, this dragon and this are going to have a connection.*' Minutes later, they were considering the dragons as a product of the characters' imaginations or dreams. Juan believed that '*it is* [was] *only the girl's imagination*'; Toni, that it was the product of the father's imagination: '*Yo creo que es de su imaginación porque a lo mejor extraña su hija y se empieza a imaginar cosas que lo hacen recordar de ella*' [I believe that it is his imagination because maybe he misses his daughter and starts imagining things that remind him of her]. Viviana, on the other hand, proposed that it was probably a dream reflecting the girl's feelings:

> *O a la mejor también es un sueño que ella tiene que en un dragón ella y su papá se agarraba, se subía a un dragón y fueron a una parte lejos. Y para que su papá no se tuviera que ir.*

> [Maybe it is a dream the girl is having about a dragon, that she and her father got hold of, they got on, a dragon and they leave to a faraway place. And so that her dad doesn't have to leave.]

The fantasy elements also led to debates about whether the story was happening in the past or in the future, such as in this exchange in GLW:

> Hassan (Somalia): *It's very high tech.*
> Ali (Afghanistan): *Uhuh. It's very high tech there cos I can see a flying boat.*
> Hassan: *It is a bit of history and a bit of future. Like this is old kind of stone. That could be part of history and those flying boats are like hi-technical stuff going down there. Could be a part of the future. I think this is a historical and future book.*

In BCN, one of the children also referred to this apparent contradiction, '*Como si fuese de una época muy antigua o demasiado moderna, o como si viniera de un país muy avanzado, ¿sabes?*' [As if he was from a very ancient era or very modern one, or as if he came from a very advanced country, you know?] (Emma).

Other comments made by children in all contexts were assessments of the verisimilitude of the main character's experience of migration, usually based on their own. In BCN, the startling authenticity of the passport-like images on the endpapers made the children think that the story was real. Verisimilitude was commonly confused with reality, and sometimes the mimetic quality of the story, the proximity of their experience to the characters', made them argue that it had really happened. Tan himself notes that 'the most rewarding feedback for me as a creator has come from those readers who are themselves migrants, commenting on how these strange pencil drawings seem truthful, recalling something of their own personal experiences' (Tan, 2009, p. 10). In both BCN and GLW, the children were inclined to evaluate Tan's work positively based on the realistic, photographic style of illustration, as if the author's style choice could be read as an eloquent commitment to the 'true nature' of the story – a story that was similar to their own and therefore had to be documented seriously and truthfully.

The fantastic element caused a particular reaction in two cases, the first an immigrant child in GLW and the second a Catalan child in BCN. We cannot claim to fully understand the meaning of their comments or the reasons for them, nor was this the aim of the analysis, but in both cases there seemed to be other issues affecting the response. We include them here because these responses stood out from the others and took the form of a strong rejection of the fictional elements of the story.

Sunil was an asylum seeker in GLW and his attitude to *The Arrival* suddenly changed just as the group reached the end of the book:

> *Because I don't like because actually I don't like it any more. I don't like magic and that's like a magic stories. I don't like the end of the story but I like the beginning.* (Sunil, Sri Lanka)

The researchers later found out that this comment was made at a time when his family had heard news about their impending deportation, which happened shortly afterwards. In this light, Sunil's use of the word '*magic*' seems to connote 'fantasy', which, linked to the 'happy ending' where the family is settled in the new country, may have, at that moment, seemed bitterly unrealistic because of his own family circumstances.

Carles made his remarks within a group of all Catalan children in BCN. His comments give the impression he is less empathetic than most of the other non-immigrant children, but whether this is due to a need for distancing himself from tragic events and even migration or to his understanding of the role of '*reality*', '*fiction*' and '*lies*' in literature would be impossible to say without further conversation with him:

> Mediadora: *¿Y este libro te recordó algo especial?* [...]
> Carles: *No me recordó nada, porque son puras mentiras. Son ficción. Esto no es real. Esto es pura ficción.*
> Mediadora: *¿Y la ficción no nos puede decir nada?*
> Carles: *A ver, sí. La ficción tiene sus partes reales pero esto no ... Esto hace como explicara qué paso en la guerra, pero es como si a lo mejor murieron veinte personas y aquí hace de cuenta que murieron mil. Lo toma muy*

> *exageradamente esto, que se destruya una sociedad tan rápido . . . Mil, ¡es*
> *imposible! ¡y ellos tan felices y todo!*
> Mediadora: *¿Y hay algo más que te gustaría decirme sobre el libro? ¿Cómo te*
> *sentiste al leerlo?*
> Carles: *No, no sentí nada porque es una ficción pura. No me sentía triste ni*
> *nada.*

[Mediator: And does this book make you recall anything special? [. . .]
Carles: It doesn't make me recall anything, because it is all lies. It is fiction.
   This is not real. This is pure fiction.
Mediator: And fiction can't show us anything?
Carles: Well, yes. Fiction has real parts but this ... This seems as if it's
   explaining what happened in the war, but it's like maybe twenty people
   died here and it says that a thousand died. It's very exaggerated. You can't
   destroy a society so quickly . . . A thousand, it's impossible! And they [are]
   so happy and everything!
Mediator: And is there something else you'd like to say about the book? How
   did you feel when you read it?
Carles: No, I don't feel anything. It's pure fiction. It didn't make me sad or
   anything.]

One issue the discussion about reality and fantasy addressed was the difficulty some children had in making the distinction between author, narrator and protagonist. The absence of written language and the use of near-photographic images contribute to the fictional transparency, and led to questions about whether the story 'really' happened. Although they were not aware of Tan's having used himself and some of his friends as models for some of the characters, the children tended to note the realistic impression made by the protagonist and his family. The discussion in BCN on this subject was very productive as the children considered the existence of a narrator, referring at times to the invisible narrator and debating whether it was the author or the protagonist who is telling their story. They also argued about the complexity of the inset stories, which are told to a character within the book as well as to the readers. They agreed that the difficulty of attributing the narrative to a third or first person was due to the lack of written text, as Ana insightfully reflected: '*No sé, puede ser "había una vez una casa" o puede ser "cuando yo tenga una casa", no se sabe*' [I don't know, it could be 'there was once a house' or it could be 'when I have a house', you can't tell]. Finally, another girl, An You, reached the conclusion that '*nadie*' [no one] was telling the story:

Yo creo que no hay . . . que no lo cuenta nadie, que es así que pasa, como
en la vida real, aquí no cuenta nadie qué está pasando ahora mismo.

[I think there is no . . . that no one is telling this [story], that it's like this tha
it happens, like here in real life, here no one is telling what is happening
now.]

The idea that there is no determined narrator because it is a reflection of how
things happen in real life is an interesting conclusion if it refers to an intentional
device of the picturebook; however, it could also be a translation of An You's
scant distinction between reality and fiction. This comment about reality and
fiction, as in the case of the other children mentioned above, shows how *The
Arrival* encouraged complex reflections about levels of fictionality and how
much further these ideas could be explored.

Using the compositional blueprint to develop visual literacy

Reading *for* compositional elements means engaging with the book as an object
and understanding that it has been put together in dynamic and intentional
ways. For the children, the compositional part of the visual journey began by
identifying and describing what pictures show and then analysing the way the
narration is constructed. One of the steps in the development of visual literacy is
being able to recognize the artist's choices and understand their narrative
function. In analysing students' written responses to *The Arrival*, Pantaleo
and Bomphray observed that 'many students reflected on Tan's artistic choices
and considered how he used specific semiotic resources to represent, convey and
evoke particular emotions in his visual storytelling' (Pantaleo and Bomphray,
2011, p. 181). When young readers explore compositional elements in texts, they
can engage with the process of storytelling in a more complex and integrated
manner, which considers some of the 'choices' the author made to generate each
page, and how those choices work in concert to reflect both a story's meaning
and the author telling it.

We found that the children were engaging with the book's affordances
whether or not they could pinpoint or label a particular artistic technique and,
regardless of background, they were bringing their 'funds' of visual knowledge
– many of them from a shared popular culture – to bear on their meaning-
making. While their immediate responses tended to concern themselves by
finding the clues that would help them solve the 'puzzle' of what these images

meant and what the story was about, as they entered more fully into Tan's surreal worlds, they also perceived the emotional atmosphere he created through the visual cues. This suggests that, when the children deepen their exploration and begin to discover more subtle relationships, they tend to respond with enthusiasm as they find that their interpretation can go far beyond what they had originally understood. Looking at how narratives function is an enjoyable novelty that encourages them to take on a venture that produces intellectual pleasure and consolidates them as a group.

While most literary practice in education identifies reading comprehension as the ability to identify key points and overarching meaning, the nuances of *how* the meaning is generated through specific, stylistic choices of the author(s) are often overlooked. Perhaps valuing certain types of comprehension (content) over others (form) in traditional literacy practices accounts for the lack of responses related to this aspect. In BCN, however, once the mediator began probing further into the artist's choice and use of colour and texture, the discussion began to include more speculation as to how the aesthetic impact had been achieved, for example, in reference to how colour is employed to inform the reader about movement or the passing of time, aspects that are usually part of the world of the written word. So, one of the benefits of focusing on the compositional elements of the text is that the children can begin to question the distinction usually made between *form* and *content*, so that they realize that *story* (characters, actions and setting) and *discourse* (the language in which the story is told) cannot be easily separated and that *form* is *content* too.

This kind of metaliterary awareness is sophisticated but, as we have stressed, Tan's text encourages readers to build on the metaknowledge they already have, for example, through their experience of other visual media. Given that this knowledge varies greatly among children and most of them lack the specific visual vocabulary to express this knowledge, throughout the sessions, mediators made sure the children's initial tentative responses were supported in a way that helped develop their visual literacy, sometimes providing the necessary metalanguage. Other forms of support are detailed in the next chapter.

In this inquiry, the affordances of Tan's wordless narrative, along with the collective meaning-making – both verbal and visual – provided paths for the children to 'cross the border', not only in the sense of appreciating images more fully, but also in the sense of helping children across the linguistic and cultural boundaries that have been traditionally limiting for immigrants, making the most of the knowledge and experiences they bring with them.

Notes

1 See http://www.shauntan.net/books/the-arrival.html. Another useful book for understanding the codes and resources of sequential art is Miller (2007).
2 We have used both letter and word here as 'letra' in Spanish can sometimes be used to refer to words, as in 'la letra de la canción' [the words of the song].

Part Three

Mediation and Pedagogy: Transforming Literacy Learning and Teaching

Fostering a Community: Mediation that Supports Learning

The responses to *The Arrival* described in Part Two draw attention to the different types of mediation that supported students' meaning-making. Chapters 4–7 offered a glimpse into the sophisticated meaning-making processes in which the children engaged to make sense of *The Arrival*. Chapters 4 and 5 highlighted how their knowledge about immigration and their experiences mediated their transactions with the text, their understanding and the inferences about characters, plot and setting. Chapter 6 expanded on the nature of the students' connections (e.g. to landmarks, popular culture), which mediated their development of intercultural understanding. Finally, Chapter 7 considered how the children responded to the visual affordances the text presented and indicated that mediation played a significant role in this interaction. Informed by a sociocultural perspective on learning and literacy, we see all these responses as not only mediated by the children's experiences and knowledge but also situated within the context we created for the research (Cole, 1996; Moll, 2001; Vygotsky, 1978). Part of the context in our inquiry included the ways in which the discussions were organized, as described in Chapter 3, the social interactions that such organization made possible, and the cultural and material resources available to them as part of our research design (e.g. the language of the discussions, the texts with its visual affordances, and the visual response strategies).

In this chapter, we focus on some of the ways adults and children mediated the discussions, paying special attention to the types of talk used during the discussions by the adults, the visual strategies and the ways children acted as mediators of each other's learning. Both the adult's and the children's mediation contributed to fostering a community that supports learning.

Mediators as facilitators and guides

The discussion of the role of the adults in the kinds of responses offered by the children needs to be framed within Vygotsky's (1978) description of interactions between children and adults or more capable peers as central to children's learning and development. His concept of mediation in the zone of proximal development highlights such a role: 'what a child can do with assistance today she will be able to do by herself tomorrow' (Vygotsky, 1978, p. 87). As Martínez-Roldán and Smagorinsky (2011) indicate, although there is an agreement on the crucial role teachers and adults play in students' learning, the nature of the assistance and mediation has been the subject of debate, and researchers are still trying to understand how much assistance and under which circumstances this assistance supports students' learning. For a book of such length and as layered and rich as *The Arrival*, it is clear that the mediation of the adult is crucial, as some of the children's responses suggest. For instance, during the first discussion, after trying to elucidate the genre of the book based on the first images, the children in AZ were asked if the images invited them to read it on their own. Some of their responses were as follows:

> Mediator: *¿Te dan ganas de leerlo al ver estas fotos? Does it make you feel like reading it?*
>
> Juan: *Yeah.*
>
> Janice: *Sí.* [Yes]
>
> Mediator: *Why? You each can say, uh, ¿te invita a leer el libro estas fotos?* [Do the images in the book invite you to read it?]
>
> Janice: *Sí, porque pienso que es muy emocionante.* [Yes, because I think it is exciting.]
>
> Mediator: *¿Sí? ¿Piensas que va a haber emoción en el libro?* [Yes? You think there will be excitement in the book?]
>
> Juan: *Como Janice porque nomás viendo la primera foto te da imaginación con los monstros [sic] y como se ve el libro de viejo.* [Like Janice, because just by looking at the first picture, it sparks your imagination with the monsters [sic] and the book looks old.]
>
> Mediator: *Mmhm.*
>
> Viviana: *Um, I think that if I were going to read this book I probably wouldn't 'cause I see that since it looks old so like most old books are thick, and I don't like reading like really thick books.*
>
> Mediator: *Uh huh. Okay. Good. Okay. ¿Y tú Toni?* [and you, Toni?] *What about you?*

Toni: *Mostly no, 'cause old books, the people who write it they write it in cursive and it's kind of complicated to read.*

Mediator: *Okay. So you anticipate that it might be complicated to read because of the letters* [type of font] *people use to write it . . .*

Toni: *Yeah . . .*

Toni's and Viviana's responses remind us of the important role teachers or other adults can have in mediating children's transactions with texts.

While we mediated the discussions in a variety of ways, as described in Chapter 3, the focus here is on specific ways of talking aimed at supporting the children's interpretative process. There are similarities in the type of talk and questions used in both research and pedagogical situation; for example, although neither Sipe (2008) nor Pantaleo (2008) asked, or had the teachers ask, a particular set of questions in their research on responses to picturebook 'readalouds' by the teacher, it was clear that those experienced teachers used open-ended questions, encouraging predictions and personal responses. Other studies examining the role and talk of teachers in literature circles have identified different ways in which teachers can support the discussions and children's literary understandings (Kauffman, Short, Crawford, Kahn and Kaser, 1996; Munita and Manresa, 2012; Sipe, 1996). In this section, we address the ways in which we mediated the discussions through two main types of talk: 1) providing language; and 2) posing questions. These questions can be further classified as including: a) open-ended and bridging questions; b) questions focused on the narrative and the literary elements that compose it; c) questions focused on the visual elements; and d) questions inviting text-to-life connections. These two categories of teacher talk can be described as 'facilitating' and, as in the case of other reader-response studies (Kauffman *et al.*, 1996), were the primary type of adult talk in the discussions.

As other researchers have found, we also facilitated by being active listeners, offering comments where we acknowledged children's statements (e.g. 'yes', 'aha', 'OK'). Although, as researchers, we tried to keep our comments to a minimum, there were times when we also naturally participated as readers, expressing our opinions, sharing our experiences of migration and/or journeys, or, like the children, choosing and talking about our favourite images. This participation occurred mostly during the first session, when the children also asked us questions about our languages or countries of origin. Finally, as one of the examples below shows, when the teachers were present, the researchers respected their interventions or leads, given that the teachers were more familiar with the needs and reactions of their students.

Providing language

The role of the adults as facilitators involved providing language for different purposes such as offering suggestions (both linguistic and in terms of paraphrasing); summarizing ideas; using restatement sentences; and inviting children to clarify or expand their ideas. It sometimes included providing specific background information or an explanation of vocabulary. This is exemplified in the following excerpt from GLW, when the teacher who was participating in this discussion gave an explanation to Claude, from Congo, and Jack, from England, who did not know the meaning of 'Caledonia', a word that appears in the peritextual documents at the beginning of the book:

> Jack: *It says 'inspection card'.*
> Sam: *'23 March 1912'.*
> Claude: *It's from Glasgow!*
> Teacher: *Ohhh, so it does, it says Glasgow* [reading …] *'Name of ship, Caledonia'.*
> Claude: *I've heard of the 'Caledonia'.*
> Teacher: *Do you know what 'Caledonia' means? It means – does anybody know? Will I tell them or?*
> Mediator: *Yes, please.*
> Jack: *'Caledonia'. I actually know the word, but I don't really know.*
> Teacher: *Do you know? It's an old name for a country. It's an old name for?*
> Jack: *I knew it, erm, is it Canada?*
> Teacher: *Scotland.*

In addition to these language (and sometimes cultural) challenges, the wordless and surreal nature of many of the images in *The Arrival* means that there are no identifiers for the many strange and fantastic objects that appear that readers can rely on. Thus, the mediator had to encourage risk-taking as well as providing new vocabulary or helping to speculate about what the objects might be.

Mediators also often made restatement sentences that summarized and tied together the responses made during the course of the discussion, providing 'orderly' interpretation of the story. This turned out to be a useful strategy because it meant that the less elaborate responses could be included and built on for a more in-depth interpretation of events and it supported the children's learning about the process of making meaning during the act of reading.

Guiding questions

Facilitating the discussions also meant guiding the reading and moving it forward through focused questions. These were usually asked at points in the narrative that we had identified as important to support their understanding of plot, character or the author's choices. Without words to use as guidance, the readers often turned to the mediator, either through words or gestures, for assurance that they were 'getting it right' or for confirmation of their ideas especially during the first sessions. As the sessions went on, however, through the mediator's questions and answers, the children realized that the researchers were neither looking for 'correct answers' nor did they hold the 'key' to the text, and this led to the creation of a more equal platform for all participants. In what follows, we highlight some of the main types of questions used by the mediators:

a) Open-ended and bridging questions

More general and open-ended questions, such as 'What can you see?' or 'Tell me about this picture', were used to start the discussion and provide a way into the text. They allowed the children to focus on what was relevant and important to them rather than every single detail of the story. We realized that asking questions such as 'What is happening here?' or 'What is he doing?' often resulted in less elaborate responses, while asking readers to 'think' or 'wonder' led to more elaboration. These open questions encouraged some rich retellings and the creation of dialogues for the characters, as we saw in Chapter 5. However, sometimes these questions could result in circular, speculative descriptions about the identity of people or things (especially the more fantastical objects), so we introduced 'bridging' questions that helped move them on to a more interpretative response in which they could elaborate on particular clues offered by the author or other elements of the visual text. Some examples of these 'bridging questions' are 'I wonder why this is here?'; 'What makes you think that?'; or 'What could this mean/represent?' It is important to note that this does not imply that for every comment or hypothesis offered by a child a bridging or follow-up question would be asked, because this would have required the children to justify their responses and perhaps prevented some of them from volunteering their interpretations.

b) Questions with a focus on the narrative and the literary elements

Mediators supported the children's learning of literary knowledge and, on occasions, ways of making this knowledge explicit. As in other studies, we found evidence that understanding the ways authors craft their stories enriches readers' literary experiences and meaning-making processes (Manresa and Silva-Díaz, 2005; Munita and Manresa, 2012; Wolf, 2004). In the following interactions from BCN, we offer an example of this type of guidance:

> Mediador: *Y por ejemplo sobre elementos de la narración esto que ustedes decían bueno no hacen falta palabras para explicar una historia, pero ¿qué hace falta para explicar una historia?*
>
> Ana: *Un tema*
>
> Mediador: *Un tema, bien, qué otras cosas, qué otras cosas hacen falta para armar una historia?*
>
> Rodrigo: *Imágenes*
>
> Mediador: *Bueno aquí podrían ser imágenes sí o palabras que también decía Denis que también con palabras, entonces- pero dentro de la historia, ¿qué tiene que tener una historia para que la podamos contar […]? a ver pensemos ¿qué tiene esta historia? un tema, ¿qué más?*
>
> Ana: *un protagonista*
>
> […]
>
> Mediador: *. . . entonces ¿qué otra cosa podría ser que . . . que se necesita para armar una narración y que encontramos aquí?*
>
> Rodrigo: *Personaje*
>
> Mediador: *Bien, personaje pero si el personaje está sólo así para . . . ¿una narración?*
>
> Rodrigo: *Una aventura*
>
> Mediador: *Bien, una aventura, sí, que hace algo, ¿no?*
>
> Ana: *El espacio, el espacio donde pasa*
>
> Mediador: *Un espacio donde pase eso muy bien; entonces el personaje es lo principal, por eso ustedes lo dijeron primero que todo, ¿sí? el protagonista, alguien a quien le pase algo, pero también necesitamos claro esto, que pase algo, digamos las acciones, en un espacio.*
>
> Ana: *El tiempo*

> [Mediator: And for example about the elements of the narrative you said that well words are not necessary to explain a story, but what is necessary to explain a story?
>
> Ana: A theme
>
> Mediator: A theme, good, what other things, what other things are needed to put a story together?
>
> Rodrigo: Images

Mediator: Well here it could be images yes, or words as Denis said that also with words, then, but inside the story, what does a story have to have so we can tell it [. . .]? Let's think, what does this story have, a theme, what else?

Ana: A protagonist

[. . .]

Mediator: . . . then what other things could it be that is needed to put a narrative together and that we find here?

Rodrigo: Character

Mediator: Good, character but if the character is only there to . . . a narrative?

Rodrigo: An adventure

Mediator: Good, an adventure, yes, that does something, doesn't it?

Ana: The space, the space where it happens

Mediator: A space where it happens, very good, so that character is the main thing, that's why you said it first of all, yes, the protagonist, someone to whom something happens, but we also need, of course, that something happens, let's say the actions, in a space.

Ana: The time]

In the process of engaging the children in this discussion, the mediator offered them metalanguage related to the literary elements and the creation of a story. Researchers such as Kiefer (1995) have demonstrated that the more children talk about books, the more conscious they become of the role of the aesthetic elements. In addition, engaging children in talks about the craft of authors and/ or illustrators also has the potential to support them in their writing (Smith and Edelsky, 2005).

c) Questions with a focus on the visual image

As we have mentioned in previous chapters, despite using many of the same questions about visual aspects such as frames, light and perspective, the mediator's role tended to vary according to the interests and research expertise of each team and this resulted in the different types of responses obtained. In BCN, and as the example above also shows, the mediators played a more direct role in encouraging readers to probe further into the visual elements and this resulted in their data being richer in this respect. One mediator in particular was eager to signal to students this type of observation. Once she had started them in exercising their metaliterary knowledge, their responses became more spontaneous and needed progressively less and less of her intervention.

Both the GLW and the AZ teams, however, focused more on the meaning-making process based on children's interpretations of the narrative, with narrative elements or the visual design as part of the general process. For instance, in their interactions, the mediators attempted to draw compositional responses towards a reflection as to why Tan had chosen to present the elements in a particular way and this led the children into more inferential comments. While compositional responses were often teased out and mediated, the fact that there were relatively few compositional responses provided by students throughout the interviews all together may also reflect the mediator's influence. The primary focus of the discussion tended to be on content over style. Nevertheless, in all contexts, the children had very rich discussions about the book as a cultural artefact.

d) Questions encouraging text-to-life connections

Because we also wanted to encourage the readers to make personal and intertextual connections, we asked questions that would support this type of response. The following example, from the children in AZ, illustrates one of the many opportunities the children had to make sense of some rather difficult experiences in their lives in light of the characters' experiences. The children were retelling and discussing the two-page spread that presents images of the immigrant, who, in search of a room, uses signs and drawing to communicate with someone who speaks a different language. The mediator asked the group *'¿Ustedes han tenido que usar ilustraciones así para que los entiendan?'* [Have any of you had to use pictures in this way to be understood?] Various students said that they had, and they talked about their experiences. Here is Ryan's experience:

> Mediador: *¿Y tú, cuando te ha pasado eso que has tenido que usar alguna clase de señal así o ilustración para darte entender?*
>
> Ryan: *Aquí, cuando mi papá estaba buscando casa, llegamos con una Americana y no sabía nada, y mi mama traía un papel y un lápiz y le hicimos así, una forma de una casa.*
>
> Mediator: *¿Y lo resolvió?* [Ryan assents] *¿Lograron comunicarse?* [Ryan assents] *Muy bien vamos a seguir con el señor, ¿qué más paso?*

> [Mediator: And you, when did it happen to you that you had to use some kind of signal or picture to be understood?
>
> Ryan: Here when my dad was looking for a house and we went where there was an American [English-speaking person] and she didn't know

anything [of Spanish] and my mom had a paper and a pencil and we did like this, a picture of a house.

Mediator: And did it solve [the problem]? [Ryan assents]. Were you able to communicate? [Ryan assents] Very good, let's continue talking about the man, what else happened?]

Ryan shared an experience not uncommon to many immigrant families in the USA, where parents engage in business transactions with the help of their children as translators, including searching for housing.

Within the research teams, there were differences of opinions and conversations regarding this kind of mediation. Some researchers wondered about the validity of responses and personal connections that were not offered spontaneously by the children but prompted by the adult and also about how 'authentic' or 'uncontaminated' these responses might be. We finally understood that this expectation of documenting 'uncontaminated' responses is not only impossible but also unrealistic, as one of the tenets of the study is that all response is socially constructed. It is also important to remember the fact that, if a child does not offer a personal connection, it does not mean that there was an absence of these but that students may choose not to share them. Some may wonder whether this kind of response may distract from focusing on the literary elements and from benefiting from the richness of the literary work. Short's words provide a response to this concern when she states that learners 'need to remain anchored in their own life experiences in order to generatively reach beyond themselves to create a productive tension between current understanding and new experiences' (Short, 2011, p. 50). It is important to invite personal connections when discussing literature, among other reasons not only because we do learn by making connections to previous knowledge and experiences, but also because sometimes the way instruction in schools is organized makes some children believe that their lives and personal experiences have no room in academic discussions. This seems particularly relevant when working with immigrant children because these connections make a sense of community and belonging more possible.

In our study, the direct questioning of the children was sometimes received with answers in monosyllables or a closing of a particular route of exploration with responses that were equally direct, for example from BCN, '*no, nunca me ha pasado*' [no, that has never happened to me]. We also observed gestures that reflected a physical closing up, shaking their head or answering, 'I don't know'. These responses remind us that, while discussions about books should offer opportunities for the students to find themselves in the literature, it is important to keep in mind, as Medina and Martínez-Roldán (2011) discuss, that readers can connect to books in very unexpected ways that challenge our sometimes oversimplified view of culturally relevant pedagogies, diversity and the role of literature in people's lives. As we have said in our article (Martínez-Roldán, 2003; Medina and Martínez-Roldán, 2011), we also believe, together with Sumara (2002), that engagement with literary texts can become a productive site for the continued interpretation of culture and the way culture is historically influenced, and we think this is true for both readers and facilitators of the discussions. We also see the personal connections and personal narratives the children brought to the discussions as potentially mediating their understandings of the text and of life, and as opportunities to develop and negotiate identities as members of the literary community of the classroom, while negotiating their place in their host countries.

Children as inquirers and problem posers

Throughout the book, we have presented examples in which the children made predictions, posed questions, considered multiple possibilities and, finally, elaborated upon each other's ideas to co-construct the narrative. While the adult's role was crucial in mediating the discussions, it is clear that the children themselves played an important role in mediating and negotiating not only their own but also their peers' interpretative process. In fact, in BCN, the researchers found that, while children offered more elaborate responses to more open questions, these increased when questions were not directly asked by the mediator but when the response was provoked in an indirect mode through the collaborative dialogue. The children formulated their own questions and they worked at engaging others in their own enquiries, mediating the group's meaning-making process in this way. Again, the role of the mediator was important here as some participants began to adopt the language and type of questions set by the mediator, using them to ask questions of both adults and peers.

In addressing the role of children's literature in the classroom, Short approaches the reading and responding to literature as a problem-posing and problem-solving process, and proposes that 'Children need to have a voice in both identifying and pursuing the tensions and questions that matter to them within a literary study' (Short, 2011, p. 50). While the mediators in this project were ready to mediate the discussions through questions and comments, the children had plenty of opportunities to pursue their own enquiries and questions and, in the process, they mediated their peers' understandings. In the following example from GLW, four children are looking at the first page with the images of the objects from the family home. The conversation turns to the family's financial situation and Lily (Scot) comments that the characters have 'loads of money'. Ruby (Rwanda) disagrees and point to the evidence for saying they are poor, especially the cracked teacup. The children then look more carefully and, when asked about how the characters on the next page might be feeling, Lily has now taken on the idea and speculates that the man has to leave to find a job and money. Ruby introduces the idea of migration, of the whole family having to leave their home, and Nadia (Pakistani/Scot) brings in her knowledge of history to conclude that something 'bad' like the Second World War has happened and this is why they are no longer rich. Later in the discussion, Alex (Sri Lanka) picks up Ruby's idea again of the family having to leave their country and the rest of the group seem to now accept this as the premise for understanding the rest of the narrative:

Mediator: *What sort of family do you think it was [. . .]? What do these objects tell you about the family?*

Lily: *I think it's an English family cos it doesn't look like Chinese, cos look, you can tell.*

Ruby: *Yeah, but they are poor, don't have money.*

Mediator: *How do you know they're poor?*

Lily: *They have loads of money.*

Ruby: *Cos look* [pointing at signs of poverty] *and they have a crack there, the things.*

Mediator: *So the cup is cracked, Ruby.*

[The children continue looking at the objects . . .]

Mediator: *How do you think they're feeling in that picture?*

Lily: *They're feeling really sad because this husband has to go and find a job and get more money for his family, poor family.*

Sunil: *Yes, that's these things are old, old, things.*

Ruby: *I think, I think they're sad because they had to leave their home and find a new one.*

Mediator: *They've had to leave. Uhuh. It looks like somebody's leaving.*

Nadia: *I think it's a Second World War* [inaudible] *broken things and they've blasted people's house, that's why they look sad. And then they're bad things happening in all around the world, and there's, they're used to be rich and now they are poor cos of all the bad things happening.*

There were a great number of interactions like this in which the children helped each other make sense of the story. In this excerpt, it was the adult who provoked the discussion with the question about the family, but in many other instances the children initiated the enquiries, with explicit questions or problems, such as Almah's enquiry in AZ: '*But, what I don't understand is why they're standing in a line, kind of like, here?*', or through more indirect enquiries, such as Ryan's: '*No sé si aquí se dan cuenta ...*' [I don't know if you notice that here ...]. In this case, Ryan, whose monolingual teacher was wondering if he could make meaning of texts given that he was not participating much in his English classroom, contributed what he observed to the discussions, raising possibilities and ideas that other more experienced readers in the group built upon. He invited the students to engage in his own inquiry on a regular basis and the group followed his questions. In return, he, too, considered the others' interpretations and began to employ some of the strategies he saw them using – such as Almah's use of dialogue for retelling the story. Through such collaborative effort, the children were learning from one another independent of their language and reading proficiencies, or of their linguistic, ethnic and/or immigration differences.

Mediation through the image-based strategies

In Chapter 9, we will elaborate on the role of image-based strategies to support the children as readers; however, here we want to briefly address how the visual responses mediated understanding as they offered children an opportunity to increase the sharing and negotiation of their interpretations. In some cases, the children seemed to be more willing to elaborate on their responses using the different media as a base (photographs, annotations, drawings and graphic strips). The paired annotations encouraged the most peer-to-peer interaction, but significant mediation also occurred when the children gave explanations and opinions and made comparisons during the sharing of the results of these strategies.

A brief example from GLW shows how the sharing of an annotation raised questions but also generated new ideas, retelling and parallel stories. Morag (Scot) and Ruby (Rwanda) worked together on annotating the image of the first inset story, where a little girl seems trapped and forced to work in a factory. Based on the details in the image, as well as the way Tan uses colour, the girls created their parallel text. Their annotation includes questions and answers, on which they based their explanation, such as:

Why does the colour change?
Why is she trapped?
What's in the book?
Is it just a memory?
The book looks a bit like a diary.
Sneaking out.
She's running away with the book.
She is cold.

The following excerpt is just part of a longer discussion from the end of the session when the girls are telling their peers and the adult mediators, a researcher and a teacher, about the image, based on the narrative they have worked out together (with a bit of occasional support from the researcher):

Mediator: *Do you want to tell us a bit about your* [annotated] *picture?*

Ruby: *That there, see how the man meets the woman and then I think he's asking her something and they start talking with each other and so then the woman starts telling him about her past, what happened to her and stuff.*

Morag: *I thought maybe it was her daughter and that's her daughter there* [the girl in the inset story image], *she's working somewhere and maybe has a diary or something.*

Claude: *See how like she's telling the man one reason she came* [...] *why did she run away because she had to work in the night over and how she ran away from her city and go to another city.*

[...]

Ruby: *those people locked her up in a big room and here she gets that* [pointing to shovel]

Morag: *shovel*

Ruby: *shovel, to try to get out and then she opens the door*

Morag: *and she tries to sneak out, like a bedroom, see, she tries to sneak by*

[...]

Morag: *we think it was her mum's secret diary or something*

Ruby: *about the book, we thought it had like secret things and the girl's mum gave it to her and the people heard about it and that's why they locked her up* [...]

The discussion continued with Morag and Ruby's retelling of the girl's rescuing her book and escaping on the train and explaining that the story goes back to the 'present' where the woman has been telling the story to the protagonist. Jack then goes back to the idea that it was the woman talking about her past, but the girls and Claude are convinced it is a story about her daughter. What they all agree about, though, is that it is a different story because, as Ruby says, '*look, the colour changes, this is the past and this is what's happening now*'. At the end of their 'presentation', the teacher responds: '*That's fabulous!*'

Fostering a community of learners

The different forms of mediation mentioned in this chapter all contributed to the creation of a community of readers in which adults and children listened to each other, expressed their opinions and engaged in the interpretative process of making sense of *The Arrival* and, sometimes, of their own lives. Within this community, the children saw how their individual responses became part of, and enriched, the collective story. Through the mediation, they also saw they could take risks not only with interpretation but also with offering their personal responses. The sharing, even if it was about small details, such as a dislike of aeroplane food, sometimes led them to realize that others had had similar experiences, and therefore stronger bonds between them were created.

The continuity offered by the sessions, looking closely at one single book and talking about it in depth, encouraged the children's sense of belonging to the group. This belonging could then be extended to membership of a 'literacy club', to use Smith's (1987) well-known term, where readers are able to engage in inquiry and discussions about literature. In a classroom that encourages an inquiry stance to the use of literature, as Short asserts, 'children gain a sense of possibility for their lives and that of the society in which they live along with the ability to consider others' perspectives and needs' (Short, 2011, p. 60). Literature discussions that create this type of community of inquiry are especially important for new arrivals and immigrant children as they try to find their place in the new school and the new society in which they find themselves.

The researchers in BCN were particularly struck by the attitude and remarks of the children, which showed them to be more confident readers of image by the end of the sessions. The researchers suspected that this was the result of the context of shared construction of meaning, which seemed to represent a novelty in terms of their usual reading practices in school. This was confirmed during a general conversation about school, when the children observed that during the research sessions they were able to talk and they were listened to, as opposed to the lack of opportunities to express themselves or to be heard that they encountered in their usual classroom routines. As we have noted, more traditional teaching practices do not often encourage the expression of opinions or feelings, but, if a genuine community is to be fostered, one that welcomes diversity and particularly experiences of migration, this needs to change.

Looking Together: Image-based Strategies for Inclusive Pedagogy

The findings of this inquiry point to the need for a more inclusive pedagogy for immigrant children, one which, as C. Suárez-Orozco argues, builds on the knowledge and skills that the children already possess and results in a more 'engaging' curriculum where 'information must be provided multimodally in order to scaffold the children's available linguistic and cultural resources' (C. Suárez-Orozco, 2001, p. 588). One of the key features of this multimodality, and which is at the core of Tan's book, is the visual image. By building on Tan's sophisticated visual art and the immigrant children's visual literacy skills, we were able to overcome some of the multiple challenges to learning as well as to cross cultural borders.

The potential of image, however, has tended to be overlooked in school curricula, including in the area of language and literature, although recent studies and curricular developments are beginning to give it a more central role, partly as a result of the explosion in digital developments, the increased publication and use of multimodal texts and the work arising as a result of New Literacy Studies. A variety of new learning and teaching approaches have been proposed, based on different artistic media such as paintings, films, advertisements, photographs, digital images and picturebooks. Their objectives are similar and usually include the promotion of analytical and critical thinking, exploring a particular visual medium and raising and enhancing enjoyment of the visual experience (Callow, 2006; Frey and Fisher, 2008; Thibault and Walbert, 2003).[1] Fleckenstein, Calendrillo and Worley argue that students must be challenged to 'to analyze critically the texts they view and to integrate their visual knowledge with their knowledge of other forms of language' (Fleckenstein et al., 2002, p. 7), but, to do so, teachers must be aware of and bring imagery and language into their teaching 'because it is by means of such integration that we create, transform and live in our world. To teach shorn of imagery is to teach shorn of vision' (Fleckenstein *et al.*, 2002, p. viii).

Based on the findings from our inquiry, this chapter addresses some of the implications for pedagogy for the greater use of image and its integration with words, through reading and talking about picturebooks. It also shows how school practices, which are often characterized by prescriptive learning and lack of contextualization, can be turned into a process that allows children to rebuild their personal history and identity as subjects and, at the same time, invites them to participate in a collective learning process where they can build on shared knowledge through dialogue and mutual listening. While our findings refer to wordless picturebooks and immigrant children in particular, they can be extended to picturebooks with words and used with all students. However, although we firmly believe that well-crafted, complex picturebooks can encourage readers to cross borders, we also agree with Hope (2008) that, for their potential to be fully realized in the classroom, they must be accompanied by critical reading pedagogies (Arizpe *et al.*, 2013). We first provide some guidelines for using the image-based strategies, which have been encountered earlier in the book (Chapter 3), as research tools, but here we explore them as *pedagogy* for the school classroom. Inevitably, there will be some repetition but, in order to set the frame of reference for the classroom practices and activities described, such repetition should be useful.

It is important to note that this does not mean neglecting engagement with language and literature; on the contrary, as Fleckenstein *et al.* point out, 'such an endeavour requires that we nuance our sense of meaning by welcoming into our classrooms the necessary transaction between imagery and language' (Fleckenstein *et al.*, 2002, p. 5). The image-based strategies utilized in this project contribute to the cognitive, emotional, aesthetic and intellectual development of all learners, not just those who are newly arrived in the country and who are language learners, and consequently are of significant importance more generally in modern classrooms. The beauty of these strategies is that they are not overly complex to manage and make use of current theory that addresses both sociocultural and visual aspects, as well as using current pedagogic practice that taps into the skills, knowledge and concepts available to most children regardless of their language history or ability to read. The children's enthusiastic engagement with these strategies during our inquiry suggests that they did not find the tasks onerous or consider them learning 'assignments' to be completed; as such, these strategies must be regarded as valuable additions to the classroom repertoire.

The second part of the chapter refers to the perspectives and reflections of some of the teachers involved in the inquiry with regard to the wordless narratives and the strategies. The third and final part describes how each team has been moving forward in their research during the writing of this book.

Image-based pedagogical tools for literary understanding

In what follows, based on our findings, we provide guidelines for using the image-based strategies in the classroom, along with other possible ideas and variations in their application.

Text selection

As has become evident, central to this particular project and set of strategies was the selection of the texts. Painter *et al.* note that texts like *Flotsam* and *The Arrival* can provide a form of 'apprenticeship' in the understanding of literature: 'Literary picture books offer a very important "training" in becoming sensitised in how to read narrative texts (including monomodal ones) in ways that are educationally valued' (Painter *et al.*, 2013, p. 156). There is a plethora of picturebooks and graphic novels that can offer this 'training' and our strategies could be used with any 'literary picturebooks', but, as we have seen, reading wordless picturebooks immediately sets up an active learning environment with student engagement at its very heart. As we have also seen, these provide a level playing field for all children, no matter their reading or language level, because there are no expectations of success or failure based on traditional reading and writing skills. In terms of our specific contexts, we selected picturebooks on the theme of journeys, migration and the visual image itself. There are plenty of possibilities on offer not only on this theme, most of them with words (there are also wordless books on many other topics).[2] Looking at a range of Tan's books would also be a stimulating activity because children could look at themes that run through his work, and consider not only intertextuality but also intratextuality, that is, the way the visual and verbal texts refer to each other. Discussions could also include one of the themes the children in this inquiry found so fascinating – the relationship between reality and fantasy – and this could be supported by the introduction of ideas of artistic style and trends such as surrealism and 'steampunk'.

Oral response to the visual text

The elicitation of oral response tends to be the first step in the reading process and this strategy forms the basis of much good teaching: the contextualization of the learning. In this case, it includes establishing the book as an aesthetic object, as well as a narrative about a particular topic. These first encounters with the text provide an opportunity to fire the imagination, create curiosity and engage attention.

For the inquiry, we used a combination of group configurations to encourage talk and discussion. Conversations can begin in pairs and move on to groups, for example. What is important, as demonstrated by the inquiry, is that the discussion occurs in an inviting space that does not replicate the traditional classroom arrangement. Even if this is only in a small way – moving to an alternative classroom or part of the school, or even sitting on the floor.

Introductory 'walkthrough'

This 'warm-up' activity focuses on activities that establish the book as an aesthetic object, such as looking at the front cover, the endpapers, title page, dust jacket and the blurb at the back. Teachers/facilitators can use prompts about the author, the main characters, the title, unusual illustrations and encourage speculation and prediction. The 'walkthrough' should be done at a reasonably brisk pace so that attention is caught and interest is piqued, encouraging more detailed 'looking' at the next stage, because, as Hunt (2011) reminds us, reading a picturebook should be read at 'picture speed' rather than word speed.

This is a good moment to explore the lack of words and what it may mean for a story. Is it true that there are no words at all? This can lead to a discussion about publishing information, blurbs and embedded text, for example, in signs. Why would an author choose to create a book without words? What difference would words make to the story? Can you describe how reading pictures is different from reading words?

Facilitators can use this opportunity to introduce some initial concepts and language related to the images. Having a 'language for talking about language, images, texts and meaning-making interactions' (New London Group, 2000, p. 24) is commonly referred to as a metalanguage. Arizpe and Styles argue that, 'providing or expanding the terms or metalanguage to discuss visual aspects is crucial to developing a better understanding of the texts' (Arizpe and Styles, 2008, p. 371). This does not mean that the texts cannot be enjoyed or discussed without knowledge of technical terms, and these terms can be used at different levels, beginning with the different types of colour, line or perspective. As we have seen in Chapter 7, children point these out but often have no words with which to describe them. The benefit of starting to introduce this language at this point is that there is a genuine context for such language.

Literary conversations or discussions

Following the initial walkthrough of the book, readers should engage in a closer, more detailed reading, which normally requires a number of sessions depending on the text. The non-linear characteristic of reading pictures usually reveals something new on each subsequent reading. It is this 'roundabout negotiation of understanding' (Bland, 2013) that makes even wordless picturebooks particularly valuable for language learning and for encouraging thinking dispositions generally.

> A progressive roundabout negotiation of meaning can lead to a generative, dialogic discussion, for clearly development takes place on many fronts between the readings: the language development of the young reader; the visual literacy of the children and teacher; the cognitive development of young learners. (Bland, 2013, p. 38)

Here are some suggestions to assist teachers in creating discussion and inquiry opportunities for their students:

- Use a small-group format similar to literature circles. After some demonstrations of ways to talk about books, the whole class can be divided into small heterogeneous groups, with everyone reading and discussing the same wordless book or choosing from various options around a personally familiar or relatable theme.
- Try having groups focus on several books by the same author and then compare various authors' styles.
- Organize students into linguistically homogeneous groups whenever possible to facilitate children's access to their own languages as they discuss the book. Heterogeneous groups may work with the right support.[3]
- Use buddy reading, pairing students to talk. The two students can take turns interpreting and commenting on the images found on alternating pages. The teacher moves to different groups demonstrating and encouraging open-ended discussion.

- Keep the conversation open – invite students to share their thinking and pose their own questions. Questions or prompts can be helpful:
  - What do you think about this page?
  - What do you notice here?
  - What is happening here?
  - Why do you think so?
  - What else would you like to say?
- Ask how they think characters might be thinking and feeling.
- Ask students to share their predictions.
- Pay attention to the elements of art present in the book (e.g. the use of perspective, light, frames, colour, lines, etc.) and learn the language of art. Ask students to deliberately incorporate some of those elements in their own work.
- Do not rush the discussion of the book; provide enough time for the students to become familiar with the book and the way the story is revealed.
- Remember that inquiry can take many forms. It does not only mean direct questions, but can include wondering and guessing, such as 'Maybe . . .' and 'I wonder if . . .'
- Ask for volunteers to narrate the story, each one telling or acting the part of one of the characters.

(Martínez-Roldán and Newcomer, 2011, p. 192)

Annotation of images

The annotation of images task emerged from the work of Bednall *et al.* (2008) with multimodal texts and bilingual children. Using annotations is a creative tool that encourages careful reading of the visuals. This task slows down the reading process and encourages a much more careful examination of the images. In the annotation task, using double-page spreads from the book effectively acts as an examination of a 'still' image from the narrative, and so it is important to realize that this is rather an unnatural 'freeze-framing' in the dynamic of a visual narrative.

Double-page spreads are photocopied and stuck to A3 paper, which leaves a substantial border around the picture. Students, either individually or in pairs, are given marker pens and encouraged to write down any questions they have about the picture; add speech or thought bubbles for the characters in the picture; write down their own thoughts, feelings and opinions about anything in the picture. They can use arrows or lines to link their comment to the images.

Initially, students can be unsure how to proceed, so provision of exemplars or teacher/mediator 'modelling' can be with teachers/facilitators using the three questions Richards and Anderson (2003) suggest for developing emerging readers' visual literacy skills: 'What do I see? What do I think? and What do I wonder?' The image can be annotated with arrows indicating their replies. Interactive whiteboards can be especially useful for the modelling of this task.

When this is done as a paired activity, it is a good strategy to give each one in the pair a different-coloured pen to allow tracking of their thought processes. If the children are working in pairs, they should be free to discuss and share ideas as well as offering support for each other, asking and answering questions, offering alternative explanations, seeking evidence to support conclusions or even assisting each other with the written element. Newly arrived students who may struggle with the writing of the 'host' language can have their comments and questions scribed for them by teachers. Alternatively, the annotations can be done in the child's home language and translated at a later stage.

The annotated texts themselves form useful tools for both student and teacher as objects for reflection and subsequent revisiting. Teachers may also find they can be used for assessment purposes as non-traditional examples of pupils' language progression. Members of the GLW team shared the research, and the annotation tasks in particular, with groups of both undergraduate initial teacher education and postgraduate teacher trainees. They served as an excellent vehicle for them to explore the needs of EAL learners. The student teachers were also asked to complete annotations, and many of them found it significantly more difficult than the children did (their annotations were often far less detailed and adventurous than the children's). The experience caused many of the student teachers to re-evaluate the power of picturebooks – wordless picturebooks in particular – and to see that image-based strategies should not be overlooked as valid learning strategies in a variety of subject areas and for all ages of learners.

Photographs

As we have discussed elsewhere, our inquiry with *Flotsam* confirmed that 'children's photographs are not just their "view of the world" but are also a construction of their identity in relation to their parents and their peers' (Sharples *et al.*, 2003, cited in Arizpe and McAdam, 2011, p. 241). The use of *Flotsam* provided an ideal opportunity to explore the potential use of photography as a learning and teaching strategy but it is not the only possible text with which to use this activity.

The use of photography as a tool in the classroom is not new and leads to a variety of possible pedagogic tasks (see, for example, Byrnes and Wasik, 2009), but its potential has not been exploited as much as it could have been, and as a vehicle for visual learning it provides an enormous range of possibilities, which have now been extended by the use of mobile phones and sites for uploading digital images. Photographs provide an obvious means of communication for children who struggle to express themselves orally or through written language or who are learning new languages. Using photographs provides another strategy to strengthen readers' comprehension and critical skills by encouraging them to reflect on how meaning is made through pictures.

The Arrival also invited the use of photography as a learning strategy, but so do many other wordless narratives (and other picturebooks). To take the photographs, children can use digital cameras, disposable cameras or their own phones. A task related to the book can be set, such as we did, asking children to take photographs of people, places and things that are important to them. Not only are the photographs themselves important, but it is also interesting to observe how the children go about the task and whether all the discussion of the visual elements of the picturebook that precede this – colour, perspective, shade and pattern, for example – feature in any of the pictures. Once the photographs are developed, the students can present their photographs to their peers and teachers using PowerPoint and talk about their selection of images and their significance.

In BCN, when working with *Flotsam*, the students actually constructed a version of the old-fashioned camera illustrated in the text, and when they had their own photographs developed they 'inserted' them into the model camera to reproduce more accurately what they would have sent on to the next recipient. To some degree, this demonstrates the degree of 'buy-in' to the premise of the story by the readers and illustrates beautifully the degree of engagement with the text. The practice of 'situating oneself in the text' is a critical aspect in engaging in the meaning-making process.

In Italy (as will be seen in the next chapter), team members combined photography and drawing. They photocopied certain pages of the book with some elements covered up leaving only the frame visible – this also included the front cover of the book. The students were asked to use the blanks on the pages to build their own story of arriving in a new country. For this task, students were not required to maintain the wordless format but were allowed to use speech bubbles to enhance their pictures. The team also generated sepia-toned photographs of the students and these were inserted in the empty frame on the front cover and another photograph taken of each individual's front cover of *The Arrival*.

Alternatively, the children can be asked to make a selection from their pictures, perhaps five or six images, and then arrange these on A3 paper, using captions underneath to explain each picture. The presentation of the photographs, in whatever format, is of particular importance because without that the photographs have no 'intrinsic meanings' (Pink, 2007); they are only given meaning when the photographers talk about why they chose to take that picture and what they think the image depicts. In doing this, the students demonstrate their understanding of image selection, of narrative structure and of the need to justify choices, and the act of presenting to their peers confirms spoken language progression and growth in confidence. Using cameras to capture images also relieves the pressure for those students who are not comfortable trying to draw the images, and the cameras give control over the images that are captured and shared.

The use of photography in the classroom does, of course, raise specific issues of ethics and of security. When setting up the photography tasks, there should be a discussion with the students about the appropriateness of taking pictures in particular places and of the necessity sometimes to ask permission before photographing people. There must be agreement at the outset about how and where any photographs will be used in the classroom and also who owns the photographs and how and where they will be stored. Parental and school approval may also be required in some cases.

Graphic strips

Another visual strategy variation did involve some drawing and took its influence from the use of graphic or comic strips. Like other image-based strategies discussed here, comics in the classroom have been an underused resource. Since the 1940s, there has been fierce educational debate, with supporters on both sides of the divide, about the effects of using comics in the classroom (Yang, 2003). That debate has continued into the twenty-first century, and only in recent years are comics being used more widely at all levels of education. Ironically, many of today's teachers use comics to develop reading and imagination skills, the very skills some educators in the 1940s feared they would suppress, according to Yang. Versaci welcomes the 'interplay of the written and the visual' (Versaci, 2001, p. 62), noting that comics can 'quite literally put a human face on a given subject' (Versaci, 2001, p. 62), resulting in an intimate, emotional connection between the students and the characters in a comic story. Tiemensma states that 'Sequential art provides plenty of opportunity for connecting the story to the children's own experiences, predicting what will happen and inferring what happens between panels' (Tiemensma, 2009, p. 6). This latter effect was of particular importance for the graphic-strip task, as it was framed in the project.

In this task, where the students draw their own graphic strip, they can include text as well as image and this can be in the form of captions underneath the pictures or as speech or thought bubbles. Templates for such tasks can be easily found, and with so many free online comic-creation tools there is a wealth of possibilities to extend the task. Alternatively, many students prefer to design their own frames to suit the story they want to tell, in the way they want to tell it. A single pane in a comic can represent paragraphs' worth of written material in a way that is enjoyable and effective for the beginning or challenged reader. The graphic strips can also provide concrete evidence of the metacognitive links the students make between their reading of the text and their language backgrounds and histories, and as such can be used for assessment purposes where appropriate. For students who lack the ability to visualize as they read – and that can include language learners – comics provide the graphic sense that approximates what good readers do as they read. In turn, students have to make use of these techniques as they try to produce graphic strips on their own. Additionally, the graphic strips themselves can be excellent vehicles for teaching writing, since a comic story has to be pared down to its most basic elements.

The teachers' perspectives

Although the students were the focus of this research, the team in GLW also sought to capture some of the teachers' responses to the learning strategies used.[4] The two teachers who participated in the inquiry, Haile and Jennifer, usually worked with EAL children in small groups, withdrawing them from the class for additional support or providing support within the main class. Both these teachers had intimate knowledge of the children, their backgrounds and their families. When interviewed, both teachers noted that the books had engaged the children in the reading process even before it was discussed or used in sessions. Speaking of *The Arrival*, Haile said, '*this book seems to surpass a lot of texts that I have used because when the children have picture books they've got ideas of their own, which they can talk to ...*'

Both teachers were excited at the freedom the wordless texts offered the children. Haile commented that '*the children's reading habits are freed up, they are not constrained in moving through the book in order, they are free to move backwards and forwards*'. Jennifer also echoed these comments, focusing on the way the texts did not impose ideas on the children: '*it's about them interpreting a story and that's like higher-order reading skills … when you are looking at something and it's not literal, it's evaluative …*'

The annotation task was viewed as another means of inviting the children to respond to the text and explore their own ideas of what was happening within the picturebook narrative. Haile valued the way in which they could be applied to print-based texts and used by children who struggle to speak, '*or don't wish to speak, they also allow children to work with their peers speaking their home language or work in groups to socially construct meaning*'.

In summing up the texts used in the project, Jennifer said, '*it's active learning as well, you are interacting with these texts, you're not just being fed something … you have to think about it and bring something to the page, rather than sitting there passively and being told this is what this book is about …*' Haile was drawn to the importance of the visual in the reading process: '*the picture is one of the main instruments of understanding the content of the story*'. He was also aware of the children using the texts to begin building up a vocabulary of terms used to describe the visual elements of text: '*terms such as perspective and zoom, angle and tone*'. Jennifer commented on how more complex visual texts can draw in older language learners and was considering using graphic novels with these students: '*it's quite difficult to find a book for the children I teach, that is going to be relevant and appropriate for them, because many books can be too young in content. I think things need to be very visual for bilingual learners*'.

From AZ, the team reported an anecdote from a teacher whose students were involved in the project, though she herself was not. In the third week of the project, one of the class teachers approached the researchers and shared her concerns about one of the children participating in the study: '*Are you doing any kind of reading assessment in your study? He seems really lost in my classroom. I would like to know if he can make meaning of texts because he is silent in my class*'. She wondered about his level of participation in the group discussions and was unsure about his reading abilities in her integrated social studies and language arts class.

Her concerns surprised the team, for, while the student had certainly not been the most talkative student at the beginning of the small-group discussions, his participation in this after-school literacy project had been steadily increasing. In fact, by the time the teacher voiced her concerns, the student had become one of the most active participants in the group. In retrospect, however, the team believed there was an explanation for the concern. The student had been in school in the USA for only three months. In addition, since he was a Spanish-speaking student, his teacher, who was not bilingual, could not communicate with him effectively. Consequently, she had no way of assessing his reading. She was left having to use standardized tests, which must be completed in English, and his limited participation in class to assess his language progress. The information provided by the bilingual team provided much more accurate information, and the class teacher was able to see the advantages of the project.

At the end of the study, Sarah Newcomer, the graduate assistant working in AZ with Carmen, and who had been a teacher at the school, wrote about what she had learned about the children through the study. We believe this insightful reflection will be useful to practitioners in any country working with EAL or ELL children, as it brings together the initial rationale for the inquiry and some of its most significant findings:

What We Can Learn From Listening to Our Students' Own Meaning-Making Process – A Teacher's Perspective

Many teachers and students across the country find themselves facing the same situation as Ryan and Ms. McDonald (the teacher) – they do not speak each other's language and the teacher is left operating within an educational system that takes a deficit approach to teaching ELLs – ELLs are regarded as being deficient in English and need to be 'caught up' with the rest of the students. In this kind of educational climate, it is easy for teachers to be concerned in the same way as Ms. McDonald, unsure of what their students may be capable of, and left with little but an AZELLA [AZ English Language Learners Assessment] score and their classroom observations to work with.

Even at a school like ours, where we take a balanced literacy approach, and strive to have literature discussions, we feel the pressure of high stakes testing and how such testing led to our former 'Underperforming' school label. As a teacher there, I always felt the yearlong pressure of needing to prepare the students to do well on the impending AIMS [Arizona's Instrument to Measure Standards] test. In order to assess where the students were in the months leading up to the AIMS, we took quarterly benchmarks to assess the children, and I often felt that these benchmarks, while certainly not valued as authentic assessments among the teachers at our school, hung over my head, precursors to the final 'judgment' of what my students knew or how 'well' I had taught them. We also used other performance-based assessments, but I think that even with these multiple measures, some of the abilities that our students possess went overlooked – especially since these multiple measures were still largely based on just reading and writing. Our study with wordless texts showed me that the students with whom we worked knew more than their AZELLA or AIMS scores said they did. When we gave them the opportunity to discuss a book that, by its very nature of being wordless, invited students' own interpretations, and to discuss that book in their native language, as well as English, then we were able to more fully see what they knew how to do.

Visual literacy is another literacy practice that we as teachers can incorporate to make connections between the literacy strategies that we teach, and the literacy strategies that the students already know. Ryan, Almah, and the other students in our study demonstrated this to be true by engaging in collaborative inquiry, in which they both explored the text's meaning and also created individual and group narratives for the story. Ryan, especially, is a great example of a student who was viewed by his teacher as having limited proficiency with reading, but, who, when given the opportunity, showed that he actually could be a sophisticated reader of a visual text.

As I participated reading and analyzing the transcripts of the discussions and reflected on the meaning-making strategies we were focusing on – the students' inquiry and 'diegetic border crossing,' I realized that the students were naturally making use of several comprehension strategies that we, as teachers, often plan to explicitly teach our students. As a teacher, I planned many lessons around the reading comprehension strategies of asking questions, making predictions, and making inferences. In writer's workshop, I taught lessons about helping readers get to know the story's characters by writing revealing dialogue and by inserting 'thought shots' or internal monologues for the characters they were writing about. Sometimes I struggled to find ways to make these concepts clear to my students. I modelled the strategies, and they practiced them, and we discussed them, but sometimes I wondered how meaningful such lessons were for my students.

Yet, in our discussions of The Arrival, the students were naturally utilizing these strategies as they worked together to make sense of what they saw in the pictures, and to co-construct the narrative by moving in and out of the text. They 'stepped out' to ask questions as they tried to understand the meaning of the pictures, and then they 'stepped back in' and continued in a more narrative style – utilizing such literary devices as third person, internal monologue, and dialogue. As Mackey (2003) puts it: 'The ability to move across fictional borders with flexibility ... is no small element in the making of a sophisticated reader' (p. 626). After listening to the students' responses to The Arrival, *I reflected that if I had focused first on eliciting these skills that my students already possessed, our learning experiences could have been much more meaningful.*

Perhaps because of the open and inviting nature of wordless picture books, and because of the open and inviting nature of our conversations, the students felt free to both figure out and create. We created a learning environment in which instead of expecting one 'right answer' the students learned to consider different alternatives and also where students could bring all of their resources to the table – their languages, their experiences, and their prior literary knowledge. While you can interpret written texts, I think sometimes it is harder for children, especially for recent immigrants, to look for clues in the written text because they have to 'read between the lines,' but with wordless picture books they can instead read 'between the pictures.'[5] *When students and teachers are engaged in this process of 'reading between the pictures' together, this can allow the teacher a clearer understanding of the literacy skills that their students already possess and how to build from there to help them expand their repertoires of meaning-making strategies.*

Sarah's reflection not only highlights the learning that is possible for students who read *The Arrival* in a supportive context and with the right mediation, but also highlights how important it is for teachers and facilitators to listen to their students and identify their strengths. The potential of the image-based strategies is only realized because these take into account the literacy knowledge that all children, regardless of background, bring with them to the classroom. Immigrant children come to classrooms with experiences of navigating a variety of texts and images from their environments; these wordless narrative and pedagogical strategies support readers as learners and meaning-makers because they provide spaces for this knowledge to emerge and be valued. Thus, working with the wordless texts offers teachers an opportunity to learn about the children's knowledge while expanding their repertoire of reading skills and strategies.

Finally, we want to mention some of the other work that has been done with *The Arrival* and which the GLW research team encountered during the course of the inquiry. These separate projects indicate that many other practitioners have recognized this text as being a rich source of material for a range of activities, including creative writing (e.g. Cliff Hodges, Binney and Evans, 2010). As part of drama and dance projects, *The Arrival* has been used in secondary schools in the UK. It has also featured during Refugee Week as a result of collaboration between libraries and museums. In another example from GLW, it was used as part of a project for transition from primary to secondary during which the deputy head teacher of a school created a visual journey of her own, based on Tan's use of textual fragments, to show the journey her grandparents made from Lithuania to Scotland. This included copies of a letter from her grandparents' parish priest in Lithuania, writing to explain that the birth certificates had been burned during the war. All the new-arrival children were invited to read the book and create similar visual representations of their own journey, which were presented to all the children arriving from primary school to emphasize the role of journeys in everyone's life.

Moving forward in each country

All the teams benefited from the process and findings of the inquiry, and they have built on them to move on to other areas of research and knowledge exchange.

Glasgow

In GLW, the research team was concerned that the findings of the Visual Journeys inquiry should have an impact at practitioner level, so efforts were made to embed the work in a range of professional development projects. The team gained funding from the Esmée Fairbairn Foundation to undertake a follow-up project: *Journeys from images to words: Examining the efficacy of visual meaning-making strategies in the development of inclusive communities of critical readers.* The team was keen to evaluate the image-based approach in a whole-class setting with children of mixed-ability literacy and language levels working with their own teachers. The project took place in two upper primary (ten- to twelve-year-olds) classrooms in GLW with a high multi-ethnic population, including asylum seekers and refugees. Workshops were held in collaboration with class teachers, EAL support teachers and members of the research team to plan and evaluate the sessions.

Three books were selected during the first workshop, which reflected the themes of migration and journeys and had different combinations of words and images: a picturebook, *The Rabbits* (2000) by John Marsden, illustrated by Shaun Tan; a non-fiction book with a balance of words and images, *Gervelie's Journey* (2008) by Anthony Robinson and Annemarie Young, illustrated by June Allen;

and a chapter book, all words, *Boy Overboard* (2002) by Morris Gleitzman. The teaching sessions were held in the mainstream classrooms with between 25 and 32 students. The evaluation methods included classroom observation, teacher interviews, focus groups with students and detailed analysis of book talk data as well as students' work. This project provided evidence on the use of the image-based strategies; developing intercultural understanding and empathy; building bridges between school and home community literacies; and developing a pedagogy for inclusion.[6]

It was found helpful to have a final group session after the paired and smaller group sessions to reflect on the project as a whole. Although these were not used as a form of assessment in this inquiry, these types of sessions can be extended to act as informal opportunities to review progress, in the way that student teachers are often encouraged to do during their training. These 'plenary sessions', as they are known in GLW, tend to include questions such as: What have we learned today that we didn't know before? What can we do now that we couldn't do before? What do we understand now that we didn't before? While the final plenary session may not be entirely about image-based strategies, the results of these strategies will provide other topics for discussion and teachers can consider how well a book 'worked': Did it grab and hold their attention? Did it provoke strong feelings of a positive or negative kind? How well do they think the author/illustrator achieved their purpose? Are they left with any questions? How do they think their language skills have improved? Have their views been changed by the process? What kind of thing would they like to move on to now?

Other topics central to the books that formed the basis for the learning, in this case the topic of immigration, should be explored again to reflect on what has been learned and how their own identity and attitudes have been affected, and students should also be encouraged to articulate any benefits they have gained through their participation in the sessions.[7]

Barcelona

In Spain, three funded projects allowed GRETEL to work on picturebooks and immigration from 2006 to 2012. This allowed the group to achieve three different aspects: analysing the publications produced in response to the migration phenomenon; observing the use of literature in the Reception Classes of immigrant children; and making proposals for discussion and other school activities with picturebooks. This culminated in an international symposium on this topic ('La literatura que acoge: infancia, inmigración y lectura', Universitat

Autònoma de Barcelona, November 2011) and the publication of an edited book (Colomer and Fittipaldi, 2012) as well as numerous conference papers, journal articles and conference outreach.[8] The accumulated knowledge on picturebooks and on children's responses in literary discussions has now led the team to move their research to the emerging field of digital children's literature. A new funded project, *Children's and Youth's Digital Literature: Productions, Reading Uses, Reception and Pedagogical Practices* (EDU2011-26141), will allow the study of the characteristics of digital production and children's responses to digital reading, both in family and school contexts (in kindergarten, primary and secondary levels), as well as in both free reading situations and shared discussions.

Arizona

The researcher from the Arizona study is working now with Latino student populations in New York City. She is currently studying children's responses to literature in small-group literature discussions, including their discussions of wordless texts, as contexts that provide opportunities for students' expansive learning. This interest has extended to include students' meaning-making of the images and stories embedded in some digital games and online sites. The researcher created a bilingual after-school programme for second- and third-grade students to offer teacher candidates opportunities to support Latino children's biliteracy development through the use of children's literature and also online games that encouraged problem solving. The theory of Expansive Learning (Engeström, 1987, 2001; Sannino, Daniels and Gutiérrez, 2009) builds on key concepts proposed by Vygotsky (1987). Within this framework, reading and meaning-making are approached not as mainly individual accomplishments but as taking place within activity systems in which learning is mediated in many ways.

An important concept within Expansive Learning theory is the role of internal contradictions as a driving force of change and development, as invitations to expand and generate new knowledge. Approaching small-group literature discussions with immigrant children as an activity system in which new or expansive learning can come out of contradictions also builds on a view of children as holders and creators of knowledge (Delgado-Bernal, 2002). Additionally, extending the study of students' meaning-making of texts to include digital texts addresses the need to provide bilingual learners with an equal opportunity to acquire the same content and high-level skills that school reform movements advocate for all students (Working Group on ELL Policy, 2010, p. 2), which in the twenty-first century includes, among other things, access to technology and the development of multiliteracies.

Notes

1 Other approaches include the Visual Thinking Skills method that involves teacher-facilitated discussion of art images (http://www.vtshome.org/), and the approach taken within the Australian Curriculum where visual literacy is integrated in all literacy syllabus documentation across states and territories (the Australian Curriculum: English, http://www.australiancurriculum.edu.au/).

2 See the IBBY Silent Books Collection at http://www.ibby.org/index.php/.

3 There are also arguments for organizing students into heterogeneous groups; this will depend on the classroom context and the facilitator's knowledge of the group participants.

4 Parts of this section are based on a longer article on the teachers' role in this inquiry and also in the project that followed (McAdam and Arizpe, 2011). Pseudonyms have been used.

5 Sarah's reflection provided the title for the article co-authored with the researcher (Martínez-Roldán and Newcomer, 2011). For reasons of space her reflection could not be included in that article in its totality.

6 The project was awarded the 2013 BCF/BERA/Routledge prize for joint development work between schools and universities. More detailed information on this project can be found by visiting the website at www.journeys-fromimagestowords.com/.

7 The work also fed into the Comenius project *Portfolio of Integration* and *Education for All* (2012), which funded the creation of courses and support networks for teachers across Europe working with new-arrival children to achieve their full educational potential (http://poiproject.org/download/17-Case-Study-Report.pdf).

8 www.gretel.cat/.

Coda: A (Visual) Journey to Italy

Giorgia Grilli and Marcella Terrusi

Having completed most of the research and analysis in Glasgow, Barcelona and Arizona, we were approached by two researchers from the University of Bologna who were keen to replicate the study in that Italian city. We welcomed them on board and proposed they added a chapter on their experience. Before describing their journey, a short section first provides a context for this work with immigrant children in Italy.[1]

The context of immigration in Italy

A changing profile

Like other European countries, Italy's migratory historical profile has been that of emigrants rather than immigrants. In the last decade, however, this profile has changed and, in spite of the economic crisis, Italy has become a major host country in Europe. The Italian National Institute of Statistics (ISTAT) struggles to monitor the situation but has provided some revealing statistics: in January 2011, foreign residents were 7.9 per cent, and 13.9 per cent of the total births in Italy in 2010 were babies born to foreign parents. Most of this foreign population lives in Northern and Central Italy.

Bologna is in Emilia Romagna, one of the regions in Italy with the largest presence of foreign citizens: in 2009, more than 500,000 foreign citizens lived in this region, 10.5 per cent of the total population in the region. The data also reflects the largest presence in Italy of 'foreign minors' who, even though they were born and raised in Italy, are not allowed Italian citizenship. During the first decade of 2000, a process of stabilization of immigration occurred, meaning that the presence of immigrants became less transitory. This stability has resulted in an increased need for educational services. From 2000 to 2010, for instance, the number of 'foreign' children attending infant school has increased more than four times (from 3.29 per cent to 13.15 per cent). In the academic year 2010/2011, the proportion of foreign students to the total amount of students has grown at every school level. In primary schools in particular, 9 of every 100 were foreign students.

Italian schools have had to adjust to this new reality of cultural pluralism. Many interventions, meant to promote integration and intercultural exchanges, have been developed over the last decades, but their complexity arises from the fact that they must accommodate pupils from over 200 countries, which is no easy task. Added to this, although in recent years there has been a decrease in newly arrived pupils, there has been an increase of second-generation 'foreigners', which also contrasts with the decrease of births from couples of Italian parents.[2] The government, having gathered an excessive concentration of foreign students in some territories, has attempted to obtain a more balanced distribution among schools of the same territory through a regulation that, from 2010, the number of pupils with non-Italian citizenship present in each classroom should not exceed 30 per cent of the total of pupils in the classroom; however, the limit can be raised or lowered according to the linguistic skills of the pupils. In state schools (the situation is different in private schools), at a national level, the percentage of classrooms with more than 30.0 per cent of foreign students is 5.3 per cent. Some of these pupils, though, were born in Italy and, removing these from the count, we obtain a reduced percentage, 1.7 per cent. It is also interesting to note how the higher the level of instruction, the higher the percentage of classrooms with more than 30.0 per cent of pupils born abroad: 0.6 per cent in primary school, 1.9 per cent in junior high school and 2.9 per cent in senior high school (Borrini and Di Girolamo, 2012).

The presence of foreign pupils varies in terms of their origin and distribution of the various ethnic groups. The citizenship of non-Italian students has been roughly consistent over the last few years with the biggest migratory influx from Romania, followed by Albania and Morocco. Among the students with non-Italian citizenship, one has to consider also the nomadic students, for example Rom and Sinti, who distribute themselves in a uniform way in different geographical areas.

The city of Bologna and the primary school 'Don Milani'

Bologna is the most populated city in Emilia Romagna, one of the most dynamic and productive regions in northern Italy. The largest immigrant community is Romanian, followed by the Moroccan, Albanian, Moldovan and Philippine communities. Other groups may have a lower percentage but have a meaningful role at social, cultural and economic levels; for example, the Eritrean and Ethiopian immigrant communities (Vieira and Zannoni, 2012). There are 112 immigrants' associations in the province of Bologna, some of which are part of a large Metropolitan Forum. There are also associations composed of the children of immigrants, committed to maintaining their specificity and diversity among other immigrants' associations, due to the divergence of their present conditions, backgrounds and expectations for the future. The network, called Rete TogethER, is very important for their actions and is coordinated collectively, including the virtual network presence (blogs, forums and groups on platforms such as Facebook).

Bologna is divided into nine districts, the largest of which is the Quartiere Santo Stefano that contains several schools. This project involved the primary school called Scuola Don Milani, which is part of a 'Didactic Circle' called XIII Circle and includes two other primary schools and two infant schools. In this Circle, in the year 2010/2011, there were 128 foreign pupils attending the three primary schools (17 per cent of the total). The largest group of immigrants was the Philippines (28 pupils) followed by Albania, Romania and Moldavia.

Scuola Don Milani was founded in 1974/1975 at the same time as the working-class neighbourhood where it is situated. The serious problems caused by the sudden massive immigration of the 1970s have eased off since then, and now many projects and actions actively aim to help immigrant children and their families to integrate and take part in the life of the community. These projects were conceived in accordance with the Education Office which, in its guidelines for the 'reception and integration of foreign students' states:

> School is in fact a central place for the construction and the sharing of common rules, as it can activate a daily life practice inspired by the respect of democratic forms of coexistence and, mainly, it can hand down the historic, social, legal and economic knowledge that is indispensable in the making of an active citizenship.[3]

The school is thus conceived as a place not only for learning but also as a space for exchange between families, children and teachers. Teachers are asked to pay attention to the so-called '*interlingua*' (Favaro, 2002; Pallotti, 2005; Adorno, 2006), which means literally 'language in between', in other words, a transitional Italian. The study of this interlanguage is important for the educational programming, because it allows for a personalized didactic approach. There is also a specialized professional devoted to the analysis of children's interlanguage, so that the proposal of projects can follow from this supervision. Projects include intensive Italian language workshops, but even these are insufficient to cover the general need.

In Don Milani, there is a 'Foreigners Project', conceived by the school itself and put into practice with its own (few) funds, which offers further help to foreign children by organizing them in groups according to their linguistic competence, for special activities. To assess which level a child belongs to, 'interlanguage' rather than age is taken into consideration. The XIII Didactic Circle is very active on these themes and there are mediators who coordinate all the work done in the field of immigration. They are not a compulsory presence but they are almost always there because they are considered very useful, for example, in meetings with the families, which are held as soon as a child enters the school in order to plan schoolwork, and Italian language courses for parents.

The school has created a network with other schools in the area and with the entire neighbourhood, in order to benefit from the intervention and assistance of an NGO (Amici dei popoli – Friends of the people). The aim of the network is to raise funds to help the children's families too, as in the case of another project financed by the Department of Equal Opportunities, which has the interesting title 'It's never too late to learn' (2011–13). The need to increase the possibilities of intervention, together with the high quality of the projects activated, expresses the desire of the region to really assist, integrate and value the presence of foreign citizens, starting from the children, and to consider the opportunities offered by immigration as stimuli to improve the school, and to think in innovative ways.

The severe cuts in funding to the Italian State School meant the Scuola Don Milani was grateful for a free offer of an activity specially directed at the school by academics. Reading promotion and addressing the themes of inclusion and immigration meant real, effective help for the teachers and families involved. Already alerted to paying full attention to the immigrant children in school, the teachers welcomed the proposal of a project on travelling through wordless or 'silent' books, as they are known in Italy.

Bewilderment, surprise and wonder in reading a 'silent book'

The 'visual journey' to Italy was born from a meeting held under the banner of both travel and reading, at the biennial IBBY (International Board on Books for Young People) conference in Santiago de Compostela in 2010. After hearing about the Visual Journeys project and talking to the researchers, we planned an Italian experience that would ideally build on and enhance the work being developed in the other countries involved. Two years later in London, at another IBBY conference, we met with the research groups again. This time, we had our own experiences and findings to share, on the crossing of boundaries between cultures, between pictures and words, between reality and imagination, and between childhood and the adult viewpoints.

We were excited about taking part in the project because the experience of working with immigrant children on a book that narrates 'migration' in such an original and fascinating way as *The Arrival* immediately offered an irresistible challenge. This challenge was inherent in our own interdisciplinary approach to studying children's books, which includes looking at the relationship between the collective imagination and children's imagination (Farnè, 2006; Grilli, 2006; Terrusi, 2012).

As a result of the involvement of the two researchers from the 'G. M. Bertin' Department of Educational Sciences of the University of Bologna, *The Arrival* and other wordless books entered this Italian school. The project initiated real and metaphoric journeys filled with surprises and valuable information on the condition of young immigrant readers, and the extraordinary possibilities offered by wordless books.

The active silence of a 'silent book'

In Italy, the almost oxymoronic expression 'silent book' emphasizes the creative, active and pre-eminent role of the reader who gives voice to the book through a 'reading event' in which the book becomes a catalyst. The wordless book presents a playground, a place that stimulates various methods of exploration and play for attributions of meaning and hermeneutical combinations. This space helps guide the readers in their understanding of how the text works, through the rhythm, the repetition of elements; the multiplication of details; and the construction of an internal grammar, which, by way of ellipsis and accumulation, finds a way to narrate a world that accepts its complexity as it tries to tell its tale. The wordless book has an active silence, perhaps similar to that of the therapist, a silence that produces language, listening, attention, vision, comparison and integration, when accepted as a place of educational relationships able to produce wonder and knowledge (Terrusi, 2013).

The silent books of our research thus came to an Italian school, but not to the desks of an ordinary classroom. Together with the teachers of two fifth-year primary-school classes, we identified eight children aged ten and eleven. We chose a special setting, that of the classroom usually adopted as the school theatre, with a giant screen which was used to project the pages. The chairs were arranged in a semi-circle and the atmosphere of the special event was very much

Figure 10.1 Group photograph

perceived and mentioned on several occasions by the children, who were very pleased to be able to leave their classes during normal school hours to take part. Six of the children selected corresponded to the sample of children who participated in the other countries, that is, who had emigrated from their home country and come to Italy halfway through their primary education (some in the second, some in the third and some in the fourth year). The other two children were born in Italy, one from a 'mixed' Italian-Thai couple and the other from Peruvian parents who had been in Bologna for some time. Both of these children had travelled extensively between countries to visit relatives. The teachers asked us to include them in the group because, in the case of the Italian-Thai child, he openly expressed feelings of being only half Italian, and bilingual (and, in his case, trilingual, given his parents communicate in English). In the case of the Peruvian girl, her difficulties in participating in the class context due to her extreme shyness were the reasons the teachers wanted to include her, as they hoped that an experience in a small group could help her to socialize more and give her an opportunity to express herself.

The stars of our journey were therefore:[4]

Gabriel (Moldova)
Nicolaj (Moldova)
Brixcio (Philippines)
Cynthia (Peru)
Alessia (Poland)
Shajjad (Bangladesh)
Joachim (Italy/Thailand)
Alessia (Italy/Peru)

After having been given formal consent by the children's parents to carry on our research, we introduced ourselves to the children as researchers from the University of Bologna and explained the project. We told the children that we would need to listen, observe and film them to see how they 'read' and interpreted some wonderful, mysterious books we would like to look at together. We told them that these books are usually not seen in primary schools and that they are books that tell stories only through pictures. The children willingly and responsibly agreed to the experience with a sense of great pride, and on several occasions they referred to their being part of a wider community of migrant children involved in the same research project in Glasgow, Arizona and Barcelona.

During the initial introductions, we worked out that the ten of us speak nine different languages: Italian, Spanish, English, Russian, Moldovan, Bengali, Thai, Filipino and Polish. We were therefore a group rich in language skills about to work with books that, from a linguistic point of view, have no readers who are privileged from the outset. This in itself was something that, unavoidably, and for these children in particular, never happened in the classroom.

We first focused on *Flotsam*, reading it in a single two-hour session, which offered a wealth of unexpected and surprising interpretations by the enthusiastic children. We then moved on to *The Arrival*, which was read over a period of five different two-hour sessions. A final session was held at the request of the children themselves to give them the opportunity to discuss their experience of the project and to present this book to their classmates, who were eager to find out what the eight lucky migrant children had been getting up to in all those hours they were out of the classroom.

'The Arrival' group conducted the reading entirely (with teachers and researchers in the 'audience'). They acted like the researchers had done (as in a role-play), seriously and jauntily posing questions and provoking a debate and a co-constructing meaning experience, as well as collecting proposals and leading the attention of the audience. They acted like expert guides, worked as a team, gave each other a role in the presentation and expressed their personal style. The other children confidently followed, enchanted: for the first time, the travellers had become the guides.

In leading the sessions, we aimed to promote the joint reading of the pictures and their possible meanings, stimulating the production of language from these wordless pages and reinforcing that which, very spontaneously, developed into the highly interesting co-construction of meaning, based on lively and active debate and discussion. By not providing any unequivocal, pre-set solutions, beyond the often deliberately ambiguous stimuli of the pictures themselves, the illustrators of the books helped produce interpretations achievable only through the building of hypotheses, the rejection of any that in retrospect were found to be weak or contradictory. This process led to the production of explanations that were coherent and convincing for everyone, right up to the final epilogue, which was also fully open to interpretation. A central role in the experience was played by the active interpretation of the child-reader (Eco, 2002), a reader who, in this experience, proved to be rich in surprising attention, curiosity, creativity, breadth and wealth of different shades of understanding of the world and of the way in which narration works, even without words.

The children showed their full awareness, for example, of the fact that reading a picturebook implies the freedom – and indeed the need – to go backwards and forwards, returning to look at previous pages in the light of new discoveries made later on, guessing meanings from the narrative sequences often beyond the single pages or spreads we focused on during each session. They repeatedly asked to go back to a particular page, to look again at something that had stuck in their minds and which seemed to be connected to something that came later, or the meaning of which was revealed by the logical combination triggered by its position in a sequence. Moreover, again in terms of the workings of narrative, we were also surprised at the ability, indeed almost the predisposition, of the children in understanding the 'rhythm' of the narration in the way the author had arranged it. This involved deliberately using a certain type of composition, a succession of frames, some small, some large, in any case varying, all punctually 'read' by the children when it came to the verbal description of the pictures, with a rhythm suited to the compositional choice – rapidly, where there was a long sequence of small vignettes, slower when the frame was wider, with different pauses, that is, generally according to the importance each picture apparently held. As audio recordings show, the 'score' of the page very precisely counterpointed the 'punctuation' of the children's voices explaining, by changing rhythm, what they think is happening in each page.

Sharing experiences of migration

Among the various working methods proposed, we also provided the children with photocopies of some pages of the book where we covered the contents of the various vignettes and left only the frames visible. The distributed sheets presented different types of page sections, including some of the cover (of which we also covered over the central image and left only the frame visible). We invited the children to take as many sheets as they wished (filled with frames of different sizes, variously distributed and with the empty centres to be filled) to build their own story told in pictures of their own 'arrival' in Italy. For this activity, we provided the children with some of their own photographic portraits taken during previous sessions. The photographs were in black and white and were printed on sepia paper. The comparison of their own photographs printed on paper similar to that in the book, and in black and white, like the pictures in the book, was an exciting experience for them, probably because they are not very familiar with printed photographs (being more used to digital ones). Seeing their own photos, and on a type of support that somehow made their image more special, was a source of amazement for them. They asked us for more copies of the photos, and were very pleased to have their pictures taken, and to be recognized and set on paper, in some way 'narrated' in pictures by our photographer.

All the children wanted to glue their own portraits on to the page that represented the book cover, thus placing themselves in the shoes of the lead character. However, it was not easy for them to arrange the story of their own journey (or journeys) of immigration using pictures. Not all the children spontaneously wanted to share their own stories with the others, partly due to the insecurity of their own graphic skills, partly due to the high emotional charge of the narrated events (in almost all cases there were tears, hugs and stories of suffering). Despite this, we saw how the children used some of the narrative strategies applied to visual images and graphic composition used by Tan, such as the zoom feature on some vignettes, the dedicated use of frames (e.g. dark for flashbacks), or a symbolic image replacing the realistic narration of a highly dramatic situation.

From the point of view of the contents of the research, we were very touched by the immediate involvement and intimate participation of the children in a

Figure 10.2 Cynthia's graphic strip

story that, from the cover page onwards, is seen by them unequivocally as a story of travel and migration. A story not only of separation, suffering, uncertainty and fatigue, but also of surprise, wonderment, adventure, mind-opening and a meeting with new things. In this sense, the animal that accompanies the traveller on the cover is immediately spotted by the children, who are incredibly curious, fascinated and reassured by it; its presence dilutes the sadness evoked by the image due to the suitcase, the bent head and the dark colours. During the story, the author continues to add strange, incongruous objects, different from those known in our own world, which, like the animal, arouse curiosity, sympathy and a sense of fun and affection in the children, along with positive feelings of openness and the desire to get to know the new world better.

The personal experience of the journey, of our readers' own migration, immediately became a fundamentally important issue, and this was clear from their ability to give a name to all the elements that are progressively linked to journeys of this kind and which allude to the possible causes underlying similar departures. For example, the children immediately saw a detail not particularly highlighted by the author: the woman's hand holding that of the man preparing the suitcase, almost as if to say '*don't leave!*', to use Gabriel's words, when there is no doubt, however, that he *must* leave. As to the possible causes behind this type of departure, the children immediately referred to poverty, the need to work or some kind of political danger. Our readers were also quick to note, as the story unfolds, those objects alluding to a special (and certainly not a touristic) journey, even if there are no specific signals to this regard: the passport, the residence permit, the money put to one side, the map used to find one's way, the dictionary, the indecipherable signs for those coming from outside – '*once my dad lit a cigarette in a place where there was a no smoking sign because he didn't know what it meant*', said Shajjad, apparently still shaken by that event.

Communication and co-construction of meaning

During the reading, the different communication styles of the children and their different interpretative approaches also came to the fore. Gabriel gave a theatrical voice to the characters, often using direct speech to make them interact according to the indications of the pictures. Shajjad, on the other hand, was strongly driven to autobiographical narration, describing himself, his family, his country, with anthropological finesse, in the situations he recognized (for example, the segregated areas of men and women on the ship). Initially, Brixcio ignored the hypotheses offered by his classmates, but progressively learned to keep them in mind and in the end took them on board as his own. Nicolaj systematically tended to assume the interpretations of the others and propose solutions based on compromise and mediation, which he offered politely, always mentioning the authors of the various options, which he had listened to carefully.

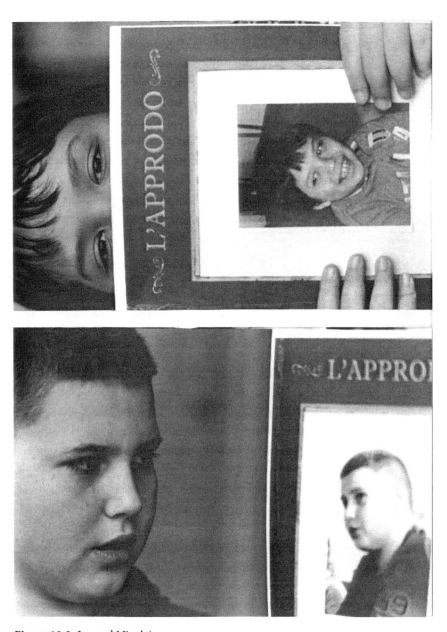

Figure 10.3 Joe and Nicolaj

There also appeared to be a difference in gender, in the less exasperated, more patient approach of the girls and, concerning the contents, in their greater capacity to hypothesize imaginative, metaphoric, symbolic levels of representation. For example, when the lead character finally reaches what seems to be a hotel in the new country, and his suitcase shows not only his folded belongings but also a woman and a girl in a small three-dimensional image, the girls interpreted this as an expression of what the man is imagining or remembering, an evocation of what he has left behind. This hypothesis left the boys speechless, caught off guard, and, in admiration at the idea, they let off cries of amazement: 'wooow!' Anchored as they were to an object-based rather than symbolic representation, at most they had linked the image to the presence of an open pop-up book in the traveller's suitcase. From the wealth of these different approaches, a co-construction of meaning (Pontecorvo, 1999; Pontecorvo, Ajello Messina and Zucchermaglio, 2004) was built, a truly surprising result, given the depth and breadth of options and alternatives offered during the process of negotiation.

A final meeting was arranged because the children insistently asked for it, even though we had finished reading the book with them. In this meeting, they wanted to show their classmates the book they had worked on so passionately and for the occasion they became the presenters, demonstrating – in a very impressive and at times entertaining manner – their acquired ability to work openly and systematically to welcome the hypotheses of each one of their classmates, to facilitate different proposals, to enhance the dignity of every contribution, and to promote negotiation (for example, often using the adjective 'possible' in considering the various interpretations of their classmates). What also came through from this experience, above and beyond the rest, was the children's acquired style of mediation, collaboration, open-mindedness towards the others and their participation in a joint project and a joint construction of meaning, which is naturally a value in its own right, as well as an element of education to citizenship. This experience of wordless book reading, targeting not the ability to technically decipher language (literacy) but rather the implementation of the whole range of knowledge involved in understanding what one sees, revealed itself as an extraordinary occasion for relationships, where identities could reveal themselves beyond pre-set paths, and participation allowed each person to assume a role or a communication style that was both personal and suited to the group.

One of the things that struck us most during this visual journey with the children was their extraordinary ability to capture even the slightest detail in the illustrations, using them to formulate coherent, solid hypotheses. Cynthia noted how the strange 'lift' the main character rides in has small wings in different positions, whether in flight or at rest. In the sequence of frames in which the man's documents are stamped, Joachim noted how the officials' cuffs are different, which not only means that many stamps were needed but also that the document passed through different hands and different offices. The similarities between faces and physiognomies are seen as a clue to possible stories, with the same open-mindedness reserved for the attempts to decipher the letters in the different alphabet that appears in some points of the book. The children start from the hypothesis that there is a guiding thread: they trust the author and Tan knows he can trust their attentiveness.

Thanks to this surprisingly attentive reading, we are led to reflect on how clearly Tan is able to represent the world as children see it. For the children, the pictures include nothing that is purely decorative, not even that which could seem a 'gratuitous' gallery of clouds arranged in order on a double-page spread, which for us researchers was simply poetic. The children, on the other hand, instantly linked them to the initial endpaper of the book, composed in the same manner but in that case with a gallery of human portraits (the same number as the clouds, they pointed out). The children told us that those clouds certainly represent the 'skies of the travellers', the weather in their own countries, or their souls, state of mind, the landscape of their interior contemplation ... For the children, everything contributed to constructing and describing the profound meaning of the story and the emotions tied to it.

Helping others finding their own way

In reading this wordless book, the children could talk about themselves while they talk of someone else, a different person who goes through what they know so well (loss, homesickness, isolation, disorientation), something that can be painful but which in the pages of this book slowly begins to make sense, and in the end also offers a clearer meaning to their own experience. The complicity emerging between the work – the vision – of the artist and the children is surprising, how they are able to tune into the figurative and compositional choices, understand them and give them full meaning, at times so far as to make *them* become the mediators. Where this complex book can easily disorient the adult, who may feel uncomfortable with the ambiguous images, our group of child-readers showed themselves willing to give unerring credit to the author because stories, in their eyes, have to *make sense*, whether they are told in words or only in pictures.

There was only one part of the book that the children initially found difficult to justify, narratively speaking: the end, where we see the traveller's daughter who, also having reached the new country and now an expert in navigating its streets, gives directions to a young woman who has evidently just arrived and who can't find her way. For some of our readers, particularly for Shajjad, the

Figure 10.4 Cynthia and Brixcio

book could have and perhaps should have ended a few pages earlier, when the character is reunited with his family in the new country (*'that's the real happy ending!'*), a moment that thrilled the children so much, after the pain of separation shared so empathetically for many pages, that they exploded in cries of joy. But

Tan is a sophisticated author, never banal, and to what the children have acknowledged as a good 'ending' he adds a tail, which carries the story and its meaning on to a deeper level. The ultimate meaning of the book, described by the children in micro-interviews in which they had to briefly summarize it in one sentence, was for them that 'even foreigners in the end can give directions and help others to find their way' (Cynthia). The children imagine that even they will one day integrate into a new context and feel at 'at home', moving around confidently and actively being of assistance.[5]

While Tan underlines how the condition of being 'foreign' is that of man in a universal sense, the children – not only as migrant children, but first and foremost as children – were able to identify themselves with that condition. Children in our world are always like Alice in Wonderland; in the same way as the traveller in *The Arrival*, they are thrown by need into a world that they cannot decipher. Growing up means learning to find our way, beginning to feel at home in a place that, when we are children, we have just reached, and makes us feel disorientated.

Alternative paths to learning

As far as the desires of the children are concerned, in their summing up at the end of the meaning of the story and also of the research experience as a whole, we were greatly surprised by the fact that they repeatedly underlined how useful it had been for them to learn new words in Italian. Throughout this project, and thanks to the constant exchange of ideas (ideas that were all expressed out loud and refined during the collective work to define the meaning), the children realized that they had enriched their own vocabularies, exposed as they had been to the expression of alternatives, synonyms and explanations posed by themselves and others. The more extreme the 'silence' of the pages, in terms of the verbal text, the greater the need to produce language (Faeti, 2005). It is as if language exploded, faced with the very stimulating complexity of pictures for which no textual indication was given. We had not set ourselves an educational objective of this kind – to promote the learning of the Italian language. However, the production of language that a wordless book helps to release, in a situation in which the children talk among themselves, with a minimum of discreet coordination by the researchers, confirms this as an excellent way of helping them to learn new words, to improve their Italian language.

Other results emerged from this experience, which could not be expressed by the children as they were not wholly aware of them during the initial phases of the work but which were reported to us by their teachers, in a final session with

Figure 10.5 Gabriel and Shajjad

them. First of all, they reported on the improvement of their self-esteem, which had a positive effect on their attitude to participation and performance in class. The possibility of participating in a group in which both the cognitive and imaginative personal interpretations of each person were enhanced literally 'opened' up the children in many directions, allowing them to launch into hypotheses, phrases, expressions, attempts to explain things and to make themselves understood. In the wordless book, progress is made slowly, and Italian native speakers, whether adults or children, are no more privileged in digging to come up with meaning. Italian was not present in the form of a written text and was not the aspect about which they were being assessed, but other competences were discovered in the children. One example among the many was when the children were talking about the woman who recalls the reasons she was forced to flee her country, and we see her as a child, forced to work in a factory, the victim of the abuse of power in which she has her book taken away and Nicolaj explains the hypothetical reasons of that gesture: '*I think they took her book away because if you study you are more intelligent, and this could be very harmful to this factory.*' '*Harmful in what way?*' we ask. '*They could be reported?*' he guesses. How many competences does the child who is able to say these things – in an imperfect Italian – possess? Political, intellectual, cultural, sociological, legal, ethical competences. School, which often evidently avoids asking children to express hypotheses or opinions because knowledge is in some way codified and has to be learned and demonstrated as such, risks not listening to what the children have to say, not knowing them truly with all that they already know, understand and think. It is fascinating to listen to what children already know, think or understand, both when it corresponds to what we adults also think and when it catches us off guard for how different it is.

The teachers were surprised when reading the materials produced in the children's recordings, learning which child showed most interest, concentration or participation in the work done during our visual journey. Gabriel, for example, untiring launcher of hermeneutical proposals concerning Tan's book, was usually considered to have difficulty in being involved in and attentive to class activities. The teachers were also surprised at Alessia, who was so shy at the start of this experience, but left it full of enthusiasm, ready to offer hugs to the new friends she had made in the group, and was more self-confident and curious about new opportunities for discussion. For the teachers, the increased interaction of these children with their classmates and greater confidence in their own ideas were immediately noted in the classroom. But it was also and above all the realization of the risk of losing something very intense and important for these children who do not master the Italian language so well, something about their being persons in their own right, that led the two extremely enthusiastic teachers, Giusi and Katia (who were always very positive towards this experience), to think about working on their own with the children on the opportunities offered by wordless books. It appeared clear that there was nothing better than a wordless book to place all readers on the same plane and facilitate the emergence of competences that otherwise the school does not notice or promote. These are competences that do not necessarily coincide with school performance in the strict sense of the word, but which, where developed, can indirectly have a positive influence. This is opposed to the more typical curricular work, in which non-native-speaking children are obviously at a disadvantage and are often wrongly considered more limited (Rosenthal and Jacobson, 1997).

Final thoughts

Taking part in a project like this, proposing it as an opportunity for learning and school activity, and venturing forth together with the children means embarking on a journey that questions the very concept of readers' skills. In this case, it suggested to us a competence that, understood according to its etymological root as a set of knowledge of the world and of oneself rather than as a collection of easily verifiable and quantifiable notions and information, becomes the deepest, sole vision of the world that each of us, from early childhood on, builds and continuously corrects (Juul, 2009). It is a vision in which the collective imagination is reflected and reinterpreted, a predisposition to filter stories, experiences, hopes and dreams in a personal way, a place of constantly evolving knowledge and vocabulary. Competence in its deepest sense has to do with the whole of us as persons. Understood as such, competence may not be easy to explain or to assess, but it can definitely be brought out and revealed by our reading of the words and images of art, of literature, of books, and also and especially of wordless books, in the interpretation of which much more of us is at stake than a simple reading ability.

A re-discussion of this term 'competence' emerged above all when the collected data was being processed: many of the children's expressions in fact belong at the same time to several categories listed for observation in the research protocol, for example, they may refer to anthropological knowledge and personal experience, or there may be inferences and mediations that result from a combination of different levels of knowledge and experience. Intertextual competences, for example, emerged immediately when, observing the variety of faces portrayed in the endpages of the book, the children had no doubt that these are travellers, but among them they thought they recognized Bin Laden, Frankenstein and Johnny Depp, citizens of the world and of the imagination. In this recognition, we see the children's need to make the unknown known.

Pictures, particularly in wordless books, produce language and stimulate interpretations that dig into the interior wealth of competences. They are able to open windows on the world told and represented by the author, but also on the worlds of the readers. In schools, they can be a source of surprise in their ability to mediate relationships, overcome stereotypes, turn the tables on the allocation of roles and offer unique opportunities for knowledge between teacher and pupils. In *Flotsam*, the readers begin to develop hypotheses, because the method is that of finding the clue, in a way incarnated by the book's lead character who likes to look at things carefully. He takes a magnifying glass and a microscope to the beach, explorer's tools that show that he is not one to stop at that which is only apparently invisible. The relationship with the invisible, the ineffable, is a pedagogically interesting lesson, which finds grounds for experience in other wordless picturebooks such as those by Iela Mari, Barbara Lehman, Istvan Banyai and others by Wiesner.

Certainly, one problem is raised in the reading of wordless books: with no written text, educators and teachers may fear not being able to punctually support or verify the children's understanding of the text. Of course, in the complexity of comprehension, which must, by obligation, be also interpretation, an active role is played by many elements, including inference. Concerning the grammatical or syntactic arrangement of a sentence, in which logical connections are expressed more or less clearly by punctuation and pronouns, in the pictures of wordless books, other aspects play equally effective roles in communication, such as the arrangement and size of the objects or the division of the page, which, as we have seen, creates scores that are similar to punctuation. The sequential structure, also used in cartoons and in films, places the elements of a visual discourse in a contiguous relationship, in sequence or repetition, guiding inferences through a more or less symbolic language and through the combination of ambiguous stimuli, which are clarified in their mutual relationship and in the action of memory and selective attention.

The reading of pictures is always an iconographic and iconological reading: they must be seen and interpreted; they demand that the reader accepts both form and meaning; they evoke the production of an overall meaning. The children spontaneously applied both iconographic and iconological analysis to their collective reading of the wordless book; they noted the tiniest details of both form and content; they produced hermeneutics, experienced identification and reflection, found a place of expression and a playground for relating with others and with each other (Farnè, 2003).

Like the girls in the last picture of *The Arrival* and *Flotsam*, we hope that, along with the encounters of the other researchers and children described in the book, our experience can lead to many other experiences of reading, viewing and meeting other worlds, cultures and readers. Readers who, particularly if they are children, are endowed with the ability to look at things from a position of alienation, which, just as wordless picturebooks do, helps to look beyond the surface of things and make reality shine with wonder and amazement: dimensions that school and places of education in general should never forgo.

Notes

1 We are grateful for the information on this topic collected by Professor Antonio Genovese (University of Bologna), Federico Zannoni (PhD student in Intercultural Education) and Michela Minelli (responsible for Interlanguage projects in XXXIII Circle, Bologna).

2 There is a campaign currently active in the region called 'Writers with children' that sees authors of children's books promoting and sustaining the right for these children to be Italian. What is advocated with this campaign is the '*ius soli*', to use the Latin expression for this kind of right.

3 'Linee guida per l'accoglienza e l'integrazione degli alunni stranieri', Ministero dell'Istruzione, dell'Università e della Ricerca – Dipartimento per l'Istruzione, Direzione Generale per lo studente, Roma (2006).

4 These are the children's real names because they were keen for their names to appear in the publication. Parental consent for this was obtained.

5 This is similar to the experience of another Italian research group, again with primary-school children (although in this case not only migrant children) that read Tan's book, starting with the assumption of disorientation understood as a human condition in the universal sense (Negri, 2012).

Conclusion: Arriving and the Journey Ahead

In this inquiry, the affordances of wordless picturebooks, along with the collective meaning-making – both verbal and visual – with mediators and peers, provided paths for the children to 'cross the border' into the picturebooks. The challenging issues raised by migration and literacy education suggest that supporting children in making this journey across the boundaries that have been traditionally limiting for immigrants, making the most of the knowledge and experiences they bring with them, is a fundamental step in the direction of a more equal, inclusive and informed society.

Tan's final 'family home' image (with the family gathered around the table in their new home in Part VI) reveals much about the author's ideological stance towards the main themes of the book, as it suggests a departure from the assimilationist agenda for immigrants that anticipates racial and cultural erasure. Instead, it more closely reflects the concept of transculturation and critical multiculturalism discussed in Chapter 1, which sees people as creatively constructing newness, reconstructing themselves, and reconstructing culture (Bueno, 1996; Pérez, 1999; Botelho and Rudman, 2009). Interestingly, the researchers in Italy found that some of the children would have been content for *The Arrival* to end with this image. Together with the series of nine frames in the previous page, it mirrors two of the initial pages in Part I of the book. The nine frames, in particular, make almost exact reference to each other starting with the origami creatures; the clock or time-keeping gadget and the hat and scarf hanging on the pegs. Yet the differences are clear: there is plenty of food in the dish, the 'pot' and crockery are not cracked; there are no travel documents or suitcases, and instead in one of the frames there is a coin being put into an extended hand. These and other differences are also noticeable when comparing the full-spread images of the interiors: one seems to be the kitchen, the other is perhaps a dining room. While the objects are arranged in a similar way, they now tell a different story in the second image, indicating a settling down in relative comfort, safety and contentment. The expressions and body language of the characters, together with the presence of the daughter and a pet, confirms this is, as one of the boys in Bologna put it, '*the real happy ending*'.

This image was annotated by several children in GLW and they took great pleasure in comparing the objects on the shelf, recognizing the similarities and also wondering what some of the new objects might be. Józef's annotations are worth describing in detail because they communicate some of this pleasure and also because they show just how much he had entered into the spirit of Tan's narrative as well as into the exploration of migration, as promoted by the questions, discussion and image-based strategies. It includes comments such as '*the man has brought this from his country*', '*this is a picture that was at the start of the book*', '*this was not there at the start of the book*'. He also notes, with an arrow pointing at the table and writing in large letters, that '*the family has supper!!!!!*' The speech bubbles (and exclamation marks) that he includes reveal his perception of the general celebratory atmosphere created by Tan: '*Hello!!*' says the father; '*Hi daddy!!!*' says the girl; and '*can I have some food please!*' says the pet. The mother's speech bubble is also revealing and, although in the image her gaze is on the daughter, the question seems to be intended for her husband, the first to emigrate: '*What were you douing* [sic] *in your journey?*'

Józef also includes two 'jokes' on his annotation. One is actually a metafictional joke: he draws an arrow to the pet and writes, '*I think the guy found the creature on the cover*' and then draws a picture of the 'creature' next to this sentence. His drawing, however, makes it look like the 'creature' is swallowing the sentence, so there is an addition in brackets underneath: '*(and it want to eat this sentence)*'. Józef also shows his sense of humour, as well as his extension of the 'happy ending' in his second 'joke': the large drawing he does on the back of the annotation page is of the '*creature it's family*' (as he described it), complete with 'wife' (note the eyelashes) and 'baby' (see Figure 11.1).

While the children tended to focus on the objects and the family relationships and we cannot tell how far children got in their understanding of the more complex concepts of multi- and transculturation, the analysis of their discussion about these last pages of the book did reveal that some of the children had started thinking and wondering about these issues and not taking dominant discourses for granted. The following excerpt from the children in AZ, in which

Figure 11.1 József's drawing

the children are noticing the differences in the objects included in the 'family home' images, offers a glimpse into this process:

Toni: *Like right here, you know, they have a picture of a family* [flipping back to the back] *but right here it has like a boat* [flipping back to the beginning]. *It's like these same things, but like how they are in this world* [indicating the back page]. *From where they originally came* [indicating first page] *from where they are right now, 'cuz right here it had like a bird*

Mediator: *mm-hmm*

Toni: *And right here it has one of those little animals and everything is really different.*

[Children continue identifying the differences until Toni notices similarities across the two contexts.]

Toni: *One thing I've noticed is that it's the same . . . like this one and the other one, it's the same.*

Mediator: *Okay. So they're the same . . . so this scarf here, or whatever, I'm not sure what it is, but this one has a pattern and this one doesn't? Okay, anything else that's the same?*

Valeria: *The picture of the family.*

Toni: *Except this one looks like it's more zoomed out.*

Mediator: *Okay. It looks like it's more zoomed out . . . Why do you guys think that the objects on this page are different?*

Valeria: *'Cause um, 'cause they changed worlds.*
Toni: *It's like a new life.*
Valeria: *For them.*
Mediator: *Okay*
Toni: *but uh, but I think they're kind of just really staying the same . . . it's them?*

From focusing on the similarities and differences between the objects from the two countries and noticing the compositional effects (zooming), these children moved to thinking of these images as a metaphor of how the immigrants' lives might have changed. But even then, at the end, Toni wondered if the immigrant family had really changed or stayed the same, an open question without a definitive answer, suggesting a sophisticated and complex thought regarding the impact of immigration on identity, which invites further inquiry.

Embracing change is an important aspect of Tan's work, as he expressed in the 2012 IBBY Congress:

> I think good stories are those that teach us to expect these changes, to embrace new and unknown things with *empathy, curiosity* and *imagination*, rather than hope everything will stay the same and that the world will continue to be 'normal' and understandable. (Tan, 2012, p. 30)

The children in the excerpt above seemed ready to accept change but were also ready to engage in new inquiries and new learning. Like any other serious work of literature, *The Arrival*'s aim is not to offer responses to questions but to present an experience in which the reader can gain insights into the complexities of life, into their own life or others' lives, and, in this case, into the immigrant experience with all the uncertainties it implies. Likewise, our purpose in analysing and discussing some of the children's responses to the book was not to describe the 'real' immigrant experience or their level of comprehension of the text but to offer a glimpse into their transactions with the visual narrative. Although the implications for language learning pedagogy are also evident, our main goal was to show the potential of mediated discussions to support children's interpretative processes, especially in the case of immigrant children. The book became not only a welcoming and inhabitable 'borrowed dwelling' for the duration of the project but also allowed for 'a transformation of the emotions and feelings, a symbolized elaboration of the lived experience', to return to Petit's words in our Introduction. This connects to the idea of a 'fostering community' because, if adaptation is a major variable in immigrants' learning, the creation of community through the literature discussions could potentially contribute to this process.

As our Italian colleagues point out, Tan adds a finale to the story, which takes the story to a further level of significance. Not only does the little girl confidently navigate the streets, the shops and the new currency in order to buy the food her father requested, but she also willingly and ably gives directions to another new arrival in the final image in the book (see Figure 11.2).

This image, as Bradford argues,

> places the child at the centre of a negotiation between self and other, shows a solitary migrant beginning the process of settlement. The girl, herself once a stranger, has developed the understanding and empathy to place herself in the place of the woman and the capacity to reach out in help. (Bradford, 2011, p. 31)

It is worth repeating what one Italian child concluded: '*even foreigners in the end can give directions and help others to find their way*' (Cynthia).

Overall, the responses of the children, both immigrant and non-immigrant, confirmed what many adult scholars and Tan himself have asserted about the way that *The Arrival* invites readers to make the journey with the protagonist or at least empathize with him (and the other migrants in the inset stories). Our findings show that this is done through a 'hook', large or small, in the narrative, with which the reader identifies and on which he or she can hang his or her own memories or experiences, or sometimes those of family or friends. In making sense of the narrative, intertextual connections play a significant role, not only as immediate analogies and as social, cultural and historical landmarks, but especially as a way of recognizing diversity itself and developing intercultural competence. The visual techniques used by Tan helped scaffold the understanding of the sequence of images but also inspired more reflective responses about intentionality and readership.

Throughout the inquiry, it became evident that adult and peer mediation, situated within the contexts we created for the research, played a crucial role in the expression and development of response because of the social and cognitive processes involved when the child-reader, to repeat Aristotle's words, 'perceives the force of an inference drawn by another' (*Oxford English Dictionary*, online). It also became evident that even what seemed to be the simplest, most 'literal' type of response was a complex interpretative act, which involved the creative acts of retelling and inventing dialogue and parallel texts. These children became aware that, even with their differing language skills, they could make meaning by bringing their own knowledge and experiences to bear on the wordless narrative and thus fully participate in a meaningful literacy event, while at the same time

Figure 11.2 Confidently helping other new arrivals

extending those literacy skills in the new language. Finally, the response strategies that were based on the visual creativity of the children proved to be beneficial as they added to the understanding of the narrative but also provided a different medium for exploring and expressing response, as was also noted by some of the teachers.

While reading *The Arrival* certainly helped those who were not immigrants to understand some of the experiences and emotions of those who were, it was the conversations between peers, supported by the mediator, that placed the immigrants in a context where they could use their knowledge and experience to enhance their peers' learning. For example, in BCN, during a complex conversation about the title of the book in Spanish, *Emigrantes*, An You provided the reply to the mediator's question about why the protagonist is nameless: '*Porque es de cualquier emigrante, es cualquier emigrante*' [Because it's about any emigrant, he is any emigrant]. This idea, which identifies the man as a sort of 'universal immigrant', raises the discussion to a more abstract, intellectual level of understanding about image, literature and the concept of migration. As Campano and Ghiso point out, this book speaks to the identity of migrants as 'cosmopolitan intellectuals because they have developed the skills to orientate themselves in new spaces' and because they are 'uniquely positioned to educate their peers and teachers about the world' (Campano and Ghiso, 2011, pp. 165–6). We cannot but repeatedly stress the significance of our inquiry for confirming the view that immigrant children's education must abandon the substractive or deficit models and instead base itself on the recognition and inclusion of the strengths that these pupils bring to the classroom – in whatever country they happen to be.

What we as researchers learned from the discussion and creative responses of the children was that, just as there is not one category of immigrant, there is not one 'model' of data collection and analysis that can categorize the responses of groups of immigrant children. Our focus was on children's meaning-making and we worked within the same broad research paradigm but we learned it was essential to keep an open mind, to be adaptable and to engage in the transcultural research conversations in order to integrate different epistemologies and research practices in ways that have not been done before in the field of literacy and migrant children. We initiated a form of collaboration during which we all learned from each other and learned to negotiate as well. It was often a 'messy' venture, where interpretations sometimes clashed and metalevels of research were often discussed, but which resulted in the opening of new routes in each of the participating countries. Just as our methodology includes guidelines for image-based strategies to support the literacy of the immigrant child that can be reproduced in alternative ways according to particular contexts, the research design also provides a model for working with picturebooks and immigrant children, but one in which flexibility is inbuilt as different countries and groups of children require different approaches.

The idea of reading as a journey through the text has been used for centuries, as Manguel reminds us. In his exploration of this metaphor of the reader as traveller, he reveals how it usually refers to the mirroring of the experience of journeying through life and the experience of reading (Manguel, 2013, p. 20). As we have seen throughout this inquiry, this metaphor is particularly apt for those children who have undergone a significant geographical transition at a stage in their lives in which reading and learning are so crucial. We have argued that it is precisely because of this experience, and its many implications, that reading a wordless narrative can support them as meaning-makers of the text and of the world, by both valuing and extending this experience within a space that both welcomes and guides. While *The Arrival* is singularly apposite for looking at (literally and metaphorically) the idea of journeys, the findings from this inquiry suggest that other wordless picturebooks or graphic novels can provide similar opportunities for reflection on the ways in which readers navigate and respond to visual narrative, as long as the reading and the responses are approached in open, flexible and creative ways, such as those proposed by this inquiry.

The last voices we hear from this inquiry should be those of the children and we end with words from Glasgow that fill us with hope for the future:

Mediator: *Why do you think he* [Tan] *is telling us this story?*

Surayya (Pakistan): *Maybe to make people think more. Think about this – like other life. See, some people, they just live in their life, they don't care if anybody else. Maybe the author wants to show a care of, like, somebody else's life.*

[...]

Sara (Kurdistan): *I don't think it's just for people only that have moved. I think it's for everybody. Because to show the people that, like, how we care, we love each other, and like care of everybody. We don't care of just our family, we care of everybody else who's alive in this place.*

Appendix: List of Participant Children

Glasgow

Pseudonym	Country	Languages
Claude	Congo	French/Lingala
Ruby	Rwanda	Rwanda
Vassily	Siberia	Russian
Sunil	Sri Lanka/Italy	Tamil/Italian
Mazin	Somalia	Somali/Arabic
Nadia	Pakistan/Scotland	Urdu/English
Ladislav	Slovakia	Slavic
Surayya	Pakistan	Urdu
Dina	Pakistan	Urdu, Punjabi
Józef	Poland	Polish
Faisal	Pakistan	Urdu
Ali	Afghanistan	Urdu/Pashto/Punjabi
Sumi	India	Gujarati/Bengali
Hassan	Somalia	Somali
Sara	Kurdistan	Pashto
Sam	Scottish	English/Scots
Andy	Scottish	English/Scots
Morag	Scottish	English/Scots
Lily	Scottish	English/Scots
Jack	English	English

Barcelona

Pseudonym	Country	Languages
Paola	Peru	Spanish
Alan	Ecuador	Spanish
Beatriz	Bolivia	Spanish
Gisela	Bolivia	Spanish
Adrián	Bolivia	Spanish
Cristina	Peru	Spanish

Barcelona – *cont.*

Pseudonym	Country	Languages
Calin	Rumania	Romanian
Naima	Morocco	Arabic/French
Carles	Catalonia	Catalan/Spanish
Emma	Catalonia	Catalan/Spanish
Hilda	Catalonia	Catalan/Spanish
Xavier	Catalonia	Catalan/Spanish
Andreu	Catalonia	Catalan/Spanish
Carolina	Catalonia	Catalan/Spanish

Other students from Barcelona who participated in groups using *The Arrival*:

Pseudonym	Country	Languages
Rodrigo	Peru	Spanish
Denis	Bolivia	Spanish
An You	Catalonia – China	Chinese – Catalan/Spanish
Antonio	Spain (Málaga)	Spanish
Tania	Catalonia	Catalan/Spanish
Ana	Catalonia	Catalan/Spanish

Arizona

Pseudonym	Country	Language
Almah	Iraq	English/Arabic
Janice	Mexico	Spanish
Juan	Mexico	Spanish/English
Ryan	Mexico	Spanish
Toni	Mexico	Spanish/English
Viviana	Mexico	Spanish/English

Bibliography

Adorno, C. (2006), 'La lingua degli apprendenti dal punto di vista delle varietà di apprendimento'. In F. Bosc, C. Marello and S. Mosca (eds.), *Saperi per insegnare*. Torino: Loescher.

Allan, C. (2012), *Playing with Picturebooks: Postmodernism and the Postmodernesque*. New York: Palgrave Macmillan.

Allen, D. (1994), 'Teaching visual literacy – some reflections on the term'. *Journal of Art and Design Education*, 13/2, pp. 133–43.

Alvermann, D. and Hagood, M. (2000), 'Critical media literacy: Research, theory, and practice in "New Times"'. *The Journal of Educational Research*, 93/3, pp. 193–205.

Anstey, M. and Bull, G. (2004), 'The picture book: Modern and postmodern'. In P. Hunt (ed.), *International Companion Encyclopedia of Children's Literature*, 2nd edn. Abingdon: Routledge, pp. 328–39.

Arizpe, E. (2009), 'Sharing visual experiences of a new culture: Immigrant children in Scotland respond to picturebooks and other visual texts'. In J. Evans (ed.), *Talking Beyond the Page: Reading and Responding to Picture Books*. Abingdon: Routledge, pp. 134–51.

Arizpe, E. (2010), '"It was all about books": Picturebooks, culture and metaliterary awareness'. In T. Colomer, B. Kümmerling-Meibauer and C. Silva-Díaz (eds.), *New Directions in Picturebook Research*. New York: Routledge, pp. 69–82.

Arizpe, E. (2013a), 'Meaning-making from wordless (or nearly wordless) picturebooks: What educational research expects and what readers have to say'. *Cambridge Journal of Education*, 43/2, pp. 1–14.

Arizpe, E. (2013b), 'Meaning-making from wordless picturebooks: An overview of historical, critical and educational perspectives'. In B. Kümmerling-Meibauer (ed.), *Aesthetic and Cognitive Challenges of the Picturebook*. London: Routledge.

Arizpe, E. and McAdam, J. (2011), 'Crossing visual borders and connecting cultures: Children's responses to the photographic theme in David Wiesner's *Flotsam*' *New Review of Children's Literature and Librarianship*, 17/2, pp. 227–43.

Arizpe, E. and Styles, M. (2003), *Children Reading Pictures: Interpreting Visual Texts*. London: Routledge.

Arizpe, E. and Styles, M. (2008), 'A critical review of research into children's responses to multimodal texts'. In J. Flood, D. Lapp and S. Brice Heath (eds.), *Handbook of Research in Teaching Literacy through the Visual and Communicative Arts*, Vol. II. London: Routledge, pp. 365–75.

Arizpe, E., Farrell, M. and McAdam, J. (eds.) (2013), *Picturebooks: Beyond the Border of Art, Narrative and Culture*. London: Taylor and Francis.

Arshad, R., Diniz, F., Kelly, E., O'Hara, P., Sharp, S. and Syed, R. (2005), *Minority Ethnic Pupils' Experiences of School in Scotland*. Edinburgh: Scottish Executive Education Department.

Atkinson, P. and Delamont, S. (2005), 'Analytic perspectives'. In N. Denzin and Y. Lincoln (eds.), *The Sage Handbook of Qualitative Research*. Thousand Oaks: Sage, pp. 821–40.

Aud, S. and Hannes, G. (eds) (2011). *The Condition of Education 2011*. IES National Center for Education Statistics. NCES 2013-033.

Aud, S. and Hannes, G. (eds) (2013). *The Condition of Education 2013*. IES National Center for Education Statistics. NCES 2013-037.

Bader, B. (1976), *American Picture Books: From Noah's Ark to the Beast Within*. New York: Macmillan.

Banks, M. (2001), *Visual Methods in Social Research*. London: Sage.

Banks, J. and Banks, C.M. (eds.) (2001), *Handbook of Research on Multicultural Education*. San Francisco: Jossey-Bass.

Bearne, E. (2009), 'Multimodality, literacy and texts: Developing a discourse'. *Journal of Early Childhood Literacy*, 9/2, pp. 156–87.

Beckett, S. (2012), *Crossover Picturebooks: A Genre for All Ages*. London: Routledge.

Bednall, J. and Cranston, L. with Bearne, E. (2008), 'The most wonderful adventure … going beyond the literal'. *English Four to Eleven*, 32, pp. 19–26.

Bellorín, B. and Silva-Díaz, M.C. (2011), 'Reading mental processes in *The Arrival*'. *New Review of Children's Literature and Librarianship*, 17/2, pp. 210–26.

Berninger, M., Ecke, J. and Haberkorn, H. (2010), *Comics as a Nexus of Cultures: Essays on the Interplay of Media, Disciplines and International Perspectives*, Vol. 22. Jefferson, NC: McFarland.

Bhaba, H.K. (1994), *The Location of Culture*. London: Routledge.

Bland, J. (2013), *Children's Literature and Learner Empowerment*. London: Bloomsbury Academic.

Bloome, D. and Egan-Robertson, A. (2004), 'The social construction of intertextuality in classroom reading and writing lessons'. In N. Shuart-Faris and D. Bloome (eds.), *Uses of Intertextuality in Classroom and Educational Research*. Greenwich (USA): Information Age Publishing.

Boatright, M. (2010), 'Graphic journeys: Graphic novels' representations of immigrant experiences'. *Journal of Adolescent and Adult Literacy*, 53/6, pp. 468–76.

Borrini, C. and Di Girolamo, P. (eds.) (2012), *Gli alunni stranieri nel sistema scolastico italiano a/s 2011–12*, MIUR, Ministero dell'Istruzione, dell'Università e della Ricerca, Direzione Generale per gli Studi, la Statistica e per i Sistemi Informativi – Servizio Statistico.

Bosch, E. (2010), 'El juego de Pululeer y juegos para releer'. *Bloc. Revista Internacional de Arte y Literatura Infantil*, 6, pp. 6–21.

Bosch, E. (2013), 'Texts and peritexts in wordless and almost wordless picturebooks'. In B. Kümmerling-Meibauer (ed.), *Aesthetic and Cognitive Challenges of the Picturebook*. London: Routledge.

Bosch, E. (in press), 'Texts and peritexts in wordless and almost wordless picturebooks'. In B. Kümmerling-Meibauer (ed.), *Picturebooks: Representation and Narration*. London: Routledge.

Bosch, E. and Duran, T. (2009), 'Ovni: Un álbum sin palabras que todos leemos de diferentes maneras'. *Anuario de investigación en literatura infantil y juvenil*, 7/2, pp. 39–52.

Botelho, M. and Rudman, M. (2009), *Critical Multicultural Analysis of Children's Literature: Mirrors, Windows, and Doors*. New York: Routledge.

Bourdieu, P. and Passeron, J.C. (1977), *Reproduction in Education, Society and Culture*. Beverly Hills: Sage.

Bradford, C. (2011), 'Children's literature in a global age: Transnational and local identities'. *Nordic Journal of ChildLit Aesthetics*, 2, pp. 20–34.

Brisk, M.E. and Harrington, M. (2006), *Literacy and Bilingualism: A Handbook for ALL Teachers*. Oxford: Psychology Press.

Bromley, H. (1996), 'Spying on picture books: Exploring intertextuality with young children'. In V. Watson and M. Styles (eds.), *Talking Pictures: Pictorial Texts and Young Readers*. London: Hodder & Stoughton, pp. 101–11.

Brooks, W. and Browne, S. (2012), 'Towards a culturally situated reader response theory'. *Children's Literature in Education*, 43/1, pp. 74–85.

Bueno, R. (1996), 'Sobre la heterogeneidad literaria y cultural de América Latina'. In J.A. Mazzoti and U.J. Zeballos-Aguilar (eds.), *Asedios a la heterogeneidad cultural: Libro de homenaje a Antonio Cornejo Polar*. Philadelphia: Asociación Internacional de Peruanistas, pp. 21–36.

Byram, M. (1987), *Cultural Studies in Foreign Language Education*. Clevedon: Multilingual Matters.

Byram, M. (1997), *Teaching and Assessing Intercultural Communicative Competence*. Clevedon: Multilingual Matters.

Byram, M. (2008), *From Foreign Language Education to Education for Intercultural Citizenship: Essays and Reflections*. Clevedon: Multilingual Matters.

Byrnes, J. and Wasik, B. (2009), 'Picture this: Using photography as a learning tool in early childhood classrooms'. *Childhood Education*, 85/4, pp. 245–8.

Callow, J. (2006), 'Images, politics and multiliteracies: Using a visual metalanguage'. *Australian Journal of Language and Literacy*, 29/1, pp. 7–23.

Campano, G. (2007), *Immigrant Students and Literacy*. New York: Teachers College Press.

Campano, G. and Ghiso, M.P. (2011), 'Immigrant students as cosmopolitan intellectuals'. In S.A. Wolf, K. Coats, P. Enciso and C.A. Jenkins (eds.), *Handbook of Research on Children's and Young Adult Literature*. New York: Routledge, pp. 164–76.

Campbell Hill, B., Johnson, N.J. and Schlick Noe, K.L. (eds.) (1995), *Literature Circles and Response*. Norwood, MA: Christopher-Gordon.

Candappa, M. with Ahmad, M., Balata, B., Dekhinet, R. and Gocmen, D. (2007), *Education and Schooling for Asylum-Seeking and Refugee Students in Scotland: An Exploratory Study*. Final Report. Edinburgh: Scottish Government. Accessed (10/1/2010) at http://www.scotland.gov.uk/Publications/2007/09/19133151/0.

Carrington, V. and Marsh, J. (2009), 'Forms of literacy'. Review for the Beyond Current Horizons Programme (Bristol, Futurelab). Accessed (6/1/2012) at www.beyondcurrenthorizons.org.uk/evidence/knowledge-creativity-and-communication/.

Cassells, J. (2006), *Effective Teaching and Learning in a Multi-Ethnic Education System*. Glasgow City Council.

Chambers, A. (1993), *Tell Me: Children, Reading and Talk*. Stroud: Thimble Press.

Christensen, P. and James, A. (2000), 'Childhood diversity and commonality: Some methodological insights'. In P. Christensen and A. James (eds.), *Research with Children*. London: Falmer, pp. 160–78.

Cliff Hodges, G., Binney, A. and Evans, E. (2010), *Planning for Innovation in English Teaching*. Leicester: UKLA.

Coatsworth, J.H. (2004), 'Globalization, growth, and welfare in history'. In M. Suárez-Orozco and D. Baolian Qin-Hilliard (eds.), *Globalization, Culture, and Education in the New Millennium*. Berkeley, CA: University of California Press, pp. 38–55.

Cole, M. (1996), *Cultural Psychology: A Once and Future Discipline*. Cambridge, MA: Harvard University Press.

Colomer, T. (1998), *La formación del lector literario. Narrativa infantil y juvenil actual*. Barcelona: Fundación Germán Sánchez Ruipérez.

Colomer, T. (2000), 'Aprendizajes literários en los libros para primeros lectores'. In *Saberes e práticas na formaçao de profesores e educadores: Actas das jornadas DCILM 2002*. Instituto de Estudos da Criança, Universidade do Minho, pp. 113–23.

Colomer, T. (2002), 'El papel de la mediación en la formación de lectores'. In T. Colomer, E. Ferreiro and F. Garrido (eds.), *Lecturas sobre lecturas*. México DF: Conaculta, pp. 2–29.

Colomer, T. (2005), *Andar entre libros. La lectura literaria en la escuela*. México: Fondo de Cultura Económica.

Colomer, T. (2012), 'La literatura que acoge: un proyecto de investigación en las aulas'. In T. Colomer and M. Fittipaldi (eds.), *La literatura que acoge: Inmigración y lectura de álbumes*. Barcelona: Banco del Libro–GRETEL, pp. 7–25.

Colomer, T. and Fittipaldi, M. (2012), *La literatura que acoge: Inmigración y lectura de álbumes*. Barcelona: Banco del Libro–GRETEL.

Coulthard, K. (2003), 'The words to say it: Young bilingual learners responding to visual texts'. In E. Arizpe and M. Styles (eds.), *Children Reading Pictures*. London: Routledge, pp. 164–89.

Crago, H. (1990), 'The roots of response'. In P. Hunt (ed.), *Children's Literature*. London: Routledge, pp. 118–30.

Crawford, P.A. and Hade, D. (2000), 'Inside the picture, outside the frame: Semiotics and the reading of wordless picture books'. *Journal of Research in Childhood Education*, 15/1, pp. 66–80.

Crouch, C. (2008), 'Afterword'. In J. Elkins (ed.), *Visual Literacy*. London: Routledge, pp. 195–204.

Cummins, J. (2000), *Language, Power and Pedagogy*. Clevedon: Multilingual Matters.

Cummins, J. (2001), *Negotiating Identities: Education for Empowerment in a Diverse Society*, 2nd edn. Los Angeles, CA: CABE.

Cummins, J. and Early, M. (eds.) (2011), *Identity Texts: The Collaborative Creation of Power in Multilingual Schools*. Stoke on Trent: Trentham Books.

Curriculum for Excellence (CfE), online at http://www.scotland.gov.uk/Publications/2009/10/16155220/13/.

Daniels, H. (2002), *Literature Circles: Voice and Choice in Book Clubs and Reading Groups*. Maine: Stenhouse Publishers.

De la Luz Reyes, M. (ed.) (2011), *Words Were All We Had: Becoming Biliterate Against the Odds*. New York: Teachers College Press.

Debes, J.L. (1969), 'The loom of visual literacy: An overview'. *Audiovisual Instruction*, 14/8, pp. 25–7.

Delgado-Bernal, D. (2002), 'Critical race theory, Latino critical theory, and critical race-gendered epistemologies: Recognizing students of color as holders and creators of knowledge'. *Qualitative Inquiry*, 8, pp. 105–26.

DfES (2002), *Supporting Pupils Learning English as an Additional Language: Revised Edition*. Annesley, Notts: DfES.

Driver, J. and Baylis, G.C. (1998), *Attention and Visual Object Segmentation*. Cambridge, MA: MIT Press.

Drury, R. (2007), *Young Bilingual Learners at Home and School*. Staffordshire: Trentham Books.

Eco, U. (2002), *Lector in Fabula*. Milano: Bompiani.

Education Department of Catalonia (2004), *Programma LIC. Llengua, Interculturalitat i Cohesió Social*. Barcelona: Generalitat de Catalunya.

Engeström, Y. (1987), *Learning by Expanding: An Activity-theoretical Approach to Developmental Research*. Helsinki: Orienta-Konsultit.

Engeström, Y. (2001), 'Expansive learning at work: Toward an activity theoretical reconceptualization'. *Journal of Education and Work* [Online], 14/1, pp. 133–56. Accessed (1/4/08) at Academic Search Premier http://www.library.dcu.ie/Eresources/databases-az.htm/.

Erickson, F. (1986), 'Qualitative methods in research on teaching'. In M.C. Wittrock (ed.), *Handbook of Research on Teaching*, 3rd edn. New York: Macmillan, pp. 119–61.

Eriksen, T.H. (2001), *Tyranny of the Moment: Fast and Slow Time in the Information Age*. London: Pluto Press.

Evans, J. (ed.) (2009), *Talking Beyond the Page: Reading and Responding to Picturebooks*. London: Routledge.

Evans, J. (2013), 'From comics, graphic novels and picturebooks to fusion texts: A new kid on the block!' *Education 3–13: International Journal of Primary, Elementary and Early Years Education*, 41/2, pp. 233–48.

Faeti, A. (2005), *Specchi e riflessi. Nuove letture per altre immagini*. Il Ponte Vecchio: Cesena.

Farnè, R. (2003), *Iconologia didattica. Le immagini per l'educazione: dall'Orbis Pictus a Sesame Street*. Bologna: Zanichelli.

Farnè, R. (2006), *Diletto e giovamento. Le immagini e l'educazione*. Torino: UTET Università.

Farrell, M., Arizpe, E. and McAdam, J. (2010), 'Journeys across visual borders: Annotated spreads of "The Arrival" by Shaun Tan as a method of understanding pupils' creation of meaning through visual images'. *Australian Journal of Language and Literacy*, 33/3, pp. 198–210.

Favaro, G. (2002), 'L'italiano L2 in azione: Esperienze, priorità, proposte'. In *Insegnare l'italiano agli alunni stranieri*. La Nuova Italia: RCS.

Fittipaldi, M. (2008), *Travesías textuales: Inmigración y lectura de imágenes*. Unpublished Master's thesis: Universitat Autònoma de Barcelona.

Fittipaldi, M. (2012), 'La categorización de las respuestas infantiles ante los textos literarios. Análisis de algunos modelos y propuesta de clasificación'. In T. Colomer and M. Fittipaldi (eds.), *La literatura que acoge: Inmigración y lectura de álbumes*. Barcelona: Banco del Libro–GRETEL, pp. 69–86.

Fleckenstein, K.S., Calendrillo, L.T. and Worley, D.A. (2002), *Language and Image in the Reading-Writing Classroom*. London: Lawrence Erlbaum.

Fransecky, R. (1969), 'Visual literacy and teaching the disadvantaged'. *Audiovisual Instruction*, 28/31, pp. 117–18.

Frey, N. and Fisher, D. (eds.) (2008), *Teaching Visual Literacy*. Thousand Oaks, CA: Corwin Press.

Garcia, E. (1988), *Effective Schooling for Language Minority Students*. Washington, DC: National Clearinghouse for Bilingual Education.

Gee, J.P. (2005), *An Introduction to Discourse Analysis: Theory and Method*, 2nd edn. New York: Routledge.

Ghiso, M.P. and McGuire, C.E. (2007), '"I talk them through it": Teacher mediation of picturebooks with sparse verbal text during whole-class readalouds'. *Reading Research and Instruction*, 46/4, pp. 341–61.

Gibson, M. and Ogbu, J. (1991), *Minority Status and Schooling: A Comparative Study of Immigrant and Involuntary Minorities*. New York: Garland Publishing, Inc.

Glasgow City Council (2007), *A8 Nationals in Glasgow*. Edinburgh: Blake Stevenson.

Glasgow City Council (2008), *Policy for Supporting Children and Young People with English as an Additional Language in Glasgow*. Glasgow City Council Education Services. Accessed (25/2/2011) at http://www.glasgow.gov.uk/.

Gleitzman, M. (2002), *Boy Overboard*. London: Puffin.

Gombrich, E. (1979), *Arte e ilusión. Estudio sobre la psicología de la representación pictórica*. Barcelona: Gustavo Pili. (1st edn.: *Art and Illusion: A Study in the Psychology of Pictorial Representation*. London: Phaidon, 1960.)

González, M.L., Huerta-Macías, A. and Tinajero, J.V. (eds.) (1998), *Educating Latino Students: A Guide to Successful Practice*. Lancaster, PA: Technomic Publishing Co.

González, N., Moll, L. and Amanti, C. (2005), *Funds of Knowledge: Theorizing Practices in Households, Communities, and Classrooms*. Mahwah, NJ: Lawrence Erlbaum Associates.

Goodman, K. (1969), 'Analysis of oral reading miscues: Applied psycholinguistics'. *Reading Research Quarterly*, 5/1, pp. 9–30.

Goodman, K. (1978), *Reading of American Children whose Reading is a Stable, Rural Dialect of English or Language Other than English*. Washington, DC: National Institute of Education, U.S. Department of Health, Education and Welfare.

Goodman, K. (1996), *On Reading: A Common-Sense Look at the Nature of Language and the Science of Reading*. Portsmouth, NH: Heinemann.

Graham, J. (1998), 'Turning the visual into the verbal: Children reading wordless books'. In J. Evans (ed.), *What's in the Picture?* London: Paul Chapman, pp. 25–43.

Graves, D.H. (1983), *Writing: Teachers and Children at Work*. Portsmouth, NH: Heinemann.

Gravett, P. (2005), *Graphic Novels: Stories to Change Your Life*. London: Aurum Press.

Gregory, E. (1996), *Making Sense of a New World: Learning to Read in a Second Language*. London: Paul Chapman.

Gregory, E., Long, S. and Volk, D. (eds.) (2004), *Many Pathways to Literacy: Young Children Learning with Siblings, Grandparents, Peers and Communities*. New York: Routledge.

Grilli, G. (2006), *Myth, Symbol and Meaning in Mary Poppins*. New York: Routledge.

Guasch, O. (ed.) (2010), *El tractament integrat de les llengües*. Barcelona: Graó.

Gutiérrez, K.D., Baquedano-López, P. and Tejeda, C. (1999), 'Rethinking diversity: Hybridity and hybrid language practices in the third space'. *Mind, Culture, and Activity*, 6/4, pp. 286–303.

Haddad, C. (2008), *Improving the Quality of Mother Tongue-Based Literacy and Learning: Case Studies from Asia, Africa and South America*. Bangkok: UNESCO.

Halliday, M.A.K. (1985), *An Introduction to Functional Grammar*, 1st edn. London: Arnold.

Heath, S.B. (1983), *Ways with Words: Language and Life in Communities and Classrooms*. Cambridge: Cambridge University Press.

Heath, S.B. (2006), 'Dynamics of completion: Gaps, blanks, and improvisation'. In M. Turner (ed.), *The Artful Mind: Cognitive Science and the Riddle of Human Creativity*. New York: Oxford University Press, pp. 133–50.

Hernández-Chávez, E., Cohen, A.D. and Beltramo, A. (eds.) (1975), *El Lenguaje de los Chicanos*. Washington, DC: Center for Applied Linguistics.

HMIe (2009), *Count Us In: Meeting the Needs of Children and Young People Newly Arrived in Scotland*. Livingstone: HMIe.

Hope, J. (2008), '"One day we had to run": The development of the refugee identity in children's literature and its function in education'. *Children's Literature in Education*, 39, pp. 295–304.

Hornberger, N. (ed.) (2003), *Continua of Biliteracy: An Ecological Framework for Educational Policy, Research, and Practice in Multilingual Settings*. Clevedon: Multilingual Matters.

Howard, E.R., Sugarman, J., Christian, D., Lindholm-Leary, K.J. and Rogers, D. (2007), *Guiding Principles for Dual Language Education*, 2nd edn. Washington, DC: Center for Applied Linguistics.

Hunt, P. (2011), 'The fundamentals of children's literature criticism: *Alice's Adventures in Wonderland* and *Through the Looking-Glass*'. In J. Mickenberg and L. Vallone (eds.), *The Oxford Handbook of Children's Literature*. Oxford and New York: OUP, pp. 35–50.

Hunter, L. (2011), 'The artist as narrator: Shaun Tan's wondrous worlds'. *Bookbird*, 49/4, pp. 10–16.

IBBY Silent Books Collection. Accessed (25/8/13) at http://www.ibby.org/index.php.

Ivanič, R. (2004), 'Intertextual practices in the construction of multimodal texts in inquiry-based learning'. In N. Shuart-Faris and D. Bloome (eds.), *Uses of Intertextuality in Classroom and Educational Research*. Greenwich (USA): Information Age Publishing, pp. 279–311.

Iser, W. (1978), *The Act of Reading*. Baltimore: Johns Hopkins UP.

Jett-Simpson, M. (1976), *Children's Inferential Responses to a Wordless Picture Book: Development and Use of a Classification System for Verbalized Inference*. Unpublished dissertation: University of Washington.

Jewitt, C. (2008), 'The visual in learning and creativity: A review of the literature'. A report for Creative Partnerships Arts Council. Accessed (20/5/13) at http://www.creative-partnerships.com/data/files/the-visual-in-learning-and-creativity-168.pdf.

Juul, J. (2009), *Il bambino è competente*. Milan: Feltrinelli.

Kapadia Bodi, M. (2008), 'Talking about immigrating: Adult immigrants read and respond to Shaun Tan's *The Arrival*'. Accessed (13/12/2012) at http://www.melissakapadiabodi.com/MKBTalkingaboutImmigrating.pdf.

Kauffman, G., Short, K.G., Crawford, K.M., Kahn, L. and Kaser, S. (1996), 'Examining the roles of teachers and students in literature circles across classroom contexts'. In D.L. Leu, C.K. Kinzer and K.A. Hinchman (eds.), *Literacies for the 21st Century: Research and Practice*. Chicago: National Reading Conference, pp. 373–84.

Kenner, C. (2000), *Home Pages: Literary Links for Bilingual Children*. Stoke-on-Trent: Trentham Books.

Kiefer, B. (1995), *The Potential of Picturebooks: From Visual Literacy to Aesthetic Understanding*. New Jersey: Prentice-Hall.

Kozulin, A. (1998), *Psychological Tools: A Sociocultural Approach to Education*. Cambridge, MA: Harvard University Press.

Kramsch, C. (1998), *Language and Culture*. Oxford: Oxford University Press.

Kress, G. and van Leeuwen, T. (1995), *Reading Images: The Grammar of Visual Design*. London: Routledge.

Kress, G. and van Leeuwen, T. (2001), *Multimodal Discourse: The Modes and Media of Contemporary Communication*. London: Arnold.

Kress, G. and van Leeuwen, T. (2006), *Reading Images: The Grammar of Visual Design*, 2nd edn. New York: Routledge.

Larrosa, J. (2002), '¿Para qué nos sirven los extranjeros?' *Educação and Sociedade*, 23/79, pp. 67–84.

Larsen, S.F. and László, J. (1990), 'Cultural–historical knowledge and personal experience in appreciation of literature'. *European Journal of Social Psychology*, 20/5, pp. 425–40.

Lassén-Seger, M. (2013), 'Reading Guide for *The Arrival*'. Accessed (17/1/2013) at http://www.alma.se/Documents/2013/L%c3%a4snycklar,%20jan%2013/Reading_guide_Tan_Arrival.pdf.

Lavin, M. (1998), 'Comic books and graphic novels for libraries: What to buy'. *Serials Review*, 24/2, pp. 31–45.

Leitch, R. (2008), 'Creatively researching children's narratives through images and drawings'. In P. Thomson (ed.), *Doing Visual Research with Young Children*. London: Routledge, pp. 37–58.

Lemke, J.L. (1992), 'Intertextuality and educational research'. *Linguistics and Education*, 4/3, pp. 257–67.

Lemke, J.L. (2004), 'Intertextuality and educational research'. In N. Shuart-Faris and D. Bloome (eds.), *Uses of Intertextuality in Classroom and Educational Research*. Greenwich, USA: Information Age Publishing.

Lewis, C. (2001), *Literary Practices as Social Acts: Power, Status, and Cultural Norms in the Classroom*. Mahwah, NJ: Lawrence Erlbaum Associates.

Lewis, D. (2001), *Reading Contemporary Picturebooks*. London: RoutledgeFalmer.

Lewis, M. (2006), *Warm Welcome? Understanding Public Attitudes to Asylum Seekers in Scotland*. Institute for Public Policy Research. Accessed (31/7/2012) at http://www.ippr.org/ecomm/files/warm_welcome.pdf.

Lindfors, J. (1999), *Children's Inquiry: Using Language to Make Sense of the World*. New York: Teachers College Press.

Lindholm-Leary, K. (2005), *Review of Research and Best Practices on Effective Features of Dual Language Education Programs*. Washington, DC: Center for Applied Linguistics.

Mace-Matluck, B. (1990), 'The effective schools movement: Implications for Title VII and bilingual education projects'. In L. Malavé (ed.), *Annual Conference Journal NABE '88–'89*. Washington, DC: NABE, pp. 83–95.

Mackey, M. (2003), 'At play on the borders of the diegetic: Story boundaries and narrative interpretation'. *Journal of Literacy Research*, 35/1, pp. 591–632.

Mackey, M. (2011), *Narrative Pleasures in Young Adult Novels, Films, and Video Games*. Basingstoke: Palgrave Macmillan.

Madura, S. (1995), 'The line and texture of aesthetic response: Primary children study authors and illustrators'. *The Reading Teacher*, 49/2, pp. 110–18.

Madura, S. (1998), *Transitional Readers and Writers Respond to Literature through Discussions, Writing, and Art*. Unpublished doctoral dissertation: University of Nevada.

Manguel, A. (2013), *The Traveler, the Tower, and the Worm*. Philadelphia: University of Pennsylvania Press.

Manresa, M. and Silva-Díaz, C. (2005), 'Dialogar per aprendre literatura'. *Articles de Didàctica de la Llengua i la Literatura*, 37, pp. 45–56.

Marsden, J. (2000), *The Rabbits*. Victoria: Lothian Children's Books.

Martínez-Roldán, C. (2003), 'Building worlds and identities: A case study of the role of narratives in bilingual literature discussions'. *Research in the Teaching of English*, 37/4, pp. 491–526.

Martínez-Roldán, C. (2005), 'The inquiry acts of bilingual children in literature discussions'. *Language Arts*, 83/1, pp. 22–32.

Martínez-Roldán, C. (2012), 'Pláticas literarias con estudiantes bilingües: La metodología de estudio de caso'. In T. Colomer and M. Fittipaldi (eds.), *La literatura que acoge: Inmigración y lectura de álbumes*. Barcelona: Banco del Libro–GRETEL, pp. 213–38.

Martínez-Roldán, C. and López-Robertson, J. (1999), 'Initiating literature circles in a first-grade bilingual classroom'. *The Reading Teacher*, 53/4, pp. 2–14.

Martínez-Roldán, C. and Malavé, G. (2004), 'Language ideologies mediating literacy and identity in bilingual contexts'. *Journal of Early Childhood Literacy*, 4/2, pp. 155–80.

Martínez-Roldán, C. and Newcomer, S. (2011), 'Reading between the pictures: Immigrant students' interpretations of *The Arrival*'. *Language Arts*, 88/3, pp. 188–97.

Martínez-Roldán, C. and Smagorinsky, P. (2011), 'Computer-mediated learning and young Latino/a students' developing expertise'. In P. Portes and S. Salas (eds.), *Vygotsky in 21st Century Society: Advances in Cultural Historical Theory and Praxis with Non-dominant Communities*. New York: Peter Lang, pp. 162–79.

McAdam, J. and Arizpe, E. (2011), 'Journeys into culturally responsive teaching'. *Journal of Teacher Education and Teachers' Work*, 2/1, pp. 18–27.

McCarty, T. (2002), *A Place to Be Navajo*. Mahwah, NJ: Lawrence Erlbaum Associates.

McCarty, T. and Watahomigie, L. (2004), 'Language and literacy in American Indian and Alaska Native communities'. In B. Pérez (ed.), *Sociocultural Contexts in Language and Literacy*. Mahwah, NJ: Lawrence Erlbaum Associates, pp. 79–110.

McGonigal, J. and Arizpe, E. (2007), *Learning to Read a New Culture: How Immigrant and Asylum Seeking Children Experience Scottish Identity through Classroom Books* (Final Report). Edinburgh: Scottish Government. Accessed (23/1/13) at http://www.scotland.gov.uk/Publications/2007/10/31125406/0.

McKinney, S., McAdam, J., Arizpe, E., Crichton, H. and Britton, A. (2012), *Portfolio of Integration (Scotland)*. Project Report. Oxfam Italia. (Unpublished.)

Medina, C. (2010), 'Reading across communities in biliteracy practices: Examining translocal discourses and cultural flows in literature discussions'. *Reading Research Quarterly*, 45/1, pp. 40–60.

Medina, C. and Martínez-Roldán, C. (2011), 'Culturally relevant literature pedagogies: Latino/a students' reading in the borderlands'. In J. Naidoo (ed.), *Celebrating Cuentos: Promoting Latino Children's Literature and Literacy in Classrooms and Libraries*. New York: ABC-CLIO (Libraries Unlimited), pp. 259–72.

Meek, M. (1988), *How Texts Teach what Readers Learn*. Stroud: Thimble Press.

Meek, M. (ed.) (2001), *Children's Literature and National Identity*. London: Trentham Books.

Mercado, C. and Moll, L. (1997), 'The study of funds of knowledge: Collaborative research in Latino homes'. *CENTRO, the Journal of the Center for Puerto Rican Studies*, 9/9, pp. 26–42.

Merriam, S.B. (2009), *Qualitative Research: A Guide to Design and Implementation*. San Francisco, CA: John Wiley and Sons.

Mill, J.S. (1843), 'A system of logic ratiocinative and inductive'. *Collected Works*, Vol. VII. London: John W. Parker.

Miller, A. (2007), *Reading Bande Dessinâee: Critical Approaches to French-language Comic Strip*. Chicago: Intellect Books.

Mines, H. (2000), *The Relationship Between Children's Cultural Literacies and their Readings of Literary Texts*. Unpublished PhD thesis. University of Brighton: Brighton, UK.

Miramontes, O., Nadeau, A. and Commins, N. (1997), *Restructuring Schools for Linguistic Diversity*. New York: Teachers College Press.

Mitchell, C. (2011), *Doing Visual Research*. London: Sage.

Moll, L.C. (ed.) (1990), *Vygotsky and Education: Instructional Implications and Applications of Sociohistorical Psychology*. New York: Cambridge University Press.

Moll, L.C. (1994), 'Literacy research in community and classrooms: A sociocultural approach'. In R. Rudell, M.R. Rudell and H. Singer (eds.), *Theoretical Models and Processes of Reading*, 4th edn. Newark, DE: International Reading Association, pp. 179–207.

Moll, L.C. (2001), 'Through the mediation of others: Vygotskian research on teaching'. In V. Richardson (ed.), *Handbook of Research on Teaching*, 4th edn. Washington, DC: American Educational Research Association, pp. 111–29.

Moll, L., Amanti, C., Neff, D. and Gonzalez, N. (1992), 'Funds of knowledge for teaching: A quantitative approach to connect households and classrooms'. *Theory Into Practice*, 31/2, pp. 132–41.

Morgado, M., Livingston, K., Ondráš, M., Tembra, J. and Blazic, M. (2008), *Visual Literacy and Intercultural European Education: European Children and Educators Look at Pictures*. Castelo Branco: IPCB.

Moss, G. (2001), 'Seeing with the camera: Analysing children's photographs of literacy in the home'. *Journal of Research in Reading*, 24/3, pp. 279–92.

Moss, J., Deppeler, J., Astley, L. and Pattison, K. (2007), 'Student researchers in the middle: Using visual images to make sense of inclusive education'. *Journal of Research in Special Educational Needs*, 7/1, pp. 46–54.

Mourão, S. (2009), 'Multilingual use of the multimodal: Picturebooks in an English language class'. In M. de L. Dionisio, J. Carvalho and R. Castro (eds.), *Discovering Worlds of Literacy: Proceedings of the 16th European Conference on Reading and 1st Ibero-American Forum on Literacies*. Braga: Littera.

Mourão, S. (2012), *English Picturebook Illustrations and Language Development in Early Years Education*. Unpublished PhD thesis: University of Aveiro, Portugal.

Munita, F. and Manresa, M. (2012), 'La mediación en la discusión literaria'. In T. Colomer and M. Fittipaldi, *La literatura que acoge: Inmigración y lectura de álbumes*. Barcelona: Banco del Libro–GRETEL, pp. 119–43.

Negri, M. (2012), *Lo spazio della pagina, l'esperienza del lettore: Per una didattica della letteratura nella scuola primaria*. Trento: Erickson.

Negrón de Montilla, A. (1970), *Americanization in Puerto Rico and the Public-School System 1900–30*. Río Piedras, PR: Editorial EDIL.

Netto, G., Rowena, A., de Lima, P., Almeida, D.F., MacEwen, M., Patel, V. and Syed, R. (2001), *Audit of Research on Minority Ethnic Issues in Scotland from a 'Race' Perspective*. Scottish Executive Central Research Unit.

New London Group (1996), 'A pedagogy of multiliteracies: Designing social futures'. *Harvard Educational Review*, 66/1, pp. 60–92.

New London Group (2000), 'A pedagogy of multiliteracies: Designing social futures'. In B. Cope and M. Kalantzis (eds.), *Multiliteracies: Literacy Learning and the Design of Social Futures*. London: Routledge, pp. 9–37.

Nières-Chevrel, I. (2010), 'The narrative power of pictures: *L'Orage* (The Thunderstorm) by Anne Brouillard'. In T. Colomer, B. Kümmerling-Meibauer and C. Silva-Díaz (eds.), *New Directions in Picturebook Research*. London: Routledge, pp. 129–38.

Nieto, S. (1995), 'From brown heroes and holidays to assimilationist agendas: Reconsidering the critiques of multicultural education'. In C. Sleeter and P. McLaren (eds.), *Multicultural Education, Critical Pedagogy, and the Politics of Difference*. Albany: State University of New York Press, pp. 191–220.

Nieto, S. (2000), *Affirming Diversity: The Sociopolitical Context of Multicultural Education*. New York: Longman.

Nieto, S. (2003), 'Challenging current notions of "highly qualified teachers" through work in a teachers' inquiry group'. *Journal of Teacher Education*, 54/5, pp. 386–98.

Nieto, S. (2009), *The Light in Their Eyes: Creating Multicultural Learning Communities*, 10th Anniversary edition. New York: Teachers College Press.

Nikolajeva, M. (2012), 'Reading other people's minds through word and image'. *Children's Literature in Education*, 43/3, pp. 273–91.

Nikolajeva, M. and Scott, C. (2001), *How Picture Books Work*. New York: Routledge.

Nikola-Lisa, W. (1994), 'Play, panache, pastiche: Postmodern impulses in contemporary picture books'. *Children's Literature Association Quarterly*, 19/1, pp. 35–40.

Nodelman, P. (1988), *Words about Pictures: The Narrative Art of Children's Picture Books.* Athens: University of Georgia Press.

Nodelman, P. (2000), 'The implied viewer: Some speculations about what children's picture books invite readers to do and to be'. *CREArTA*, 1/1, pp. 23–43.

Nodelman, P. (2010), 'On the border between implication and actuality: Children inside and outside of picture books'. *Journal of Children's Literature Studies*, 7/2, pp. 1–21.

Orellana, M.F. (1999), 'Space and place in an urban landscape: Learning from children's views of their social worlds'. *Visual Sociology*, 14/1, pp. 73–89.

Orellana, M., Thorne, B., Chee, A. and Lam, W. (2001), 'Transnational childhoods: The participation of children in processes of migration'. *Social Problems*, 48/4, pp. 572–91.

Osler, A. and Yahya, C. (2013), 'Challenges and complexity in human rights education'. *Education Inquiry*, 4/1, pp. 189–210.

Oxford English Dictionary, online. Available from http://www.oed.com/.

Painter, C., Martin, J.R. and Unsworth, L. (2013), *Reading Visual Narratives*. Sheffield: Equinox.

Pallotti, G. (2005), 'Le ricadute didattiche delle ricerche dell'interlingua'. In E. Jafrancesco (ed.), *L'acquisizione dell'italiano L2 da parte di immigrati adulti*. Atene: Edilingua.

Pantaleo, S. (2005), 'Young children engage with the metafictive in picture books'. *The Australian Journal of Language and Literacy*, 28/1, p. 19.

Pantaleo, S. (2008), *Exploring Student Response to Contemporary Picturebooks*. Toronto: University of Toronto Press.

Pantaleo, S. (2009), 'Exploring children's responses to the postmodern picturebook, *Who's Afraid of the Big Bad Book?*' In J. Evans (ed.), *Talking Beyond the Page: Reading and Responding to Picturebooks*. Abingdon: Routledge, pp. 44–61.

Pantaleo, S. (2011), 'Grade 7 students reading graphic novels: "You need to do a lot of thinking"'. *English in Education*, 45/2, pp. 113–31.

Pantaleo, S. and Bomphray, A. (2011), 'Exploring grade 7 students' written responses to Shaun Tan's *The Arrival*'. *Changing English: Studies in Culture and Education*, 18/2, pp. 173–85.

Parsons, M.J. (1987), *How We Understand Art*. Cambridge: Cambridge University Press.

Peal, E. and Lambert, W.E. (1962), 'The relationship of bilingualism to intelligence'. *Psychological Monographs*, 76/27, pp. 1–23.

Pennac, D. (1994), *Reads Like a Novel*. Daniel Gunn (transl). London: Quartet Books.

Pennycock, A. (2010), *Language as a Local Practice*. New York: Routledge.

Pérez, E. (1999), *The Decolonial Imaginary: Writing Chicanas into History*. Bloomington: Indiana University Press.

Perkins, D. (1994), *The Intelligent Eye: Learning to Think by Looking at Art*. Cambridge, MA: Harvard Graduate School of Education.

Peterson, R., and Eeds, M. (1990), *Grand Conversations: Literature Groups in Action*. New York: Scholastic.

Petit, M. (2009), *El arte de la lectura en tiempos de crisis*. Barcelona: Océano.

Pink, S. (2007), *Doing Visual Ethnography*, 2nd edn. London: Sage.

Pontecorvo, C. (1999), *Come si dice? Linguaggio e apprendimento in famiglia e a scuola*. Rome: Carocci.

Pontecorvo, C., Ajello Messina, A.M. and Zucchermaglio, C. (2004), *Discutendo si impara: Interazione sociale e conoscenza a scuola*. Rome: Carocci.

Poplack, S. (1980), 'Sometimes I'll start a sentence in Spanish and termino en español: Toward a typology of code-switching'. *Linguistics*, 18/7–8, pp. 581–618.

Portes, A. and Rumbaut, R.C. (1996), *Immigrant America: A Portrait*. Los Angeles, CA: University of California Press.

Prosser, J. and Loxley, A. (2007), 'Enhancing the contribution of visual methods to inclusive education'. *Journal of Research in Special Educational Needs*, 7/1, pp. 55–68.

Rama, A. (1987), *Transculturación narrativa en América Latina*. México DF: Siglo XXI Editores.

Raney, K. (1998), 'A matter of survival on being visually literate'. *English and Media Magazine*, pp. 37–42.

Reedy, D. (2010), *Agenda for Action: UKLA's Vision for Future Literacy Education*. [Online] Accessed (1/10/10) at http://www.ukla.org/news/.

Richards, J.C. and Anderson, N.A. (2003), 'What do I See? What do I Think? What do I Wonder? (STW): A visual literacy strategy to help emergent readers focus on storybook illustrations'. *The Reading Teacher*, 56/5, pp. 442–4.

Robinson, A. and Young, A. (2008), *Gervelie's Journey: Diary of a Refugee*. London: Frances Lincoln.

Rosenblatt, L.M. (1968), *Literature as Exploration*. London: Heinemann.

Rosenblatt, L.M. (1978), *The Reader, The Text, The Poem: The Transactional Theory of the Literary Work*. Carbondale, IL: Southern Illinois University Press.

Rosenblatt, L.M. (1982), 'The literary transaction: Evocation and response'. *Theory Into Practice*, 21/4, pp. 268–77.

Rosenblatt, L.M. (1988), 'Writing and reading: The transactional theory. Technical report no. 416'. Available from the Center for the Study of Reading, University of Illinois at Urbana-Champaign: Champaign, Illinois.

Rosenblatt, L.M. (1995), *Literature as Exploration*, 5th edn. New York: The Modern Language Association of America.

Rosenthal, R. and Jacobson, L. (1997), 'Pigmalione in classe'. In E. Morgagni and A. Russo (eds.), *L'educazione in sociologia: Testi scelti*. Bologna: CLUEB.

Rowe, A. (1996), 'Voices off: Reading wordless picture books'. In M. Styles, E. Bearne and V. Watson (eds.), *Voices Off: Texts, Contexts and Readers*. London: Cassell, pp. 219–34.

Ruiz, R. (1984), 'Orientations in language planning'. *National Association for Bilingual Education Journal*, 8/2, pp. 15–34.

Rutter, J. (2003), *Working with Refugee Children*. York: London Metropolitan University. Accessed (18/7/2013) at http://open.tean.ac.uk/bitstream/handle/123456789/566/Resource_1.pdf?sequence=1.

Rutter, J. (2006), *Refugee Children in the UK*. Maidenhead: Open University Press.

Saguisag, L. (2010), 'Strangely familiar: Shaun Tan's *The Arrival* and the universalised immigrant experience'. *IBBYLink*, 27, p. 20. Accessed (13/12/12) at http://www.ibby. org/fileadmin/user_upload/IBBYLink_27_Spring_2010.pdf.

Salazar Parreñas, R. (2005), *Children of Global Migration*. Stanford, CA: Stanford University Press.

Sankoff, D. and Poplack, S. (1981), 'A formal grammar for code-switching 1'. *Linguistics*, 14/1, pp. 3–45.

Sannino, A., Daniels, H. and Gutiérrez, K.D. (eds.) (2009), *Learning and Expanding with Activity Theory*. New York: Cambridge University Press.

Schwarz, G. (2006), 'Expanding literacies through graphic novels'. *English Journal*, 95/6, pp. 58–64.

Serafini, F. (2010), 'Reading multimodal texts: Perceptual, structural and ideological perspectives'. *Children's Literature in Education*, 41/2, pp. 85–104.

Sharples, M., Davison, L., Thomas, G.V. and Rudman, P.D. (2003), 'Children as photographers: An analysis of children's photographic behaviour and intentions at three age levels'. *Visual Communication*, 2/3, pp. 303–30.

Sherif Trask, B. (2010), *Globalization and Families*. New York: Springer.

Shklovskij, V. (2004), 'Art as technique'. In J. Rivkin and M. Ryan (eds.), *Literary Theory: An Anthology*. New York: Blackwell Publishing, pp. 15–21.

Short, K.G. (1992), 'Researching intertextuality within collaborative classroom learning environments'. *Linguistics and Education*, 4/3, pp. 313–33.

Short, K.G. (1997), *Literature as a Way of Knowing*. Los Angeles, CA: Stenhouse Publishers.

Short, K.G. (2011), 'Reading literature in elementary classrooms'. In S. Wolf, K. Coats, P. Enciso and C. Jenkins (eds.), *Handbook of Research on Children's and Young Adult Literature*. New York and London: Taylor and Francis and Routledge, pp. 48–62.

Short, K.G. and Pierce, K.M. (eds.) (1998), *Talking about Books: Creating Literate Communities*, 2nd edn. Portsmouth, NH: Heinemann.

Short, K.G. and Thomas, L. (2011), 'Developing intercultural understandings through global children's literature'. In R.J. Meyer and K.F. Whitmore (eds.), *Reclaiming Reading: Teachers, Students, and Researchers Regaining Spaces for Thinking and Action* New York: Routledge, pp. 149–62.

Silva-Díaz, M.C. (2005), *Libros que enseñan a leer: albumes metaficcionales y conocimiento literario*. Unpublished dissertation: Universitat Autònoma de Barcelona. Accessed (14/8/13) at http://www.tesisenxarxa.net/.

Sinatra, R. (1986), *Visual Literacy Connections to Thinking, Reading and Writing*. Springfield, IL: Charles C. Thomas Publisher.

Sipe, L. (1996), *The Construction of Literary Understanding by First and Second Graders in Response to Picture Storybook Readalouds*. Unpublished doctoral dissertation: Ohio State University.

Sipe, L. (1998), 'How picture books work: A semiotically framed theory of text-picture relationships'. *Children's Literature in Education*, 29/2, pp. 97–108.

Sipe, L. (1999), 'Children's response to literature: Author, text, reader, context'. *Theory Into Practice*, 38/3, pp. 120–9.

Sipe, L. (2000), '"Those two gingerbread boys could be brothers": How children use intertextual connections during storybook readalouds'. *Children's Literature in Education*, 31/2, pp. 73–90.

Sipe, L. (2008), *Storytime: Young Children's Literary Understanding in the Classroom*. New York: Teachers College Press.

Siqués Jofré, C. (2008), *Les aules d'acollida d'educació primària a Catalunya: descripció i avaluació dels resultats*. Doctoral dissertation: University of Girona. Accessed (5/4/11) at http://www.tdx.cat/TDX-0716108-130234.

Siro, A. (2005), 'El desafío de la continuidad: una mirada sobre la intervención del mediador en la formación de lectores de álbumes'. In M.C. Silva-Díaz and A. Siro (eds.), *Lecturas sobre lecturas*. México DF: Conaculta, pp. 47–91.

Smith, F. (1987), *Joining the Literacy Club: Further Essays into Education*. Portsmouth, NH: Heinemann.

Smith, K. and Edelsky, C. (2005), 'Different lenses for looking at the writing of English language learners'. In J. Cohen, K.T. McAlister, K. Rolstad and J. MacSwan (eds.), *ISB4: Proceedings of the 4th International Symposium on Bilingualism*. Somerville, MA: Cascadilla Press, pp. 2133–42.

Smith, V. (2009), 'Making and breaking frames: Crossing the borders of expectation in picturebooks'. In J. Evans (ed.), *Talking Beyond the Page: Reading and Responding to Picturebooks*. London: Routledge, pp. 81–96.

Smyth, G. (2003), *Helping Bilingual Pupils to Access the Curriculum*. London: David Fulton Publishers.

Smyth, G. (2006), 'Multilingual conferencing: Effective teaching of children from refugee and asylum-seeking families'. *Improving Schools*, 9/2, pp. 99–109.

Street, B. (2003), 'What's "new" in New Literacy Studies? Critical approaches to literacy in theory and practice'. *Current Issues in Comparative Education*, 5/2, pp. 77–91.

Suárez-Orozco, C. (2001), 'Afterword: Understanding and serving the children of immigrants'. *Harvard Educational Review*, 71/3, pp. 579–89.

Suárez-Orozco, C. and Suárez-Orozco, M. (2001), *Children of Immigration*. Cambridge, MA: Harvard University Press.

Suárez-Orozco, M. (2001), 'Globalization, immigration and education: The research agenda'. *Harvard Educational Review*, 71/3, pp. 345–66.

Suárez-Orozco, M. (2008), 'Migraciones hoy: aspectos globales, retos locales'. *Jornades d'Educació, globalització i interculturalitat*. CIIMU, Institut d'infància i món urbà: Barcelona.

Sumara, D. (2000), 'Critical issues: Researching complexity'. *Journal of Literacy Research*, 32/2, pp. 267–81.

Sumara, D. (2002), *Why Reading Literature Still Matters: Imagination, Interpretation and Insight*. Mahwah, NJ: Lawrence Erlbaum Associates.

Tabachnick, S.E. (2009), *Teaching the Graphic Novel*. New York: The Modern Language Association of America.

Tan, S. (n.d.), *The Arrival*. Accessed (24/4/2012) at http://www.shauntan.net/books/the-arrival.html.

Tan, S. (2001), 'Picture books: Who are they for?' Accessed (25/6/2011) at http://www.shauntan.net/essay1.html.

Tan, S. (2006), *The Arrival*. Melbourne: Lothian Books.

Tan, S. (2007), *Emigrantes*. Granada: Barbara Fiore.

Tan, S. (2009), 'Silent voices: Illustration and visual narrative'. Colin Simpson Memorial Lecture. Accessed (6/10/2011) at http://www.asauthors.org/lib/images/ColinSimpson/2009/Colin_Simpson_2009_Shaun_Tan.pdf.

Tan, S. (2010), *Sketches from a Nameless Land*. Sydney: Lothian.

Tan, S. (2011a), 'The accidental graphic novelist'. *Bookbird*, 49/4, pp. 1–9.

Tan, S. (2011b), 'Masterclass'. Talk presented at the Edinburgh International Book Festival. Edinburgh, Scotland.

Tan, S. (2012), 'Strange migrations'. *IbbyLink*, 35, pp. 22–31.

Terrusi, M. (2012), *Albi illustrati. Leggere, guardare, nominare il mondo nei libri per l'infanzia*. Roma: Carocci.

Terrusi, M. (2013), 'L'orizzonte nelle pagine'. In *Nei libri il mondo*. Bologna: Giannino Stoppani editore.

Thibault, M. and Walbert, D. (2003), *Reading Images: An Introduction to Visual Literacy*. Accessed (12/1/24) at http://www.learnnc.org/lp/pages/675.

Thomson, P. (ed.) (2008), *Doing Visual Research with Young Children*. London: Routledge.

Tiemensma, L. (2009), 'Visual literacy: To comics or not to comics? Promoting literacy using comics'. In *World Library and Information Congress: Proceedings of the 75th IFLA General Conference and Council*. Milan, Italy.

Torres-Guzmán, M.E. and de Jong, E.J. (in press), 'Looking back, sideways, and forward: Language and education in multilingual settings'. In M. Bigelow and J. Ennser-Kananen (eds.), *Handbook of Educational Linguistics*. New York: Routledge.

UNHCR (2012), *Asylum Trends 2012*. Accessed (9/7/2013) at http://www.unhcr.org/5149b81e9.html.

United Nations (2008), *International Migrant Stock: The 2008 Revision*. Accessed (9/7/13) at http://esa.un.org/migration/.

Versaci, R. (2001), 'How comic books can change the way our students see literature: One teacher's perspective'. *The English Journal*, 91/2, pp. 61–7.

Vertovec, S. (2010), 'Towards post-multiculturalism? Changing communities, contexts and conditions of diversity'. *International Social Science Journal*, 61/199, pp. 83–95.

Vertovec, S. (2011), 'The cultural politics of nation and migration'. *Annual Review of Anthropology*, 40, pp. 241–56.

Vieira, I. and Zannoni, F. (2012), *Immigrants' Associations and the 'Culture of Silence': The Case of Ethiopian and Eritrean Communities in Bologna*, Acts of the congress 'Civil Society Organizations in the Mediterranean Area: Societal Role, Challenges, Dynamics', Sassari.

Vila, I., Siqués, C. and Roig, T. (2006), *Llengua, escola i immigració: un debat obert.* Barcelona: Graó.

Vygotsky, L.S. (1978), *Mind in Society: The Development of Higher Psychological Processes.* Cambridge, MA: Harvard University Press.

Vygotsky, L.S. (1986), *Thought and Language.* Cambridge, MA: MIT Press.

Vygotsky, L.S. (1987), *The Collected Works of L.S. Vygotsky: Problems of General Psychology, including the Volume Thinking and Speech*, vol. 1. New York: Springer.

Walsh, M. (2000), 'Text-related variables in narrative picture books: Children's responses to visual and verbal texts'. *The Australian Journal of Language and Literacy*, 23/2, pp. 139–56.

Walsh, M. (2003), '"Reading" pictures: What do they reveal? Young children's reading of visual texts'. *Reading*, 37/3, pp. 123–30.

Walsh, M., Cranitch, M. and Maras, K. (2012), 'Into the deep end: The experience with Flotsam in Australia'. In *TESOL in Context. Special Edition S3.* Accessed (13/9/12) at http://www.tesol.org.au/Publications/Special-Editions.

Wiesner, D. (1992a), 'Foreword'. In V. Richey and K. Puckett, *Wordless/Almost Wordless Picture Books.* Englewood, CA: Libraries Unlimited, pp. vii–viii.

Wiesner, D. (1992b), *Tuesday.* New York: Clarion.

Wiesner, D. (2001), *The Three Pigs.* New York: Clarion.

Wiesner, D. (2006), *Flotsam.* New York: Clarion.

Winder, R. (2004), *Bloody Foreigners: The Story of Immigration to Britain.* London: Abacus.

Wolf, S. (2004), *Interpreting Literature with Children.* Mahwah, NJ: Lawrence Erlbaum Associates.

Working Group on ELL Policy (2010), *Improving Educational Outcomes for English Language Learners: Recommendations for the Reauthorization of the Elementary and Secondary Education Act.* Washington, DC: Center for Applied Linguistics. Accessed (7/8/10) at http://www.cal.org/topics/ell/ELL-Working-Group-ESEA.pdf.

Xu, S.H. (2003), 'The learner, the teachers, the text, and the context'. In D.M. Barone and L.M. Morrow (eds.), *Literacy and Young Children.* New York: The Guilford Press, pp. 61–80.

Yang, G. (2003), Comics in Education. Accessed (18/7/2013) at http://www.geneyang.com/comicsedu/index.html.

Yang, G. (2008), 'Graphic novels in the classroom'. *Language Arts*, 85/3, pp. 185–92.

Yenawine, P. (originally published 1997), 'Thoughts on Visual Literacy'. http://www.vtshome.org/system/resources/0000/0005/Thoughts_Visual_Literacy.pdf.

Young, L. and Barrett, H. (2001), 'Adapting visual methods: Action research with Kampala street children'. *The Royal Geographical Society*, 33/2, pp. 141–52.

Index